T0285431

My Mets Bible

My Mets Bible

Scoring 30 Years of Baseball Fandom

EVAN ROBERTS

TRIUMPH
BOOKS

Library of Congress Cataloging-in-Publication Data available upon request

This book is available in quantity at special discounts for your group or organization. For further information, contact:

Triumph Books LLC
814 North Franklin Street
Chicago, Illinois 60610
(312) 337-0747
www.triumphbooks.com

Printed in U.S.A.
ISBN: 978-1-63727-335-7
Editorial production and design by Alex Lubertozzi

To Mom, Dad, Sylvia, Jett, and Spence

CONTENTS

THE 2010S

THE 2020S

THE MISSING SCORECARDS

INTRODUCTION

IN 1992, at the age of eight, I started scoring Mets games. It went from a thing I did when my dad brought me to Shea into an absolute obsession. Despite decades upon decades going by and plenty of life changes, I remained completely dedicated to scoring just about every Mets game played. At age nine, I played with wrestling figures; I don't anymore. At age 14, I collected baseball cards; I don't anymore. At age 22, I would go to karaoke bars and sing my lungs out; I don't anymore. But through all of those hobbies, one has remained constant—my absolute love affair with sitting down and scoring a baseball game.

This was not an easy process in the days before DVRs. There were times I had to hide my scorebook under the covers to make my parents think I was sleeping, because it was after midnight on a Tuesday evening and I had school the next day. But I couldn't just go to sleep. The Mets were battling the Padres, and Eric Gunderson just came in to try and record a huge out against Tony Gwynn. So, even though it was well past my bedtime, my pen and book needed to record what would happen next.

When I lived the dating lifestyle in the early 2000s, I needed to DVR every single Mets game because God forbid I miss scoring a pitch from the Mets-Pirates game on a Friday night while I searched for the girl of my dreams! Scoring was a constant in my life from the age of eight until the present day, and nothing would get in the way. Upon working full-time at WFAN in 2007, I noticed that my insane habit was a real positive. When breaking down a Mets game the following day on WFAN with Joe Benigno, having the entire game in front of me was a major help. But let's not kid ourselves...whether it was going to help me do my job or not, scoring Mets games was something that would continue no matter what my life's work was.

Flash forward to 2021. I was sitting in the WFAN radio studios doing my old show with Craig Carton. He was mocking my scoring infatuation and threw out the idea that would stop me dead in my tracks: "Evan, you should write a book and publish them." Craig said it half-sarcastically but half-seriously. "Why not go through the thousands and thousands of games you have scored and pick out your favorites?" As soon as that thought came out of his mouth, a light went off in my head. *Oh, hell yeah!* My brain started going into overdrive—I could finally take all these games sitting in books and put them to good use.

How many games should I pick? was a question I asked myself immediately. The only number that made sense to me was 81. Why 81, you ask? When I went to games as a kid with my father, we always had the unrealistic goal of going to all 81 home games of a Mets season. While we never accomplished that mission, we certainly came damn close. So I spent hours and hours going back through scorecards I hadn't looked at in decades to pick my favorites. Actually, *favorite* is the not the correct word, because a lot of these games elicit pain and tears. So they're the most memorable— both good and bad from more than 30 years of scoring Mets games. The mission of going through all these scorecards was therapeutic; I not only had baseball memories flash back into my mind, but all of my life experiences along the way. I realized that each scorecard not only told a baseball story but also explained the story of my life. Laugh with me, cry with me, and wonder what the hell is wrong with me as we take a trip through my life, viewed through the lens of scoring Mets games.

My *Mets* *Bible*

The

1990s

MY "FIRST GAME"

PIRATES 3 METS 2

JUNE 13, 1992, at SHEA STADIUM

WE START with a Mets game that I have zero recollection of. I was eight years old when this game took place, and after exhaustive research this is the oldest, living, breathing scorecard from me that I could find, which makes it the first! It is simultaneously the George Washington of my scorecard collection for the being the first, and the Millard Fillmore, because I have no memory of it ever happening. I'm also taking the leap of faith that this is the genuine article, because I trust that my parents never threw out an earlier scorecard that could have been my first. So, for the sake of my psyche, I assume this is legit the first time I ever laid pencil to scorecard.

I have asked my father what got me into scoring games, and the truth is scoring games actually got me into baseball. My dad has been a diehard Mets fan since their inception in 1962 and a season ticket holder since the late 1970s, so I obviously grew up in a household where the Mets were religion. But my older sister was the one who went to games with my dad and sat there for all nine innings without an issue.... I was the opposite. Apparently (as I've been told), I could not sit still, and my dad eventually abandoned the idea of taking me to games alone. Granted, I was between the ages of one and six at that time, but my sister, who is only a few years older than I am, was

3

a real trooper. I, on the other hand, was a terror to take to games. I would cry, complain, and just flat-out not watch the game, while my sister was a little angel. So, while I would still go to games, it would only be if my mother was there too, so she could keep an eye on me. As nuts as my dad was about the Mets, my mom could not possibly care less, so she was the absolute perfect person to essentially babysit me while my dad and sis would enjoy the Mets game uninterrupted.

I got a lot of my craziness from my dad, including my propensity for keeping records on everything; he actually kept a complete list of games we attended as kids. I was able to look at this list and study it, and I noticed a trend. Starting in 1991, when I was seven, the games I attended started to increase, while my mom and sister were going less and less. It started to become just me and my dad. What the heck happened? Well, I started pounding him with questions about baseball, and somewhere along the line he brought up scoring games to me. He probably figured it would distract me from losing interest in the game. Little did he know he was slowly creating a monster. I went to 21 games in 1992, and the ninth game I went to is apparently the first game I scored. His master plan worked to perfection. Learning about scoring the game and then perfecting my process of doing it got me into baseball in a big way. Based on the stories my dad has shared, baseball didn't get me into scoring, but scoring got me into baseball.

I can tell by the handwriting that my dad contributed big time to this inaugural game. My hand clearly got tired toward the end of the game, because he is the one writing in the pinch-hitters and new pitchers that came into the game. My spelling is simply awe-inspiring! As you can see in the old Shea Stadium scorecard, they conveniently supplied the rosters of both the New York Mets and visiting Pittsburgh Pirates, but that didn't stop me from butchering every freakin' name. Eight-year-old me also apparently decided to create a new baseball player named Andy Slyke, as I got rid of the *Van*. I really wish I had an answer for the doodling that featured "Peace and Love." I'm going to just blame either my mother or sister for this one, as they were also at this game. What is pretty cool about looking back is that,

NEW YORK METS
OFFICIAL SCORECARD

Pittsburgh

Pirates Numerical Roster
2 Gary Redus, of
3 Jay Bell, if
6 Orlando Merced, if
7 Jeff King, if
10 Jim Leyland, MGR
11 Don Slaught, c
12 Mike LaValliere, c
14 Jose Lind, if
15 Doug Drabek, rhp
17 Bob Walk, rhp
18 Andy Van Slyke, of
22 Steve Buechele, if
23 Lloyd McClendon, of
24 Barry Bonds, of
26 Dennis Lamp, rhp
29 Randy Tomlin, lhp
31 Ray Miller, coach
32 Denny Neagle, lhp
37 Tommy Sandt, coach
38 Bob Patterson, lhp
39 Milt May, coach
41 Zane Smith, lhp
42 Terry Collins, coach
45 Rich Donnelly, coach
48 Roger Mason, rhp
49 Jerry Don Gleaton, lhp
50 Stan Belinda, rhp
51 Carlos Garcia, if
56 Cecil Espy, of
58 Vicente Palacios, rhp
61 Victor Cole, rhp
68 Dave Clark, of

Mets

Mets Numerical Roster
1 Vince Coleman, of
2 Mackey Sasser, c
3 Junior Noboa, if
4 Mike Cubbage, coach
8 Daryl Boston, of
9 Dave Gallagher, of
9 Todd Hundley, c
10 Jeff Torborg, MGR
11 Dick Schofield, if
12 Willie Randolph, if
13 Kevin Elster, if
16 Dwight Gooden, rhp
17 David Cone, rhp
18 Bret Saberhagen, rhp
19 Anthony Young, rhp
20 Howard Johnson, if
22 Charlie O'Brien, c
25 Bobby Bonilla, of
26 Barry Foote, coach
27 Tom McCraw, coach
28 Dave LaRoche, coach
29 Dave Magadan, if
30 Mel Stottlemyre, coach
31 John Franco, lhp
32 Bill Pecota, if
33 Eddie Murray, if
34 Chico Walker, if
35 Lee Guetterman, lhp
39 Steve Rosenberg, lhp
44 Jeff Innis, rhp
45 Paul Gibson, lhp
47 Wally Whitehurst, rhp
48 Pete Schourek, lhp
50 Sid Fernandez, lhp

• Disabled List

P. Rets 3   Mets 2   6/13/92

while the Pirates defeated the Mets that day, it was Barry Bonds who hit the game-tying home run in the top of the eighth inning. I have said many times on the radio that Bonds is the greatest baseball player I've ever laid eyes on, so it was only fitting that he played a key role in the first game I officially scored. It would take some time, but my scoring would get better and so would my spelling!

KEEPING SCORE: The Mets had taken a 2–1 lead on Howard Johnson's two-run double in the bottom of the sixth before Bonds connected off reliever Wally Whitehurst, leading off the eighth. Two outs later, Orlando Merced doubled home the go-ahead run.... Bonds hit 38 of his major league–record 762 home runs against the Mets. That is the 10th highest total for any opposing player.... The 1992 Mets went 72–90 under new manager Jeff Torborg and finished 24 games behind the Pirates, who won their third straight NL East title.

HITTING THE ROAD FOR THE FIRST TIME

METS 7 CARDINALS 1

JULY 25, 1994, at BUSCH STADIUM, ST. LOUIS

THE FIRST SEASON I truly remember from start to finish was 1993, but 1994 was when my fandom really began taking off. Each summer from 1990 to 1993, I went away for two months to attend a sleep-away camp called Camp Chen-A-Wanda in Pennsylvania. I had a ball at camp, but every year that went by I started to miss the Mets a little bit more and more. Even though 1993 was a historically bad season for the Mets, as they lost 103 games and became famously known as "The Worst Team Money Could Buy," I still needed the Mets in my life. So in 1994 I had a pretty simple request: *Can I retire from sleepaway camp and just go to Mets games all summer?* My dad was going to games all summer anyway—in fact, during the summer of 1992 while I was away, he went on a road trip to see the Mets in Chicago and Pittsburgh. You can look this up if you don't believe me, but during that six-game road trip the Mets went 0–6! Even as I look back now as a 40-year-old father of two myself, I must commend his level of fandom for wanting to travel and watch that crap. Considering all the games he was going to, if I didn't go to camp, my dad would have someone to join him.

As my love for baseball and scoring continued to explode, we went on our first road trip during the late summer of 1993 to see the brand-new Camden Yards in Baltimore for the first time. Since this was a few years before interleague play, we clearly didn't see the Mets, but it was still an awesome time. In 1994 there would be no Chen-A-Wanda, which meant there was plenty of time to plan out some Mets road trips, so my dad came up with two for us: St. Louis and Chicago. Nineteen ninety-four was a spectacular season for the Mets.... Okay, well, really only spectacular in my naïve little eyes. All I had known so far in my young Mets-loving life was pathetic, awful, overpaid, washed-up-stars baseball. The Mets lost 90 games in 1992 and then 103 in 1993. In 1994 the Mets were beginning a long rebuilding process. We began to hear about the young arms in the farm system and also saw young players such as Todd Hundley, Ryan Thompson, Jeremy Burnitz, Bobby Jones, and Jason Jacome break in. But more than just the youth was the fact that the Mets were actually winning some games and were far improved from the abysmal showing of a year earlier. It was a fun season, and we were about to see the upstart Mets on the road for the first time.

You know what excited me the most about seeing Busch Stadium? The carpet! Even though artificial turf was universally hated by just about every baseball fan, including myself, I thought it would be so damn cool to see it in person. As we walked into Busch Stadium, I was in awe. The place I had watched on TV was in front of my eyes, and I loved it. The game itself would become incredibly pivotal in my fandom as it was the day I truly fell in love with Rico Brogna. Despite spelling his name incorrectly in this scorecard, Rico was a guy I was already sort of intrigued with. Right before the start of the season the Mets traded Alan Zinter, a former first-round pick, to the Tigers for Brogna, a minor league first baseman who had played a few games for Detroit a couple of seasons earlier. At the time, my dad and I would check *Baseball Weekly* to get updates

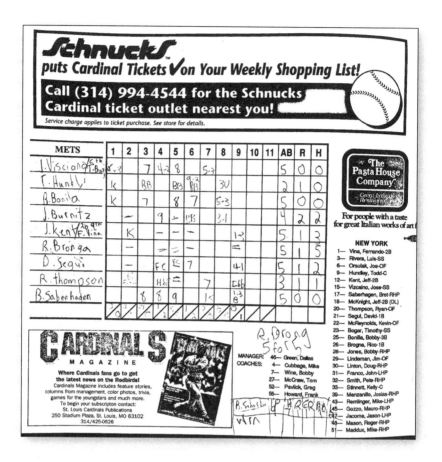

on Mets prospects, and I had read about Zinter and Butch Huskey as potential future infielders for the Mets. The only thing I knew about Rico is that he had a cool name. About a month earlier David Segui had gotten hurt, and Rico got the call to fill in and play first base. Rico was playing really well offensively and his glove work was something to behold. In this game, just one month into his Mets tenure, Rico put together a signature performance that would stick with me. He went 5-for-5, including a two-run double, and made a great defensive play. I found out many years later when Rico came on my Mets podcast (which happens to be called *Rico Brogna*), that that particular game happened to have a profound effect on his confidence, especially when Mets starter Bret Saberhagen, who pitched a complete game that night, complimented him on his sparkling

defensive play. The Mets won the game, and Rico had won my sports heart. The '94 season was a blast and so was this road trip, but there was one major cloud hovering over all of us. The impending doom of a players' strike was all the talk around baseball, and little did we know that while the St. Louis trip was a raging success, our big Chicago trip would not happen.

KEEPING SCORE: The Mets went on to sweep that three-game series in St. Louis, but the season came to an end a little more than two weeks later after the players did go on strike.... They finished third in the National League East at 55–58, and their winning percentage of .487 was a 123-point improvement over the previous season.... Brogna ended up batting .351 with seven home runs and 20 RBIs in 39 games after being called up from the minors that season. He went on to have a strong 1995, batting .289 with 22 home runs and 76 RBIs, but after injuries cut short his 1996 season, he was traded to the Philadelphia Phillies for relievers Ricardo Jordan and Toby Borland, both of whom had short and ineffective Mets careers.... Saberhagen went 14–4 with a 2.74 ERA in 1994, made the All-Star team, and finished third in Cy Young Award voting.

BASEBALL IS BACK!

METS 10 CARDINALS 8

APRIL 28, 1995, at SHEA STADIUM

THE PLAYERS' strike of 1994 came at the worst time for a blossoming baseball fan like myself. I turned 11 years old in July 1994, and my baseball fandom was exploding as rumors persisted about a potential stoppage. At first I didn't want to believe the rumors. I didn't think it was possible that baseball would just stop in the middle of a season like that. My dad would tell me stories about the 1981 strike and how damaging that was to the integrity of that season, but I just wouldn't believe something as foolish as that would happen again. Well, let's be honest. Since I was 11 years old, I wasn't using some kind of rigorous logic, I just had a hard time picturing a summer without baseball. When August 12 finally came and baseball shut down, my new form of denial was that it would only be temporary. There was no way they would wipe out the postseason and not declare a 1994 World Series champion, right? The news of baseball's cancellation was absolutely devastating. Even though the Mets weren't going anywhere, I still had hoped to see if the Montreal Expos could win their first title, or if the Cleveland Indians could get to their first World Series in my lifetime, and sure, to see if the New York Yankees could go on a deep October run. It caused me to learn the names of Dick Ravich, Donald Fehr, and Bud Selig. I wasn't an expert on the issues, but I knew that those three guys were responsible for taking baseball away from me.

While people would talk about not forgiving baseball for its sins, and potentially boycotting the sport when it came back, I was

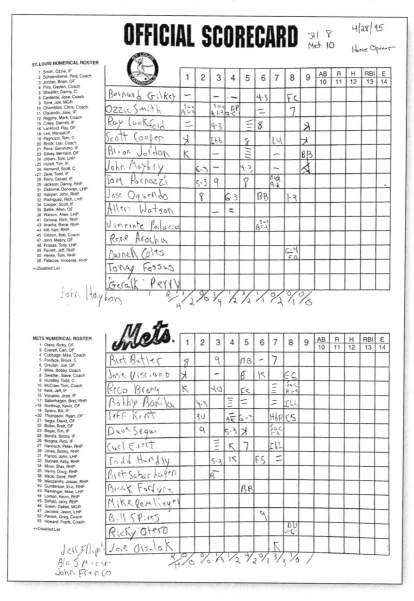

not partaking in any of those thoughts. I was desperate for baseball to come back and would hold no grudges once the game returned. Even when the awful plan was hatched by the owners to try and break the players union by using replacement players, I was ready to watch. While it wasn't ideal, it was baseball—the sport I was learning and watching religiously. Luckily, right before the season was set to begin, future Supreme Court justice Sonia Sotomayor issued an injunction that effectively ended the strike as well as the owners' attempt to stage a season with replacement players. The Mets were actually scheduled to play the first replacement regular season game in Miami against the Marlins to open the 1995 season. Luckily, it didn't happen, and the Mets would open the season a few weeks later in Denver instead.

I remember staying up very late on that midweek night to watch the Mets open the brand-new Coors Field in a very Coors Field–like game. I can still see Dante Bichette shaking his fist as he knew he'd ripped one out for a game-winning, walk-off home run off Mike Remlinger in the 14th inning. Two days later I would walk into a baseball stadium for the first time in eight months and I was ecstatic. The Mets played the Cardinals on a Friday night that opened up the home season in 1995. Everything about the scene was so freaking weird. First off, the game didn't sell out, and they didn't even come close. (The announced attendance was just 26,604—just two years earlier, the opener had drawn more than 53,000.) Apparently, most people weren't as forgiving as I was, or my father, who couldn't wait to walk into Shea Stadium. The game was ugly and sloppy but damn entertaining. Bret Saberhagen pitched poorly, allowing home runs to Ray Lankford and future Mets killer Brian Jordan. I guess that was to be expected, as there was a very short spring training and pitchers were certainly behind the eight ball. My man Rico Brogna was hitting third in the order as the Mets were fully believing in him after his red-hot 1994 that was stopped short because of the strike. The Mets trailed 5–1 in the fourth inning, 7–2 in the fifth, and 8–6 in the seventh before Brogna homered and Todd Hundley hit a two-run double later in the inning to give the Mets a lead they wouldn't relinquish.

The amazing Mets comeback on Opening Night was certainly not the most memorable thing about this game, however. All these years later I can still picture a few gentlemen running onto the field shirtless with the word GREED written on their chests. But that wasn't all...they then threw money at Bobby Bonilla and Jeff Kent. Despite my father and I running back to Shea, it didn't mean we weren't pissed about what had happened a year ago, so we stood up and cheered the men on. The crowd also roared in approval, and that wasn't the only fan interference from this game. While not as vivid in my memory, I also recall numerous other fans showing their disgust by jumping onto the field and making a scene. But all these years later I have to credit the GREED guys. It was creative, sent a message, and has stuck with me all these years later. What I forgot about was the fact that baseball wasn't all the way back either. The umpires in this game were replacement umpires because of a labor issue between the owners and umpires. You can't make it up...here we were finally seeing real players play baseball, and there was still something MLB couldn't get right. But on that night, I couldn't give a rat's ass. Baseball was back, and I was pumped to watch it from our seats in loge box 325 at Shea again.

KEEPING SCORE: Winning pitcher Blas Minor had been claimed off waivers from the Pittsburgh Pirates the previous off-season and went 4–2 in 35 appearances in '95.... Saberhagen would be traded to the Colorado Rockies at the trade deadline for righty Juan Acevedo and minor leaguer Arnold Gooch.... The Mets beat the Cardinals again the day after the home opener to even their record at 2–2, but after dropping the final game of the three-game series, they fell below .500 and stayed there for the remainder of the season.

JASON ISRINGHAUSEN'S DEBUT AND MY FIRST GAME AT WRIGLEY

METS 7 CUBS 2

JULY 17, 1995, at WRIGLEY FIELD, CHICAGO

IT'S VERY TOUGH to remember the exact moment I became an obsessed baseball fan. There are certain moments from 1991 as a seven-year-old that I vaguely recall and a few more from 1992 and 1993. But 1994 is the first year where I can almost recall the entire season. During the spring months of '91 to '93, I went to a bunch of games with my father, but come summertime I would be out of commission as I was shipped off to sleepaway camp. I had a fun experience at Camp Chen-A-Wanda, but I knew something was missing. *Baseball.* This wasn't 2023, when I could simply check my phone or sneak an iPad into my bunk and watch every game. We would get baseball updates every few days, and my dad would send an occasional letter updating me on the status of the '93 Mets. (The status reports were not positive.) When the 1994 season was about to start, I made a request of my parents: no more camp! Hey, I wanted to go to as many Mets games as possible, and while all those summer camp activities were fun and all, I needed to be laser-focused on my baseball team, even though they were coming off a 103-loss season.

Nineteen ninety-four was the year of watching and scoring the Mets! To take things up a notch, my father booked us a trip to Chicago to see the Mets on the road and make my first ever pilgrimage to the legendary Wrigley Field in late August. I was so pumped up. Early in the 1994 season, the team already felt like Murderers' Row compared to the previous year's team, so I had my calendar marked for August 26–28, when the Mets would visit Chicago for a weekend series at Wrigley. Unfortunately, Donald Fehr, Dick Ravitch, and Bud Selig conspired to devastate baseball fans all over the country. The 1994 strike was brutal. I cried like a baby when games started to be canceled and cried a little more when I knew the Wrigley trip would not happen. While the 1994 baseball strike turned many away from baseball, all it did to me was reaffirm my love for the sport, because not having it made me miss and appreciate it more.

The Chicago trip would still happen, though. How, you ask? Well, in one of the all-time coincidences that you couldn't make up, the New York Football Giants happened to be in Chicago that very same

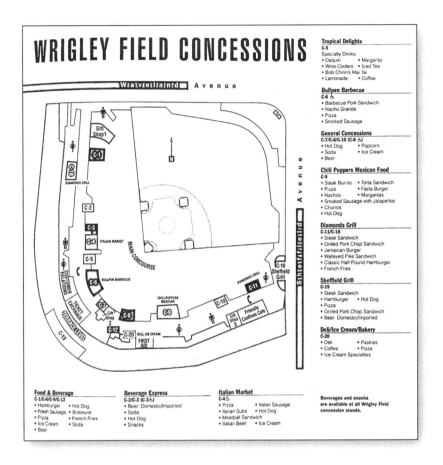

weekend to play the Bears. That was cool and all, but I'm a Jets fan, so while I was excited to go, it would have been a tad more awesome if I got to see Boomer Esiason instead. What really saved the Chicago trip was the fact that SummerSlam 1994 was taking place at the brand-new United Center. This turned out to be the first event at the new arena, and I got to see Bret Hart battle Owen Hart for the WWF title and the Undertaker vs. the Undertaker. I could write a whole piece on how dopey the Undertaker–Undertaker match was, but I digress. All was not lost in Chicago in 1994, but my dad and I both knew we were going to have try again whenever baseball came back.

Nineteen ninety-five was the reprieve. The labor dispute may have been the ultimate bad luck the year before, but in 1995 we felt like we hit the jackpot as prized Mets pitching prospect Jason

Isringhausen was set to make his anticipated MLB debut, and we would be there live! As Mets fans, our excitement wasn't wrapped up in what we were watching on the field that season. Instead, we were being sold on what was to come. What was to come were young pitching phenoms Bill Pulsipher, Paul Wilson, and Jason Isringhausen. "Generation K," as they were nicknamed, was the hope we needed to cling to. Pulse had made his MLB debut a month earlier at Shea Stadium, and it was a rare game that we missed. So after missing out on his debut, the fact we were lucky enough to see Izzy make his debut on the road made it even more special.

Early on when we made road trips, I wouldn't use my regular scorebook but instead buy one at the stadium we were visiting. So I have my cool 75¢ scorecard from Wrigley Field. It's funny...all these years later my most vivid memory of that afternoon in Chi-town was how Izzy flirted with a no-hitter. Yet when I look back at the scorecard, he only took it into the fourth inning when he gave up a single

FRONT ROW (left to right): Paul Derringer-P, Mickey Livingston-C, Stan Hack-3B, Roy Johnson-Coach, Milt Stock-Coach, Charlie Grimm-Manager, Jimmie Chalikis-batboy, Len Rice-C, Lennie Merullo-SS, Phil Cavarretta-1B, Claude Passeau-P SECOND ROW (l to r): Lloyd Christopher-OF, Paul Gillespie-C, Don Johnson-2B, Andy Pafko-OF, Peanuts Lowrey-OF, Bill Schuster-IF, Ed Sauer-OF, Dewey Williams-C, Ray Prim-P, Hy Vandenberg-P THIRD ROW (l to r): Paul Erickson-P, Frank Secory-OF, Ed Hanyzewski-P, Bill Nicholson-OF, Hank Wyse-P, Andy Lotshaw-trainer, Heinz Becker-IF, George Hennessey-P, Red Smith-Coach, Bob Chipman-P, Mack Stewart-P Not Pictured: Cy Block-IF, Hank Borowy-P, Jorge Comellas-P, Roy Hughes-IF, Johnny Moore-OF, John Ostrowski-IF, Reggie Otero-IF, Walter Signer-P, Ray Starr-P, Lon Warneke-P

to Mark Grace. It shows how desperate I was to see a no-hitter, even at the tender age of 12. The Cubs lineup that day makes me chuckle. You have a couple future key Mets in Todd Pratt and Todd Zeile, not to mention Brian McRae, and Shawon Dunston, who would play a key role in a future epic Mets moment. You have a beloved former Met in Howard Johnson (playing second base!)...and you have Luis Gonzalez. Yes, that Luis Gonzalez. The man who would go on and hit a shockingly high 57 home runs for the Arizona Diamondbacks in 2001 and deliver a walk-off hit against Mariano Rivera, the greatest closer in history, to beat the Yankees in Game 7 of that year's World Series. As for this game, Izzy went seven innings, allowing just two hits and two walks while striking out six, but took a no-decision as the Mets broke a 2–2 tie in the ninth inning with five runs, keyed by run-scoring hits by Bill Spiers, Chris Jones, and Jose Vizcaino. The winning pitcher was Jerry DiPoto, now the general manager of the Seattle Mariners.

KEEPING SCORE: The Mets completed a sweep of the brief two-game series the next day, with a 12–3 victory over future Met Steve Trachsel.... Generation K never panned out, as Isringhausen, Pulsipher, and Wilson all battled injuries and went on to win a combined total of only 31 games between them for the Mets.... Three of Izzy's victories came in his second stint with the club in 2011, 11 years after he was traded to the Oakland Athletics, where he became one of the best relievers in the game.

TODD HUNDLEY: HOME RUN KING OF CATCHERS

METS 6 BRAVES 5 (12 INNINGS)
SEPTEMBER 14, 1996, at SHEA STADIUM

YOU KNOW HOW certain things don't age very well? Well, Todd Hundley chasing and eventually becoming the short-lived home run king among catchers fits the bill perfectly. Nineteen ninety-six was such an odd year in Mets history. The team's win-loss record was atrocious and the much-ballyhooed Generation K was clearly becoming a bust. Jason Isringhausen had taken a major step back from his promising rookie season of 1995; Bill Pulsipher was out for the season due to injury; and Paul Wilson, the crown jewel of pitching prospects, was awful. Consequently, the Mets were a bad team that finished the 1996 campaign 71–91 and fired its manager, Dallas Green, late in the season. But the Mets got career seasons from three different players who would etch their names all over the Mets record books. Lance Johnson, in his first season over from the Chicago White Sox, led the majors with 227 hits (still a team record), was a triples machine, and stole a ton of bases. Bernard Gilkey, acquired via trade during the off-season from the Cardinals,

Braves W-L 86-59 GB None HOME 50-24 ROAD 36-36 VS DIV.
VISITOR
Mets W-L 66-81 GB 20½ HOME 90-35 ROAD 26-46 VS DIV.
HOME
STANDINGS

	R	H	E	LOB
ATL	5	13	1	12
NYM	6	11	1	14

WP Derek Wallace (2-1)
LP Joe Borrowski (2-4)
SV —
UMPIRES   Hirschbeck

DEFENSE

Ryan Klesko   Marquis Grissom   Andruw Jones
Chipper Jones   Mike Mordeci
Terry Pendleton   Steve Avery   Fred McGriff
Williams   Corrales
Javy Lopez

N.Y. 44 83-63
Bal 13½
Bos 8½
Tor 16½
Det 33
Cle 87-58
Chi 9½
Min 13½
Mil 17½
KC 20½
Tex 83-63
Sea 8
Oak 13
Cal 19

Atlanta Braves	1	2	3	4	5	6	7	8	9	10	11	AB 12	R 13	H 14	BI 15
9 Marquis Grissom CF .305												6	0	0	0
5 Terry Pendleton 3b .240												5	3	5	0
10 Chipper Jones SS .311												6	1	2	0
27 Fred McGriff 1b .295												3	1	1	2
18 Ryan Klesko LF .373 / 35 Greg McMichael P .201												4 2	0 0	1 0	0 0
8 Javy Lopez C .281												0	1	0	
25 Andruw Jones RF .235												0	0	0	0
16 Mike Mordeci 2b .222												3 2	0 0	0 0	1
33 Steve Avery P .256												0 0 0	0 0	0 0 0 0	0 0

when he had a career season. But 1996 was special, and as Mets fans we ate up every second of it.

It became obvious by mid-July that Todd Hundley was going to likely break not only the team record for home runs in a season, but the major league record for home runs by a catcher (40), set by Roy Campanella of the Brooklyn Dodgers in 1953. The Mets team home run mark at the time was held by Darryl Strawberry who hit 39 in both 1987 and 1988, and Hundley had reached 38 home runs on August 21, so it seemed like a mortal lock that Todd would eclipse both the Mets mark and the catching mark. Then Todd stopped hitting home runs. The only reason to watch the Mets in 1996 was the trifecta of guys having career seasons, but mostly Todd's home run chase. Yet, starting in late August, he stopped hitting them out. But, as ashamed as I may be to admit this all these years later, it didn't damper my enthusiasm for his chase. I knew Mike Piazza and Ivan Rodriguez were clearly better players, but Todd was our guy and he was chasing some kind of history.

He finally broke the team record and tied the catching mark on the road in Atlanta. But as I sat at Shea Stadium on September 14, the pressure was on. The Mets only had three more games left on the homestand, and if he didn't hit one soon, I'd risk not seeing it in person. This was a Saturday afternoon at Shea, and like most games against the Braves it started out as a complete disaster. Mark Clark gave up two runs in the first inning on a dropped fly ball by Lance Johnson. The Braves raced out to a 5–0 lead...but baseball is a real funny game, isn't it? When Todd Hundley strode to the plate in the seventh inning, he was set up for an incredibly special moment. The score was now 5–2 and he was the tying run with two on and two outs in the inning. Not only did Todd pick the most dramatic time to hit his record-breaking home run, but he did it in the most unusual way possible. When Todd hit left-handed he never, and I mean *never* would go the other way for a home run. Yet on this 0–2 pitch from future Met Greg McMichael, that's exactly what he did. Off the bat, I didn't think it had a chance, but, boy, was I wrong. The ball kept carrying and carrying and eventually hit off the retired numbers in the left-field corner. The Mets dramatically tied the game, and Todd finally passed Campanella for most home runs by a catcher in a single season. The entire dugout came out to greet him, and he was given a curtain call. Oh, by the way, the Mets would win the game in the 11th on a Lance Johnson walk-off single, but Todd had finally done it. Looking back all these years later, it's sorta pathetic I cared this much about him chasing this record. The Mets' home run record has been shattered many times over, and a few short years later we acquired a catcher who didn't need the single-season catching record for all of us to know he was clearly better then Hundley. But in the moment, this was very, very cool.

KEEPING SCORE: Hundley's record lasted only until 2003, when Javy Lopez of the Atlanta Braves hit 42 home runs while catching.... Mike Piazza came within one homer of tying Hundley's mark in 1999 during his first full season with the Mets when he hit 40, all as a catcher.... In 2021, Salvador Perez of the Kansas City Royals slammed 48 long balls, but only 33 came while he was in the lineup as the catcher, and Hall of Famer Johnny Bench hit 45 for the Cincinnati Reds in 1970, 38 as a catcher.... All 41 of Hundley's home runs in '96 came when he was catching.... His 41-homer season is tied with Carlos Beltrán (2006) for third on the Mets' single-season home run list behind Pete Alonso's 53 in 2019 and his 46 in 2023, while his 124 homers from 1990 to 1998 puts him in 10th place on the team's career list.

JACKIE ROBINSON NIGHT

METS 5 DODGERS 0
APRIL 15, 1997, at SHEA STADIUM

IT WAS NOT a normal Tuesday night in April at Shea Stadium... something was very different and unique. All we knew going into this game between the Mets and Dodgers is that Major League Baseball was going to celebrate the life and legacy of the great Jackie Robinson. April 15, 1997, was the 50th anniversary of one of the, if not *the* most important moment in sports history as well as American history. Jackie Robinson broke the color barrier and forever changed baseball in the process. So, on this landmark anniversary,

Dodgers — W-L 8-3 GB +0 HOME 6-3 ROAD 2-0 VS DIV. ___
VISITOR
Mets — W-L 3-9 GB 6 HOME 0-3 ROAD 3-6 VS DIV. WWWW
HOME
tied
STANDINGS

	R	O	H	8	E	LOB 11
LA	5		9			
NYM	5		9			4

WP Armando Reynosa (1-0)
LP Ismael Valdez (1-2)
SV Toby Borland (1)

UMPIRES Pulli
Davidson 2B
3B · 1B Gereman
HP
Gregg

DP/OPP 2   DEFENSE   1 E

Todd Hollinsworth   Bret Butler   Raul Mondesi
Greg Gagne   Wilton Guerrero
Todd Zeile   Ismael Valdez   Eric Karros
J. Amalfatano   Mike Piazza   M. Mota

Standings:
Bal 8-2
Bos 3
Det 3½
Tor 3½
NY 4 4
Mil 5-3
KC 1
Min 1
Cle 1½
Chi 3½
Oak 7-5
Sea 7-5
Ana 1½
Tex 1½

Los Angeles Dodgers .239

	1	2	3	4	5	6	7	8	9	10	11	AB	R	H	BI
22 Bret Butler CF .216												3	0	1	0
30 Wilton Guerrero 2b .225												4	0	2	0
43 Raul Mondesi RF .244												3	0	0	0
31 Mike Piazza C .344												3	0	0	0
23 Eric Karros 1b .286												4	0	1	0
28 Todd Hollinsworth LF .267												4	0	0	0
27 Todd Zeile 3b .162												4	0	2	0
7 Greg Gagne SS .286												4	0	2	0

59 Ismael Valdez P .000
61 Chan Ho Park P .000
5 Chip Hale PH .167
36 Scott Radinsky P .000
38 Todd Worrell P .000
46 Nelson Liliano PH .000

	1	2	3	4	5	6	7	8	9	10	11
R/ER	0/0	0/0	0/0	0/0	0/0	0/0	0/0	0/0	0/0	0/0	
H	0	1	2	2	1	1	0	1	0		
E	0	0	0	0	0	0	0	0	1		
LOB	2	1	2	2	0	1	0	1	2		

LH BENCH RH
Juan Castro
Bill Ashley
Wayne Kirby
Chip Hale
Tom Prince
SH
Nelson Liliano

Runs/game
3.33

PITCHERS	IP	R	ER	H	W	K	MISC.
1-1 4.05 Ismael Valdez (59)	5	2	0	6	1	4	
Chan Ho Park (61)	1	0	0	0	0	1	
Scott Radinsky (36)	1	3	3	4	0	0	
Todd Worrell (38)	1	0	0	0	1	1	

LH LA BULLPEN RH
Tom Candioti
Pedro Astacio
Mark Guthrie
Scott Radinsky
Darren Hall
Todd Worrell
Darren Dreifort
Chan Ho Park

ERA 2.21

MLB planned a grand ceremony to take place at Shea Stadium. The setting had perfect symmetry in honoring Jackie—though he played for the Dodgers, he played in New York City, so having the current New York National League team play the team he played for made complete sense. The other thing we knew going into the night was that President Bill Clinton would be a part of the ceremony. My fascination around presidents and the history of the American presidency was not something that hit me quite yet. I really got into it during the election of 2000. That not only made me interested in the process, but the history of those who held the office as well. So, at the time, seeing a real-life president in front of me was not something that would have excited me nearly as much as it would a few short years later.

Nineteen ninety-seven was the year the Mets unveiled their non-pinstriped, all-white jersey and matching white cap. You may not remember the all-white cap, because it did not last long. The Mets looked, as Howie Rose once described them, like "ice cream men." I don't think they wore that combination for very long, but on this night they did. Armando Reynoso made his Mets debut, and whenever I think of Armando I always think of what he wore and how he looked on this night. White jersey, white cap...as if he were about to sell me ice cream. The Mets were off to a dreadful 3–9 start as the season looked doomed even before it really got started, but the importance of this game was secondary to what awaited us. There was a different feel at Shea that night. First off, there was a very big crowd, which was unusual for a Tuesday night in April. But there was also a large security presence, including Secret Service agents who guarded the tunnel we walked through to get to our seats in the loge section.

In the top of the second inning, my dad made a huge mistake he would soon regret. Nature called and he needed to run to the bathroom real quick. Usually when my dad would go to the bathroom at Shea, he wouldn't even miss a pitch. He would get up as soon as the previous inning had ended, and by the time the following half inning was to begin he would be settled back down. On this night, going to the restroom would be a national security risk apparently. He missed the second inning, the third inning...and finally returned in the bottom of the fourth. I had assumed that it wasn't a normal bathroom visit, and look, when you have to go, you have to go. But no, he waited for multiple innings in line just to walk down our tunnel and return to this seat. On this night each person was being checked for ammunition, or anything else they might possess that would pose as a risk to the president, who wasn't even visible at this point.

The game itself turned into a pitchers' duel between Reynoso and Ismael Valdez and was still scoreless in the bottom of the fifth inning. We all knew the game would stop after that inning, and that's when the on-field ceremony would take place. Lance Johnson picked up a two-run infield single that broke the tie right before the game stopped. Baseball commissioner Bud Selig was joined on the field by President Clinton and Rachel Robinson. The commissioner immediately made the surprise announcement that the No. 42 would be retired throughout baseball. He used the Mets' Butch Huskey and Boston's Mo Vaughn as examples of guys who could keep the number for the rest of their careers, but from this day forward the No. 42 would not be handed out. This was a very cool gesture by Major League Baseball. Part of the intrigue around President Clinton was the fact he was going to have a tough time getting on the field. The president had had a tendon tear off his right kneecap a few weeks earlier and would appear on the field with the help of crutches. The whole story behind his injury is very bizarre and is probably ripe for a good conspiracy theory, but at the time I just wanted to see how he would waddle out behind home plate. President Clinton was met with mostly cheers but a handful of boos as he joined the commissioner. He made a nice speech about the importance of Jackie and his legacy in American culture. The game resumed after about 25 minutes, and the Mets would go on and cruise to a 5–0 victory over the Dodgers. It was very cool to be a part of history that night, and the evening left with me a few specific memories I'd never forget. The ugly white Mets hats, the surprise announcement of retiring 42 throughout baseball, my dad's hour-long bathroom break and the sight of a limping Bill Clinton.

KEEPING SCORE: Huskey (1995–98) and Vaughn (2002–03) were the final two of the 10 players to wear No. 42 for the Mets.... Notably, Ron Hodges (1973–83) had it the longest, and Roger McDowell wore it for the 1986 world champions.... Reynoso, acquired from the Colorado Rockies for reliever (and current Seattle Mariners general manager) Jerry DiPoto after the 1996 season, went 13–6 in two seasons with the Mets, but is remembered most for his final appearance, starting and losing the final game of the 1998 season at Atlanta, which eliminated the Mets from playoff contention (*see* "Welcome to a World of Pain," p. 59).

FIRST EVER SUBWAY SERIES GAME

METS 6 YANKEES 0

JUNE 16, 1997, at YANKEE STADIUM

MORE THAN 25 years later, I'm a bitter "get off my lawn" baseball fan who shouts into the clouds about how much I hate interleague play. This may sound nuts to those who hear me on the radio ripping the Subway Series and longing for the days when the Mets and Yankees didn't play during the regular season, but 13-year-old Evan couldn't wait for the advent of interleague play! When MLB announced their intention to experiment with this new concept for the 1997 season, I was a kid in a candy store. The thought that jumped into my head immediately was how wild it would be to see the Mets wearing their road grays at Yankee Stadium. The Mets playing the Yankees in games that counted—not some fugazi "Mayor's Trophy Game" that had lost fan interest decades before I was born—was going to be epic. Back then, the "Subway Series" was a concept that only applied in some crazy scenario where both teams were good enough to meet in the World Series. The early 1990s was not a time I could imagine that as a young Mets fan. Being in a pennant race was a foreign enough concept, let alone winning the NL pennant! So if we can't get the real thing, sure, why not a made-up concept like interleague play? As soon as the 1997 schedule was released, I couldn't wait to see the answers to the questions that were popping into my head all off-season: *When? Where?*

The *when* was June 16, 1997, a day after the Mets broke the interleague seal by losing two of three to the Red Sox at Shea in a rematch of the 1986 World Series. The *where* was Yankee Stadium in the Bronx. You know how you will routinely hear Mets fans chant "Yankees Suck!" at Citi Field even when the Mets are playing an April game against the Phillies? Well, I'm convinced the first time

Mets / Yankees scorecard

- VISITOR: Mets W-L 36-30 GB 5½ HOME 18-14 ROAD 18-16 VS DIV. 11-7
- HOME: Yankees W-L 37-29 GB 9 HOME 18-14 ROAD 19-15 VS DIV. 7-8

NL STANDINGS

	R	H	E	LOB		
NYM	6	9	2	6	DP/OPP 0	2 E
NYY	0	9	1	10		

WP Dave Mlicki 3-5
LP Andy Pettite 8-4
SV

UMPIRES: Shulock
2B
Everett 3B · 1B DeKinger
HP
Tschider

DEFENSE

- Bernard Gilkey (LF) — Lance Johnson (CF) — Carl Everett (RF)
- Luis Lopez — Carlos Baerga
- Matt Franco — 4.70 Dave Mlicki — John Olerud
- C. Rojas — Todd Hundley — M. Wilson

AL STANDINGS:
- Atl 42-25, Fla 2½, Mon 3½, NYM 5½, Phi 19
- Hou 33-35, Pitt 32-34, StL 1, Cin 5, Chi 6½
- SF 38-29, Col 2½, LA 6, SD 9
- Fla 39-27, Mon 1, NYM 3, Col 4

Batting: New York Mets — Avg 263 HR 60 H 587

Mets			1	2	3	4	5	6	7	8	9	10	11	12	13	14	15	AB	R	H	BI
1 Lance Johnson CF .296 0 13																					
23 Bernard Gilkey LF .203 6 28																					
5 John Olerud 1b .315 11 46																					
9 Todd Hundley C .294 15 44																					
42 Butch Huskey DH .292 9 34																					
3 Carl Everett RF .256 7 24																					
9 Carlos Baerga 2b .296 2 19																					
15 Matt Franco 3b .333 2 9																					
17 Luis Lopez SS .118 0 1																					

Dave Mlicki
2-5 4.70 GS 13 GR 0
IP 74.2 H 77 BB 37 SO 61

	R/ER	3/3	0/0	0/0	0/0	0/0	0/0	2/2	0/0	1/0
H	3	0	0	0	1	1	3	0	
E	0	0	0	0	0	0	0	0	1 E 1
LOB	1	0	0	6	0	1	2	0	1

LH BENCH RH
Beisel — Castillo
Morgan
Ochoa
Alfonzo
Mets bring up Hartkke — Gilbert DL
JH
Hartkke
Place Gilbert on DL
Take Johnson off DL

NYM PITCHERS	IP	R	ER	H	W	K	MISC.
2-5 4.70 Dave Mlicki (33)	9	0	0	9	2	8	37 BF

BULLPEN
LH NYM RH
Jordan — McMichael
Franco — Lidle
Kashiwada

Metsrealest Barry Manual

©1996 Bob Carpenter Communications, Inc. All Rights Reserved

I ever heard "Yankees Suck!" chants at Shea Stadium was a few weeks before the first Subway Series when the Mets were playing a three-game series against the Marlins. Mets fans were so giddy and fired up for the first incarnation of the crosstown battle that the chants started to rain down in a regular season game weeks before the first showdown. It definitely rang through Shea Stadium in the

Monday
DATE June 16, 1997   STADIUM/CAP. Yankee Stadium   ATT. 56,188
GAME # NYM67/NY467   WEATHER Clear 59°   START/FINISH 7:37, 10:21   TIME 2:44

AL STANDINGS

©Bal 45-19	DP/	OPP 1	DEFENSE 1 CS	1 E	SERIES Interleague Play
NY4 9					Subway Series 1 of 3
Tor 13½	Mark	Chad	Paul		First ever regular season
Det 16	Whitten	Curtis	O'neil		meeting.
Bos 18					Mets 300/000/201 6
©Cle 34-29		Derek	Pat		Yankees 000/000/000 0
KC 3½		Jeter	Kelly		
Mil 4½					
Chi 5	charlie	3.14	Tino		LETS ROCK!!
Min 5½	Hayes	Andy	Martinez		
⊘Sea 38-29		Pettitt			yesterday yesterday
Tex 2	W. Randolf		J.Cardenal		NYM Yankees
Ana 3½					Bos 10 GI NY48 GI NY15
Oak 11		Joe Girardi			NYM 1 Fla5 Fla6
©NY4 37-24					
Tex 1½					
Ana 3					
Tor 4½					

New York   Ave HR u
Yankees 280 80 666

# Player	1	2	3	4	5	6	7	8	9	10	11	12	13	14	15	AB	R	H	BI
2 Derek Jeter SS 266 4x30	E8	④		⑨				⑩	⑧										
14 Pat Kelly 2b 267 0x1	① 5-3	③			①														
21 Paul O'neil RF 320 11x47	② K		① 4-3		BB		⑤-4 ⑧												
45 Cecil Fielder DH 265 6x40	③ K				②														
24 Tino Martinez 1b 304 21x61	① 4-3	② 5-3	③ Y	③ 8															
13 charlie Hayes 3b 279 4x18	② 8	③ L4		BB		7-4													
22 Mack Whitten LF 278 5x20	④ 4-3		①	⑥ 4		⑧ 5-4													
28 Chad Curtis CF 229 3x5			① 5-3	② 9	② 9		FC												
25 Joe Girardi C 231 1x26				E4		③ 1-3													

	R/ER	H	E	LOB
8-3 3.14 GS14 GR 0	0/0		1 ES	

	1	2	3	4	5	6	7	8	9
R/ER	0/0	0/0	0/0	0/0	0/0	0/0	0/0	0/0	0/0
H	1	0	1	1	1	0	0	2	3
E	0	0	10	1	0	0	0		
LOB	1	0	1	1	1	1	1	2	2

IP 101.2 H95 BB37-50 G3
Andy Pettite

LH	BENCH	RH
Boggs	Sojo	
	Duncan	
SH		
Williams		
Posada		

NY4 PITCHERS	IP	R	ER	H	W	K	MISC.
8-3 3.14 Andy Pettite ⊗	7	5	5	8	2	4	1 HbP
Graem Loyld ㉗	2	1	0	1	0	0	8 BF

LH	NY4 BULLPEN	RH
Boyd		Rivera
Stannton		Nelson
Rogers		Mecir

©1996 Bob Carpenter Communications, Inc. All Rights Reserved

days leading up to the Subway Series as Red Sox fans joined in on the chorus. There was no doubting the city was fired up.

So here we are: June 16, 1997. I remember walking into Yankee Stadium on this Monday night with butterflies I had never before had for a baseball game. Remember at this time I had never seen the Mets play a meaningful game, let alone a postseason game. This felt like the World Series—before the game even started the crowd was chanting back and forth: "Let's go, Yankees!" *clap-clap-clap* vs. "Let's go, Mets!" This was an atmosphere I'd never seen before. The other thing that shouldn't be forgotten is that the Mets for the first time in my lifetime were actually a competitive team. They had been defying expectation with a 36–30 record, doing so despite the fact that two guys who had career seasons the year before, Lance Johnson (227 hits) and Bernard Gilkey (.317 batting average, 30 home runs, and 117 RBIs) were not producing anywhere close to their 1996 totals. So here are the overachieving New York Mets visiting not only the crosstown team who was more popular in the city, but the defending world-champion New York Yankees. My biggest memories from this game were the top of the first and the bottom of the ninth innings. The Mets portion of the crowd erupted in the first when Gilkey hit a double off Yankees starter Andy Pettitte. (I wish I somehow noted on my scorecard that the Gilkey double was a check-swing bloop.) John Olerud drove him in with another double, Butch Huskey followed with an RBI single, and then Todd Hundley was credited with a steal of home, eluding catcher Joe Girardi's tag after Huskey was caught off first base. I remember fearing that when Derek Jeter led off the bottom of the first with a clean single, the euphoria of an early 3–0 lead would probably evaporate really quickly. I had no idea that Dave Mlicki would go on to throw the game of his life, which was capped off by freezing Jeter with a nasty curve to end the game. By the time Mlicki was toeing the rubber in the ninth, most Yankees fans had abandoned ship, so Yankee Stadium had become Shea Stadium Bronx. The memory of that sound all these years later is still so damn beautiful. The back-and-forth chant battle had been replaced by a universal "Let's go, Mets!" chant. After Mlicki K'd Jeter, I stood up from my seat and let the moment soak in. The little brother Mets had kicked the big brother's ass in their own building. Little did I know that it would be all downhill from there.

KEEPING SCORE: The Subway Series went off the rails for the Mets starting with the rest of the three-game set, a routine 6–3 loss the next night and an excruciating 10-inning 3–2 loss on Wednesday afternoon (*see* "The Yankees Win the First Subway Series" below)…. For the record, the first Met to bat in a regular season interleague game was Lance Johnson, who grounded out to Jeter at short preceding Gilkey's double…. Pitching hero Dave Mlicki finished 1997 with a record of 8–12 and was sent to the Dodgers early the following year in a deal for Hideo Nomo.

THE YANKEES WIN THE FIRST SUBWAY SERIES

YANKEES 3 METS 2 (10 INNINGS)
JUNE 18, 1997, at YANKEE STADIUM

MY MOM MADE a huge mistake with my sister and me…actually it wasn't a mistake, it was a blessing for us. She was very honest about what kind of student she was and would tell us stories about her days in grade school and high school. Both my sister, Stacy, and I knew that my mom didn't take school that seriously as a teenager. She was known to skip school back in her day, which she told us about and my grandmother confirmed. You can't tell your kids that! You know exactly how we'd respond upon hearing those stories…it would open us up to doing exactly what Mom taught us. As a mother she had learned the error of her ways and stressed the importance of school, and overall I think we did just fine. Stacy became a successful dietitian and completed her degree at the University of Delaware. I, on the other hand, had decent grades, but schooling isn't what got me where I am today. Skipping school for the most important sports games is what contributed a hell of a lot more! So thank you, Mom,

A baseball scorecard filled in by hand. Key details visible:

- VISITOR: Mets — W-L 37-31, GB 6½, HOME 18-14, ROAD 19-17, VS DIV. 11-7
- HOME: Yankees — W-L 38-30, GB 9, HOME 19-15, ROAD 19-15, VS DIV. 7-8
- NYM: R 2, H 3, E 1, LOB 4
- NYY: .3, 8, 1, 8
- WP Mike Stannton 3-0
- LP Greg McMichael 3-6
- UMPIRES: Tschida 2B, Dekinger 3B • 1B Everett, HP Shulock

DEFENSE: Bernard Gilkey, Lance Johnson, Carl Everett, Luis Lopez, Carlos Baerga, Matt Franco, Rick Reed (260), John Olerud, C. Rojas, M. Wilson, Todd Hundley

NL STANDINGS: Atl 44-25, Fla 2½, Mon 4½, NYM 6½, Phi 2l; Hou 34-36, Pitt 33-35, StL 2, Cin 5½, Chi 5½; SF 39-29, Co 3½, LA 6, SD 10; Fla 44-27, Mon 2, NYM 4, Col 5½

New York Mets batting lineup:
- 1 Lance Johnson CF 290 0 613 — AB 4, R 0, H 0, BI 0
- 23 Bernard Gilkey LF 210 7 31 — AB 3, R 0, H 0, BI 0
- 5 Jon Olerud 1b 316 11 49 — AB 3, R 1, H 1, BI 0
- 9 Todd Hundley C 285 15 44 — AB 4, R 0, H 0, BI 0
- 8 Carlos Baerga 2b 291 2 19 — AB 4, R 0, H 0, BI 1
- 42 Butch Huskey DH 291 9 35 — AB 4, R 0, H 0, BI 0
- 15 Matt Franco 3b 343 2 14 / 29 Steve Beiser PR / 3 Edgardo Alfonzo 3b 303 4 24 — AB 3, R 1, H 1, BI 0 / 0 0 0 0
- 3 Carl Everett RF 246 7 24 — AB 4, R 0, H 1, BI 0
- 17 Luis Lopez SS 182 0 cl — AB 3, R 0, H 0, BI 0

Rick Reed: 4.4 2.60 65 13 GR2
R/ER 0/0 0/0 0/0 0/0 0/0 0/0 1/1 1/1 0/0 0/0
H 0 0 0 0 0 0 1 1 0 1
E 0 0 0 0 0 0 0 0 0 16Y
LOB 0 0 0 1 0 1 6 0 0 2

BENCH: LH Brisser, Castillo, Ochoa, Alfonzo; RH; SH Hartke
Mets send down ZF Kevin Morgan.

PITCHERS table (NYM):
Pitcher	IP	R	ER	H	W	K	MISC.
Rick Reed (35)	6	2	2	5	2	3	2 HR
Juan Acevedo (39)	2⅔	0	0	1	2	3	
Greg McMichael (9k)	1	1	1	1	1	0	
Jon Franco (31)	0	0	0	1	0	0	

BULLPEN: LH — Franco, Jordan, Kashiwala; RH — McMichael, Acevedo, Cible
Mets bring up RHP Juan Acevedo.

for realizing that taking my Regents exams wasn't nearly as important as being in the South Bronx on June 18, 1997.

Everything was on the line that Wednesday afternoon: the Mets had shockingly taken the opener of the first-ever Subway Series behind a sterling performance by Dave Mlicki (as detailed in the previous chapter). They lost Game 2 as Armando Reynoso was chased

DATE Wednesday June 18, 1997 STADIUM/CAP. Yankee Stadium ATT. 56,278

GAME # NYM69/NYY69 WEATHER Rain 74° START/FINISH 1:07, 4:39 TIME 3:32

AL STANDINGS

Bal 46-20
NYY 9
Tor 14½
Bos 17
Det 17

Cle 35-30
KC 3½
Mil 3½
Chi 5
Min 5½

Sea 38-30
Tex 3½
Ana 3½
Oak 10

NYY 38-30
Tex 1
Ana 3½
KC 5

DP/OPP 1   DEFENSE   1 E

Mark Whitten   Chad Curtis   Paul O'neil

Derek Jeter   Luis Sojo

Wade Boggs   2-21 David (Cone)   Tino Martinez

W. Randolf   J. Cardenal

Joe Girardi

SERIES Interleague Play
Subway Series 3 of 3
Cone pitches 6 no hit innings.

Mets   000/000/100/0 2
Yankees 001/100/000/1 3

HR in 5th doesn't count!!
Umpires say foulball.

yesterday NYM NYM3/NYY4 Acevedo makes Mets leave. yesterday NYM NYM3/NYY6

New York Yankees .250 68 680

	Ave	HR	H	1	2	3	4	5	6	7	8	9	10	11	AB 12	R 13	H 14	BI 15
2 Derek Jeter SS .271 4 132															5	0	2	0
19 Luis Sojo 2b .307 1 12															5	0	1	0
21 Paul O'neil RF .323 11 47															3	1	0	0
45 Cecil Fielder DH .261 6 40 / 14 Pat Kelly PR .263 0 1															5	1	2	1
24 Tino Martinez 1b .294 21 61															5	0	1	1
12 Wade Boggs 3b .257 2 14															4	0	1	0
22 Mark Whitten LF .273 5 30															2	0	0	0
26 Chad Curtis CF .230 3 16															3	1	1	1
25 Joe Girardi C .243 1 02															3	0	0	0

David Cone
7-3 2.21 GS 15 GE 0
IP 106 H 84 BB 44 SO 120

	1	2	3	4	5	6	7	8	9	10	11
R/ER	0/0	0/0	1/1	1/1	0/0	0/0	0/0	0/0	0/0	1/1	
H	0	0	2	2	1	0	1	0	0	2	
E	0	1 5 5	0	0	0	0	0	0	0	0	
LOB	0	0	1	2	2	0	2	0	1	2	

LH BENCH RH
Pos   Hayes
                   Duncan
                   Kelly
SH
Posada

NYY PITCHERS	IP	R	ER	H	W	K	MISC.	LH NYY BULLPEN RH
7-3 2.21 David Cone (26)	8	2	2	2	2	11	18K 1WP	Rogers Mesir
Mike Stannton (29)	2	0	0	1	2	0		Stannton Nelson
								Loyld Rivera

©1996 Bob Carpenter Communications, Inc. All Rights Reserved

in the second inning, and other than a Bernard Gilkey home run, they couldn't figure out David Wells. So bragging rights would come down to one game, and we would be gifted with an excellent pitching matchup on paper. David Cone, who had become a fan favorite of the Mets a few years earlier, was on the mound for the Yankees. Just five years earlier, the Mets had dealt David to Toronto in a deal for Ryan Thompson and Jeff Kent. Rick Reed had been pitching well in the early going of 1997 with a 2.60 ERA coming into the game. After all the excitement of winning the opener, the thought of losing this series to the defending champions made me sick to my stomach. While the deep-seated hatred for the Yankees was still growing at the time, this would be a very tough pill to swallow. Chad Curtis and Cecil Fielder would hit solo home runs against Reed to stake the Yankees to a 2–0 lead. In the days before instant-replay review, Joe Girardi hit a ball right down the right-field line that was initially ruled a home run. After a long conference the umpires reversed the call, ruling it a foul ball, which caused major pain to my scorebook! But it was well worth the scorebook issue, because the way the Mets couldn't figure out David Cone, 3–0 would have felt like 10–0. Our seats that afternoon where in the upper deck along the third-base line at the old Yankee Stadium. So when the Mets trailed 2–1 in the eighth with a runner on third base I stared as the base runner danced toward home, and shockingly enough the next thing I noticed was a large reaction from the Mets contingent. The home-plate umpire pointed at David Cone and called a balk. Steve Bieser, a rookie outfielder pinch-running for Matt Franco, would become a name recognized by Mets fans because he somehow coaxed a game-tying balk out of Cone. This felt like a World Series game…the crowd was electric all afternoon and hit a fevered pitch when Bieser touched home plate to tie the game.

My next and lasting memory from this game was the conclusion. In the bottom of the 10th inning, after Greg McMichael allowed a base hit to Cecil Fielder, the Yankees were set up with runners at first and third with one out and Tino Martinez coming to the plate. Bobby Valentine did something he rarely did, but showing the importance of this game, he summoned closer John Franco to enter the game in the middle of an inning. Franco was the native New Yorker who had not yet pitched in this Subway Series. Mlicki had pitched all nine innings in Game 1 and Franco wasn't used in a loss in Game 2. So here was the New Yorker entering the all–New York series for the first time in the toughest of spots. Franco either needed a K or a double play if he wanted to extend this game. He got ahead of Tino 1–2 before the heartbreaking climax. Tino hit the ball to left field, which was right underneath where I was sitting. We had one blind spot, which was down the left-field line. As the ball flew through the air, I begged the baseball gods for a foul ball and a reprieve. It felt like that ball hung in the air for hours before I heard a large roar from the Yankees fans. I never saw the ball land, but I knew the outcome. The Yankees had walked off the Mets to officially win the first-ever Subway Series. As we trudged our way out of Yankee Stadium and went down the endless runway, all I could hear was loud "Let's go, Yankees!" chants. This was my first real taste of Mets vs. Yankees, and it would be a good lesson for the future. Get used to this, kid, you'll essentially never beat them bastards.

KEEPING SCORE: The Yankees hold an 80–62 edge in regular season games, not to mention a 4–1 edge in World Series games…. The Amazins have managed to win the season series just four times in 27 seasons with 12 splits…. Non-Yankees interleague games have gone better for the Mets as they have gone 190–173 (.523) in those contests…. Bieser, signed as a six-year minor league free-agent by the Mets the previous off-season, appeared in only four more games with the Mets before being sent to the minors by the end of June. He played one more major league season for the Pittsburgh Pirates and is now the head baseball coach at the University of Missouri.

BUY THOSE DAMN PLAYOFF TICKETS!

METS 9 EXPOS 6 (11 INNINGS)

SEPTEMBER 13, 1997, at SHEA STADIUM

WHAT CONSTITUTES being in a pennant race? Well, when you are 14 years old and don't remember any winning seasons in your lifetime, the threshold of what actually is a real race is insanely low. At this moment in my fandom, though I was super desperate for any kind of postseason relevance, I think I was wise enough to know that the 1997 Mets were not a great team. They were not really capable of winning anything. But I had been walking long miles in the Sahara Desert desperate for a sip of water, so waking up and seeing the Mets five games out of a playoff spot felt as if I were watching a legit title contender.

As a full-season-ticket holder, one of the great benefits is that you get access to any potential home playoff games. As I have learned with my own personal experience, a team is desperate to send you a playoff bill, even if the odds of making the playoffs are very low. If a team is within a realistic mathematic probability of making the playoffs, they will most definitely send out that huge playoff bill. My old radio partner, Joe Benigno, told me the story many times about walking out of Giants Stadium after the Jets shockingly won the division in 2002. He would share with me that, while many Jets fans were pumped about the win over the Packers (and the help the Jets got when the Dolphins beat the Patriots), which secured the Jets the AFC East championship, many of them were also depressed because they did not send in their playoff bill when the Jets sent it. They figured it was a waste of money to pay for a playoff game that they thought had no chance of happening. So why let the Jets hold their money?

Expos — W-L 74-72 — GB 17 — HOME 43-32 — ROAD 31-40 — VS DIV. 16-23

VISITOR

Mets — W-L 79-67 — GB 12 — HOME 45-29 — ROAD 34-38 — VS DIV. 21-13

HOME

AL STANDINGS

Five years earlier, my dad had the same thought. A few days before this game, my dad had received a letter, one I had never seen in my life. A letter that pumped me up and made me dream the glorious dream. "Dear Joel Roberts," it began, "here is your 1997 playoff bill." The idea that that the Mets were sending out a bill for the Division Series, NLCS, and dare I say, the World Series was psychedelic. At the bottom of the letter they did include a friendly warning that "not paying this bill makes your account subject to not having access to playoff tickets." For a 14-year-old like myself, that was a threat I could not take lightly. My dad, on the other hand, thought the threat was BS and secretly didn't really think it would matter anyway, because he knew what I didn't want to admit—the 1997 Mets were not a playoff team.

The Mets' playoff hopes remained very unlikely as we drove up to Shea Stadium on this late Saturday afternoon. There were only 15 games to go in the season, and the night before the Mets had lost a brutal 15-inning marathon, 3–2, that essentially ended when Rondell White hit a home run in the top of that inning. The next night, things didn't start very well, either. Mike Lansing hit a first-inning, two-run homer, and that man Rondell White was at it again, adding a solo shot to make it 3–0 Expos early. What I didn't remember until looking back at this scorecard was how good Dustin Hermanson was early in this game. He took a no-hitter into the sixth inning and was allowed to start the ninth looking to put the finishing touches on a complete-game shutout. This game was over, and so were the Mets playoff hopes as they trailed 6–0. What followed was the wildest, craziest, and most awe-inspiring few innings of my young Mets fanhood.

Hermanson allowed two singles while also getting two outs. So imagine this: the Mets are down by six runs and down to their final out with runners on second and third. They would need three consecutive baserunners from that moment on just to get the tying run to the plate. Roberto Petagine (the epitome of a "Quadruple A" player) picked up a two-run single to make it 6–2. Rey Ordóñez and Matt Franco both singled, and the stage was set: 6–2 and the bases loaded with two outs for Carl Everett. The Expos closer, Ugueth Urbina, finally entered the game and was locked into a battle with Carl before Everett hit a 3–2 pitch into the right-center-field night. The Mets had miraculously tied the game, and you know what I was screaming to my father: "We gotta get those tickets, babbyyyyyyy, wow!" Well, the Mets still needed to close the deal and win this game. Remember a night earlier, they lost a 15-inning game, in which they also staged a comeback, to even force extra innings. Though that rally was nothing like this one. I mean, how often is a team down six runs while down to their final out and final strike numerous times before coming back on a game-tying grand slam!? John

Franco danced through a bit of trouble in the 10th and 11th, before Bernard Gilkey sent us home happy and stunned by hitting a walk-off, three-run home run off Mike Thurman. The Mets had completed an insane comeback that I figured would 1,000 percent convince my dad to send that playoff bill in. Even he had to be caught up in the excitement and told me as much. Unfortunately, the Mets could not catch the Marlins and finished short in their pursuit of a playoff spot. I apologized to my dad after the season for even insisting on sending in the bill. "Don't worry Ev...I never did." He knew what I never wanted to admit. Despite this enthralling win, the Mets were not making the playoffs. Later on, I got Jason Isringhuasen to autograph the scorecard, which was a curious choice on my part. Izzy started this game for the Mets but was responsible for them even being down to begin with. Teenage me was excited and even wrote "Holy Macrel" next to his signature. Yes, *Macrel*. Wasn't I adorable?

KEEPING SCORE: The Florida Marlins, in only their fourth season, not only won the wild-card, they went on to win the World Series as well.... The Mets did beat the Marlins three out of four in late September in Miami to temporarily stave off elimination and keep the Marlins from clinching a playoff spot.... Everett, a former first-round pick of the Yankees who spent three seasons with the Mets from 1995 to '97, was traded after the season to the Houston Astros for reliever John Hudek.

MARATHON OPENING DAY WIN

METS 1 PHILLIES 0 (14 INNINGS)

MARCH 31, 1998, at SHEA STADIUM

I WAS SO hyped going into the 1998 season! The Mets had given me my first taste of a pennant race in 1997 as they remained relevant into September and won 88 games, far and away the largest number of my short Mets fandom life. So I really thought they could take things to another level in 1998, especially considering they went out and made some big off-season deals. The Mets fell short the previous season mainly because the Florida Marlins existed. But after winning it all, Wayne Huizenga decided to sell off the entire team. Despite sharing the NL East, the Mets took advantage of the fire sale by acquiring lefty reliever Dennis Cook and Jersey guy Al Leiter. I remember Al thoroughly dominating the Mets late in the 1997 pennant race, so my biased eyes were even more excited about bringing him in since the Mets wouldn't have to face him again.

Opening Day 1998 was one of the most memorable openers in my lifetime. Why, you ask? Well, let's start with the weather. I wrote in my scorecard that it was 85 degrees, but all these years later I think I shortchanged the actual temperature. Because in my memory it was more like a sweaty 95. It was also the first regular season game the Mets ever played in March. They were scheduled to open the 1995 season on March 31, but due to the neverending work stoppage the opener was pushed back a month. My dad was ecstatic about the weather because he's always been more of a warm weather guy, but to me Opening Day is about a brisk chill in the air. That's part of what makes Opening Day special. I still feel that way about the playoffs as well all these years later. I don't want an unseasonably warm October day because then it won't feel like the actual playoffs. This day was way too warm to be Opening Day, but hey, I got to miss school and it was baseball for the most anticipated season of my life—so let's go!

Bobby Jones went toe to toe with Phillies ace Curt Schilling, and we had a classic pitchers' duel on our hands. Or maybe it was the inept Mets offense that was the real problem. We were waiting on the return of Todd Hundley, who was hurt, and had to deal with the catching tandem of Tim Spehr (who got the Opening Day nod, batting seventh) and backup Alberto Castillo (who couldn't hit a lick—more on him later). But even without the catching issue, the Mets' Opening Day lineup wasn't exactly reminding anyone of Murderers' Row. Carlos Baerga batted fifth and Bernard Gilkey third, both coming off of bad offensive seasons. Luckily, Jones navigated through six innings before handing it over to the pen. Not only did the Mets not hit in this game, they wouldn't even threaten, but that just added to the drama of this "pitchers' duel." There were two former Mets returning to Shea on this day. You had the hated Gregg Jefferies, who got a resounding boo as he strolled to the plate and had a 1-for-5 day. Then there was the beloved Rico Brogna, who had been traded to Philly after the '96 season. I loved Rico and hated the return they got for him (two ineffective relievers, Rico Jordan and Toby Borland), but it did make room for John Olerud, who was a clear upgrade at first base.

This game would...not...*end*. Every single arm who came into this game found a way to pitch a scoreless inning, including the much-maligned Mel Rojas, who somehow threw two scoreless frames. The defense was awesome in this game, especially Rey Ordóñez, who made an outstanding play on Mark Lewis in the seventh inning (hence my "GP" label on the ground-out). The sun started to set at Shea, and I began to wonder if anyone would ever score. Finally, in the bottom of the 14th, the Mets had the best opportunity of the game. They had the bases loaded with one out when Olerud came to the plate. Though John had a quiet game, he and Edgardo Alfonzo were probably the most trusted bats you could have up in a situation like that. When Olerud popped up to the third baseman, I truly wondered if this game would ever end. Alberto Castillo was the last man on the bench, and so Bobby Valentine had no other choice with two outs and reliever Turk Wendell due up. He had to send up his backup catcher, who couldn't hit a lick (just .203 with seven RBIs in 59 at-bats in 1997). I was now convinced we were going to the 15th inning scoreless, which would mean my scorebook would only have one more inning left before the dreaded "turn the page" option. This final play I can still see in my mind all these years later. Alberto was very late on a Ricky Bottalico pitch and lined a ball right over first base down the right-field line. The Mets won the game, and the least likely bat was the hero. It took over 4½ hours, but the Mets were 1–0 and put the finishing touches on an Opening Day I would remember for decades.

KEEPING SCORE: Castillo ended up batting .205 in 1998 with two homers and seven RBIs in 83 at-bats in his fourth and final season with the Mets in 1998. He ended up playing 12 major league seasons for a total of eight teams (including both the Mets and Yankees) between 1995 and 2007.... Mike Piazza would take over as catcher after being acquired from the Marlins in late May with Hundley moving to left field.... It was Jones's third Opening Day start in four seasons since 1995. The only one he missed was in 1997, the only year he made the All-Star team (Pete Harnisch got the nod that season).

"I CAN'T BELIEVE MIKE PIAZZA IS A MET"

METS 3 BREWERS 0
MAY 23, 1998, at SHEA STADIUM

THE METS have made many acquisitions over the years, but for those of us who grew up learning about and watching baseball in the mid-1990s, nothing may ever match the shock and euphoria of finding out the Mets traded for Mike Piazza. After Darryl Strawberry left as a free agent, Keith Hernandez and Gary Carter aged and eventually departed, and Doc Gooden battled his demons before being exiled by the Mets, who was our hero? Bobby Bonilla? Bobby Bo was the guy who told us he'd show us the Bronx. No one could wipe this smile off his face, and he was a large disappointment as a big-ticket free agent signing. The closest hero we had was the homegrown Todd Hundley. Todd had the good looks, the charm, and had a historic season on his résumé after breaking the single-season home run record for catchers in 1996. But the truth was Todd was good, but he wasn't great. He was *our* guy, but around baseball he was considered a solid player, nothing more. Plus, after his record breaking

1996 season, he wasn't able to build on it, as he battled injury and wasn't nearly as productive in 1997. Going into 1998 the Mets were missing something. They had overachieved in 1997 when they won 88 games, but with Hundley on the DL to start the '98 campaign they lacked two things—offensive firepower and a star attraction. Was there anyone out there who would fill that hole in one fell swoop?

I was playing basketball at the old No. 6 school in Woodmere on Long Island when the boom box that was blaring *Mike and the*

Mad Dog revealed to us the news that Mike Piazza was being traded to the Mets. I dropped the basketball and sprinted the three blocks home so I could call my dad at work and tell him the shocking news. If only this news had broke in the 2010s, life would've been so much simpler. I'd read a tweet on my phone, calmly text my dad, and then go back to bricking free throws. But in 1998 as a 14-year-old, my only option was to run as fast as I could back home. "Dad, you aren't going to believe it...Mike Piazza is a Met." Even before Twitter, baseball trade rumors existed. Between WFAN and the local tabloids, most trades didn't come out of nowhere; we would usually get a hint of some smoke before the fire started burning. But this one was freakin' shocking! Sure, Mike and Chris had pushed the Mets to get involved in the Piazza sweepstakes, but just because they suggested it, didn't mean I thought the Mets would push Todd Hundley to the curb and trade a huge haul of prospects (outfielder Preston Wilson and pitchers Geoff Goetz and Ed Yarnall) to the Florida Marlins for the free agent to be. (Piazza had been a Marlin for only a week after being acquired from the Los Angeles Dodgers along with Todd Zeile for a package including Gary Sheffield, Charles Johnson, and... Bobby Bonilla.) Needless to say, I was beyond ecstatic as this was the first time in my short sports lifetime that my team made such a high-level, franchise-changing, blockbuster deal. I couldn't believe it...Mike Piazza was a Met.

Both my dad and I were euphoric. But he reminded me that the upcoming Saturday afternoon game against the Brewers would be a game he could not attend. The deal went down on a Friday, and it was unrealistic to think Mike would show up that night at Shea Stadium, as cool as that would be, so his likely debut would be the following day. This was the height of being spoiled by going to almost every single Mets home game with my dad. So not going to a game was stunning news, but there was no way I could miss this game. I begged and pleaded and somehow convinced my parents to allow me as a 14-year-old to go with a friend from school. I mean, that was a special occasion—Mike Piazza was a Met! I had to see that debut live and in person.

DATE May 23, 1998 (Saturday) STADIUM/CAP. Shea Stadium ATT. 32,908

GAME # Mil 47 NYM 45 WEATHER Sunny 69° START/FINISH 4:11 / 6:40 TIME 2:29

NL STANDINGS

SERIES 2 of 3 — Season — Series 3-1 NYM

Brewers	000	000	000	0
Mets	000	111	00X	3

Mike Piazza Makes Mets Debut.

New York Mets	Ave	HR	H	1	2	3	4	5	6	7	8	9	10	11	AB	R	H	BI
56 Brian McRae CF	.248	3													4	0	1	0
15 Matt Franco 3b	.269														4	1	0	0
31 Mike Piazza C	.281														4	0	1	1
5 John Olerud 1b	.345														3	1	2	0
8 Carlos Baerga 2b	.261														4	1	2	0
42 Butch Huskey RF	.247														4	0	1	1
23 Bernard Gilkey LF	.235														4	0	2	1
10 Ray Ordonez SS	.224														3	0	0	0
22 Al Leiter P	.125														3	0	2	0

		PITCHERS	IP	R	ER	H	W	K	MISC.
	NYM	Al Leiter (22)	9	0	0	4	1	7	

©1996 Bob Carpenter Communications, Inc. All Rights Reserved

Reading my scorecard from this game reminds me that this was the period of tiny writing. I mean, I'm a tiny writer to begin with but, boy, did I make these names so damn small in the scorebook. If you squint your eyes you can see that Bernard Gilkey, two years removed from his career season, was batting seventh and sporting his pathetic .235 average. I have three lasting memories from this game: the dominance of Al Leiter (a six-hit shutout with seven strikeouts and only one walk), who was authoring a tremendous first season as a Met; the loud ovation Mike got upon being introduced; and his fifth-inning double off Jeff Juden, a screaming line drive that picked up steam as it split the outfielders in right-center to score Matt Franco, giving the Mets a 2–0 lead. When I thought of Mike Piazza the hitter from afar, I would think of line drives off the bat like that. I walked around for months—actually, if I'm being honest, I walked around for *years*—saying the phrase, "I can't believe Mike Piazza is a Met." That afternoon in Flushing was where it all began!

KEEPING SCORE: The Mets were 23–20 at the time of the trade using five different starting catchers—Tim Spehr, Alberto Castillo, Jim Tatum, Todd Pratt, and Rick Wilkins.... Preston Wilson, the stepson of Mets favorite Mookie Wilson, had made his major league debut for the Mets two weeks earlier. Leading off and playing left field, he went 3-for-4 with an RBI in a win against the Cardinals. Wilson had a few good years for the Marlins before moving on to the Rockies, Nationals, Astros, and Cardinals.... Florida ended up trading Yarnall to the Yankees in 1999 for third baseman Mike Lowell, who helped them beat the Yanks in the 2003 World Series.... Goetz never advanced past Double A ball.

THE BEGINNING OF A COLLAPSE

EXPOS 3 METS 0
SEPTEMBER 23, 1998, at SHEA STADIUM

WHILE THE 1997 Mets season gave me the false hope of a pennant race, the 1998 season was a legit, full-blown, edge-of-your-seat battle for the National League wild-card. This was the first one of my young baseball life, and it featured all the ups and downs of a

Expos W-L 63-94 GB 38½ HOME 39-42 ROAD 24-52 VS DIV. 25-23
VISITOR Mets W-L 88-70 GB 14 HOME 47-33 ROAD 41-37 VS DIV. 32-22
HOME

Mtl	R 3	H 7	E 1	LOB 4	DP/OPP 0
NYM	0	3	1	8	

WP Carl Pavano 6-8
LP Bobby Jones 9-9
SV Ugueth Urbina 34

UMPIRES
Rieker
2B
Layne 3B • 1B Wendlestedt
HP
Kellogg

DEFENSE

R/ER 0|0 2|2 0|0 0|0 0|0 6|0 0|0 0|0 1|1
H 0 4 0 0 0 1 0 0 2
E 0 0 0 166 0 0 0 0 0
LOB 1 2 0 0 0 0 0 0 1

PITCHERS	IP	R	ER	H	W	K	MISC.
Carl Pavano (45)	6+	0	0	3	2	1	2 BF
Tim Young (43)	0	0	0	0	1	0	1 BF
Mike Mahome (57)	1⅓	0	0	0	0	2	5 BF
Rick DeHart (33)	⅔	0	0	0	0	0	1 BF
Anthony Telford (52)	⅓	0	0	0	0	1	2 BF 1 wP
Ugueth Urbina (41)	1	0	0	0	0	1	11-23

©1996 Bob Carpenter Communications, Inc. All Rights Reserved

regular race for a playoff spot. Most of the season it was a clear, two-team battle between the Mets and the Chicago Cubs. The San Francisco Giants would soon enter the fray, but the Cubs were the No. 1 focus. In the days before the MLB.TV package and the ability to watch any game, any time you want, being in a race with the Cubs was beneficial because at the time their games would be shown on WGN. WGN was a national superstation that I had access to, so for

DATE September 23, 1998 (Wednesday) STADIUM/CAP. Shea Stadium ATT. 29,728

GAME # MH 158 NYM 159 WEATHER Clear 64° START/FINISH 7:40 / 10:40 TIME 300

NL STANDINGS

		AB	R	H	BI
New York Mets	Ave .260 HR 136 H 1896				

SERIES 2 of 2
Season Series 7-4 MTL
Mets play final REGULAR Season home game of the year.

Expos 020/000/001 3
Mets 000/000/000 0

	1	2	3	4	5	6	7	8	9	10	11	12	13	14	15
R/ER	0|0	0|0	0|0	0|0	0|0	0|0	0|0	0|0	0|0						
H	0	0	1	1	0	0	0	0	0						
E	0	0	0	0	0	0	0	1|5	0						
LOB	1	0	1	1	0	0	3	2	0						

	PITCHERS	IP	R	ER	H	W	K	MISC.
Bobby Jones (35)		7	2	2	5	1	3	24BF 1HR
Turk Wendell (99)		2	1	1	2	1	2	9BF

©1996 Bob Carpenter Communications, Inc. All Rights Reserved

most of the summer I would watch Chip Caray and Steve Stone root their team on in the midst of a race. Most of the focus in 1998 wasn't necessarily on the Cubs' chase of a wild-card spot but the epic home run pace that Sammy Sosa was on. What was also cool about battling the Cubs was the fact that most of their games were played in the afternoon, so it wasn't exclusively scoreboard watching at Shea. Following the race for a playoff spot featured a lot of watching the

Cubs at home before going to the ballpark. The 1998 season made me absolutely hate Caray and Stone. No offense to them, because they were just doing their jobs, but there were no more obnoxious hometown shills than these two. I understand they certainly weren't broadcasting for a 15-year-old New Yorker's enjoyment, but their constant begging for big hits when the Cubs were up, or pleading for a big double play when closer Rod Beck would get into trouble was nauseating. On this particular Wednesday afternoon, I was glued to the TV before my dad and I would depart for Big Shea.

New York and Chicago were tied for the wild-card lead entering action, and the days on the calendar were dwindling. The Mets were about to play their final home game of the regular season before they went down to Atlanta to wrap up the 162-game slate. The Mets were sitting at 88–70, as were the Cubs, who were playing a road game in Milwaukee on this particular afternoon. Unfortunately, things were not going our way as the Cubs had jumped out to a 7–0 lead over the new National League combatant. Sammy Sosa had continued his torrid season by hitting two home runs in the game, which were his 64th and 65th of the season. It seemed to be a *fait accompli* that the Mets would go into the final home game needing a win to keep pace. Then all of a sudden, something magical started to happen. The Brewers cut into the seven-run deficit by scoring three runs in the seventh, one run in the eighth, and then with the bases loaded and two outs in the ninth, Geoff Jenkins came to the plate. Beck got Jenkins to hit a fly ball to left field to essentially end the game, but then we witnessed Luis Castillo (*see* "The Luis Castillo Game," p. 248) on steroids. The left fielder, Brant Brown, proceeded to drop the ball. All three runs scored and the Brewers had insanely walked the Cubs off. I jumped up and down and then ran through my old house in Woodmere screaming for joy. I'm not joking...to this point in my life, there was no Mets game that gave me as much joy and hope as watching Brant Brown drop that fly ball and complete an epic collapse by the Chicago Cubs. The Mets were now a half-game up, and with a win in a few hours would have a full game lead heading to Atlanta.

I walked into Shea Stadium that night with confidence and a swagger. The Mets had lost the night before, but they were by no means playing bad baseball and showed no signs of a collapse. The pitching matchup for the home finale was Bobby Jones for the Mets and Carl Pavano for the Expos. Naïve Evan had a confidence that tonight would not be not my last time at Shea that season despite the home regular season schedule concluding that night. I figured I'd be back for my first NLDS...but early on things didn't feel right. Bobby Jones gave up a solo home run to Bob Henley in the second inning and then an RBI double to the opposing pitcher, Carl Pavano. The Mets offense went completely limp and couldn't figure out Pavano, a rookie who entered the game with a record of 5–8. They finally staged what appeared to be a game-turning rally in the seventh when they loaded the bases with no one out. Former Met and all-around terrible pitcher Mike Maddux came into the game and somehow escaped the jam by retiring Matt Franco on an infield popup, then striking out Todd Hundley and Luis Lopez. The Mets couldn't hit Mike Freakin' Maddux?! The bats never woke up and the Mets lost the game to the Expos to close out the home campaign. As I walked out of Shea that night my confidence took a hit, but I wasn't completely down yet. They were still tied for the wild-card spot and had everything right in front of them. The Cubs were the ones who should be done, *they* looked like the team collapsing! Little did I know what was about to hit me. The collapse of the 1998 Mets was on.

KEEPING SCORE: In his next start on the final day of the season, Pavano allowed Mark McGwire's 70th home run of the year. Sosa finished with 66.... The Expos had acquired Pavano the previous winter when they traded future Hall of Famer Pedro Martinez to the Boston Red Sox.... Brant Brown would be traded four times over the next two seasons and finished his major league career back with the Cubs in 2000.... He is now the hitting coach for the Miami Marlins.

THE BEGINNING OF THE "HOUSE OF HORRORS"

BRAVES 6 METS 5

SEPTEMBER 25, 1998, at TURNER FIELD, ATLANTA

TURNER FIELD would become known as the House of Horrors for us as Mets fans, but back in 1998 it was just the site of the premier team in baseball. The Atlanta Braves had cruised to their fourth straight NL East title and seventh straight division title overall. They had not yet morphed into this hated devil-like creature that stood in our way of team success quite yet. Believe it or not, in 1997 when the Mets stunningly won 88 games, they actually beat the Braves seven out of 12 times during the regular season. While the Braves had won six of nine against the Mets to this point, they were simply an elite team, not a blood rival quite yet. The final weekend of the regular season in 1998 would be the beginning of my deep-seated hatred for the Atlanta Braves that continues to this day.

While the Mets went into the weekend showdown with Atlanta to close the regular season tied for the wild-card spot with the Cubs, the Braves had long ago wrapped up the division and were poised to finish with the best record in the National League. They stood at 103–56 and essentially had nothing to gain, while the Mets had the world to play for. One day earlier, the Mets had blown a golden opportunity to take command of the wild-card lead after the Cubs had melted down and blew a 7–0 lead and lost the game on a dropped fly ball by their left fielder, Brant Brown. The Mets couldn't hit Carl Pavano and the Expos bullpen, so they remained stuck on 88 wins. Luckily for the Mets, the Cubs had to deal with a superior divisional rival as well. Chicago was slated to play three games in Houston against the Astros, who had wrapped up the division title and won 100 regular season games. The San Francisco Giants had become a major factor in this race as they were only one game behind and

Mets — W-L 88-71 GB 15 HOME 47-34 ROAD 41-37 VS DIV. 22-23
VISITOR
Braves — W-L 103-56 GB +15 NYM HOME 53-25 ROAD 50-31 VS DIV. 27-18
HOME
WC - Wild Card Winner

AL STANDINGS

	R	H	E	LOB
NYM	5	11	1	12
Atl	6	10	0	4

WP Odelis Perez 1-1
LP Rick Reed 16-11
SV John Rocker 2

UMPIRES
Rippley
2B
Pulbone 3B • 1B Darling
HP
Wendelstedt

DP/OPP
DEFENSE

©1996 Bob Carpenter Communications, Inc. All Rights Reserved

---

were set to play three games in Colorado. Either way it was all in front of the Mets: win their games and they are assured of at least a 163rd game and beyond.

I loved the pitching matchup going into this Friday night showdown. Rick Reed had been a model of consistency throughout the season and was our clear No. 2 starter behind Al Leiter. His opponent would be a little-known lefty (and future Met) Bruce Chen,

DATE September 25, 1998 — Friday STADIUM/CAP. Turner Field ATT. 48,443

GAME # N4M 160 A+1 160 WEATHER Clear 75° START/FINISH 7:42 / 10:53 TIME 3:11

NL STANDINGS Y- Clinch Division

	1	2	3	4	5	6	7
Mets	0 0 1	1 1 0	0 1 1	5
Braves	2 0 0	2 1 0	0 1 x	6

SERIES 1 of 3 — Season series 6-3 A+1

	IP	R	ER	H	W	K	MISC.
Bruce Chen (48)	4+	3	3	8	1	0	1HBP 2RBF
Odalis Perez (45)	1⅔	0	0	1	2	1	7BF
Dennis Martinez (32)	1⅓	0	0	0	0	2	4BF
Rudy Seanez (40)	1	1	1	2	1	1	5BF
Kerry Ligtenberg (40)	⅔	1	1	0	2	0	4BF
John Rocker (49)	⅓	0	0	0	0	1	1BF

©1996 Bob Carpenter Communications, Inc. All Rights Reserved

who had only made three starts prior to this one. Fifteen-year-old Evan felt very good about taking Game 1 and putting the pressure on the Cubs and Giants to keep up. Rick Reed was not Mr. Dependable on this night. His bread and butter was throwing strikes, and of course, a two-out walk in the first inning followed by a hit batsman would inflict damage. He would dance his way through trouble in the second and third innings, but got bitten by the long ball, allowing home runs to Andruw Jones and Keith Lockhart. Every time the Mets would fight back, the Braves would respond. Down 2–0, the Mets came back to tie the game in the fourth inning but ruined a golden opportunity to take the lead when they failed to score after loading the bases with nobody out.

In fact, the story of this game was how many times they missed out on big scoring chances. The biggest gut punch at the time came in the sixth inning when Mike Piazza came to the plate with the bases loaded and two outs. Bobby Cox summoned "El Presidente" Dennis Martinez out of the bullpen, and he struck Mike out to leave the runners stranded. But if I thought that was the most painful part of the game, I was sorely mistaken. That moment would occur in the top of the eighth inning and remains an image I can't wipe out of my mind all these years later. One of the Mets' top prospects, Jay Payton, was a September call-up. Jay was there for defense and speed, not much else. He was inserted into the game as a pinch-runner for Tony Phillips as the Mets trailed 5–3 and had runners on first and second with one out. After Edgardo Alonzo struck out, John Olerud came to the plate. For all the good Jay Payton gave to the Mets over the next few years, it's tough to look past what he was about to do as a rookie. On the first pitch, Olerud ripped a base hit up the middle to make it 5–4. Payton raced to second base and didn't stop there. For some reason he attempted to run on the best defensive center fielder in my lifetime as he tried to go first to third. There are two outs, Andruw Jones is the center fielder, Mike frickin' Piazza is on deck, and yet this dope is trying to go first to third. Payton was thrown out by the largest amount I've ever seen a base runner thrown out in the history of baseball. I'm not joking, go look for this game on YouTube and you'll see what I'm talking about. This was the worst and dumbest base-running display I've ever witnessed. The pain would not end there, however, because after the Braves tallied an insurance run, the Mets would again tease us. They got the first two runners on base in the ninth down two runs, and after Lenny Harris laid down a bunt, Carlos Baerga grounded out to make it a one-run game. But then Todd Pratt struck out to end our misery.

The last out of the game was recorded by a lefty named John Rocker. The future would tell me what this night would mean to my fandom in the long term. The hatred for the Braves would begin, as would my dislike for the unknown lefty who entered the game to record his second career save.

KEEPING SCORE: Rocker was the sixth Braves pitcher of the night.... Reed finished the 1998 season with a record of 16–11, a 3.48 ERA, and the first of two All-Star selections. He never had a losing record for the Mets from 1997 to 2001.... As for Payton, he would finish third in Rookie of the Year voting in 2000 behind Rafael Furcal and Rick Ankiel, and homered off Mariano Rivera in the World Series that year.

WELCOME TO A WORLD OF PAIN

BRAVES 7 METS 2

SEPTEMBER 27, 1998, at TURNER FIELD, ATLANTA

AFTER LOSING the first two games to the Braves in Atlanta, which had followed back to back home losses to the Expos, the Mets season was on life support. I knew the cold, hard truth—the season was over and a once-promising year had turned into a nightmare. But the thing about being a sports fan is that, even when all hope appears lost, you can hang on to something ever so tiny that may give you a sliver of light. As the Mets entered the final regular season game of the 1998 season, there was a scenario that would send them to a 163rd game. The Cubs were playing in Houston, and the Giants were in Colorado. If both teams lost and the Mets won, the regular season would end in a three-way tie for the National League wild-card spot. Seems simple, right? The scenario wasn't that nuts, considering neither Chicago nor San Francisco was running away with the wild-card race down the stretch of the season. The Mets

Mets W-L 88-73 GB 17 HOME 47-34 ROAD 41-39 VS DIV. 22-25
VISITOR
Braves W-L 105-56 GB +17 NYM HOME 55-25 ROAD 50-31 VS DIV. 34-19
HOME
WC = Wild Card Winner
AL STANDINGS

NYM R 2 H 8 E 2 LOB 11 DP/OPP 0 DEFENSE 2 E

Atl 7 14 0 12

WP Greg Maddux 18-9
LP Armando Reynoso 7-3
SV ~~~~~

UMPIRES Winters
2B
Darling 3B • 1B Ponino
HP
Rippley

Defensive positions: Tony Phillips, Brian McRae, Lenny Harris, Ray Ordoñez, Carlos Baerga, Edgardo Alfonzo, Armando Reynoso, John Olerud, C. Rejas, M. Wilson, Mike Piazza

New York Mets	Avg	HR	H	1	2	3	4	5	6	7	8	9	10	11	12	13	14	15	AB	R	H	BI
6 Tony Phillips LF	.259	136	1417																			
13 Edgardo Alfonzo 3B	.275	17	877																			
5 John Olerud 1B	.353	22	592																			
31 Mike Piazza C	.327	32	111																			
56 Brian McRae CF	.265	21	79																			
19 Lenny Harris RF	.261	8	57																			
3 Carlos Baerga 2B	.268	7	53																			
10 Ray Ordoñez SS	.247	1	43																			
15 Matt Franco PH	.275		13																			
26 Ralph Milliard SS	.000	0	0																			
40 Armando Reynoso P	.173	0	0																			

R/ER	0/0	0/0	1/1	0/0	0/0	0/0	1/1	0/0	0/0
H	0	1	3	0	1	0	3	0	0
E	0	0	0	0	0	0	0	0	1
LOB	0	3	2	0	1	1	2	1	1

LH BENCH RH

PITCHERS		IP	R	ER	H	W	K	MISC.
Armando Reynoso	7-3 3.24 (40)	1 1/3	5	5	6	3	0	17 BF
Rigo Beltran	(43)	1/3	0	0	0	1	1	2 BF
Hideo Nomo	(16)	4	0	0	3	0	3	15 BF
Turk Wendell	(99)	1	1	1	2	1	0	6 BF
Dennis Cook	(37)	1/3	1	1	2	1	0	4 BF
Greg McMichael	(35)	2/3	0	0	1	0	2	3 BF

LH NYM BULLPEN RH

©1996 Bob Carpenter Communications, Inc. All Rights Reserved

game in Atlanta would start at 1:10 PM while the other games would begin a little later in the day. So win this game, hope for the best, and maybe we encounter a wild, never-before-seen, three-way tie for a playoff spot.

The pitching matchup wasn't favorable as Armando Reynoso took on Future Hall of Famer Greg Maddux. Since the Braves had wrapped up not only the division, but the best record in the

National League, maybe Bobby Cox would pull Greg early, and that would give the Mets hope that they could beat up on the Braves pen. How many times can you get kicked in the balls over the first few innings? Well, let's count the ways. Was it a two-out first inning rally by Atlanta capped by Andres Gallarraga's two-run double? Was it Maddux hitting a two-out RBI double in the second inning? Or maybe it was Chipper Jones picking up his second hit in as many innings and driving Reynoso out of the game and ending his Mets career. Down 5–0 after only two innings insured this would be a three-hour funeral and put us out of our misery early. The Mets did have one pretty good opportunity in the seventh inning with the score 5–2. Mike Piazza came up as the tying run against Dennis Martinez. Much like the game two days earlier, Mike struck out, and all hope as gone. When Piazza came up again with two outs in the ninth and hit a popup to Braves second baseman Tony Graffanino, the game and the season was officially over. The 1998 regular season ended with five consecutive losses and being swept by an Atlanta Braves team that had nothing to play for. I was beside myself as I tried to cope with the reality of what had just happened. A year earlier, the Mets lost a pennant race they really had no business being in. But in 1998 the expectations started to change once they traded for Piazza and had every chance in the world to take control of the wild-card spot.

I remember sitting down for dinner later that day with my family and my dad asking if I wanted to know what was happening in the Cubs and Giants games. Since both teams were tied, those games still had major importance in a playoff race, but obviously no longer for the Mets. I responded that I didn't want to know. But who the hell was I kidding? Of course, I was curious for a few reasons. As a baseball fan I wanted to see if we would have a rare one-game playoff to determine who would make the playoffs, but then the masochist in me wanted to find out if the Mets blew a chance. In a twist that caused major pain in my stomach, both the Cubs and Giants lost within five minutes of each other in insane ways. The Cubs blew a two-run lead in the eighth inning and lost in the 11th on a walk-off sacrifice fly by Richard Hidalgo. The Giants blew a 7–0 lead and eventually lost the game in the bottom of the ninth on a walk-off home run by Neifi Perez. My mind was racing...could you imagine if the Mets had won and this is how they forced a three-way tie?! After spending the last few months hating everything about the Cubs and Giants, my natural reaction was still to be excited about these dual outcomes. Instead I was left with pain...and wondering...what could have been? The 1998 season ended in collapse and dreams about an alternate universe where the Mets win one more freakin' game. All for naught—1998 was my indoctrination into collapsing.

KEEPING SCORE: If there had been a three-way tie, the Mets would have played the Giants at Shea Stadium the following afternoon, with the winner hosting the Cubs for the wild-card spot. Since the Mets' loss on Sunday eliminated that possibility, the Cubs ended up playing the Giants in Chicago and winning that game to advance to the NL Division series where they were swept by...the Atlanta Braves.... Reynoso had missed the first half of the season after undergoing arthroscopic procedures on his shoulder and elbow. Coming into the game, he had a lifetime 0–6 record against Atlanta with a 6.37 ERA. After signing with the Arizona Diamondbacks before the next season, finished his career in 2002 with an 0–10 record against the Braves with an almost identical ERA of 6.38.

STOPPING STREAKS IN THE BRONX

METS 7 YANKEES 2

JUNE 6, 1999, at YANKEE STADIUM

EVER SINCE the Mets won the first-ever Subway Series game in 1997, it had been all downhill as a Mets fan when facing the Yankees. They lost the final two games of the 1997 series, dropped two of three in 1998, and had been defeated in the first two games of the 1999 showdown. Let's do the math together...the Yankees had beaten the Mets six out of seven times after losing the inaugural game. But on this night in 1999, it was more than the Subway Series, it felt like the Mets were fighting for their lives in early June.

The 1999 season began with huge expectations! They went out during the off-season and added Robin Ventura as a big-money free agent, plucked future Hall of Famer Rickey Henderson out of free agency, and even added former rival Orel Hershiser to bolster the back of the rotation. After the way the 1998 season ended, the hope was 1999 would be the year the Mets would make a big jump. Unfortunately, things started to spiral in late May/early June as the team dropped eight consecutive games to fall under .500. As the Mets prepared to wrap up the Subway Series at Yankee Stadium, my father and I heard some shocking news as we began our trek to the Bronx. Mets GM Steve Phillips decided to shake things up by cutting off Bobby Valentine's legs and removing three of his coaches—Bob Apodaca (pitching), Randy Neimann (bullpen), and Tom Robson (hitting). While there was talk of changes, whether firing coaches or removing even the manager himself, when it finally happened it came as a shocking jolt. I was glad Bobby wasn't fired, because despite the team's recent struggles, I'd grown to trust Bobby V and found him to be more important to the Mets' success than even the GM. Valentine had overachieved with the '97 team, and to a degree the '98 team too, despite the late-season collapse. But firing the coaches was a clear sign that if things didn't turn around quick, Bobby would be next.

My dad is probably the one responsible for giving me what my former radio partner, Craig Carton, has called "Roberts-itis," so I wouldn't classify him as a confident fan. But he would sometimes have very strong premonitions around our teams. As we walked into Yankee Stadium on that Sunday night, he made a grand one to me. "Not only will the Mets win tonight, but they are going to stop Clemens's win streak and Jeter's on-base streak." The streaks he mentioned were pretty damn impressive. Roger Clemens had not taken a loss in more than a year. The last L he took in a game was in May 1998. So, dating back over a year, Roger had won 20 consecutive decisions. Jeter's streak was reaching base in *every* single game the Yankees had played in 1999. That number had reached 54 consecutive games entering the finale of the Subway Series. Yet my dad had an odd confidence that the under .500 Mets, who had lost eight consecutive games and just had a bloodletting of coaches, were going to

Mets   W-L 27-28   GB 6½   HOME 13-15   ROAD 14-13   VS DIV. 12-7

VISITOR

Yankees   W-L 32-21   GB Tw Bos   HOME 18-10   ROAD 14-11   VS DIV. 11-4

HOME

	R	H	E	LOB
Met	7	8	1	6
NYY	2	6	0	8

WP Al Leiter 3-5

LP Roger Clemens 5-1

SV ~~~~~

UMPIRES Binkman

2B

Cousins 3B • 1B Scott

HP

Shulock

DEFENSE

Shane Spencer   Bernie Williams   Paul O'Neill

Derek Jeter   Chuck Knoblauch

Scott Brosius   (4-11 Roger Clemens)   Tino Martinez

C. Rojas   M. Wilson

Joe Girardi

STANDINGS

New York	Ave	HR	H	1	2	3	4	5	6	7	8	9	10	11	AB 12	R 13	H 14	BI 15
Mets	273	66	507															
17 Roger Cedeno LF 321 188															4	0	0	0
13 Edgardo Alfonzo 2b 297 7827															5	0	0	0
5 John Olerud 1b 333 9239															4	1	1	0
31 Mike Piazza C 318 9231															5	2	2	2
4 Robin Ventura 3b 263 9242															3	2	2	0
56 Brian McRae CF 265 6314															3	1	0	0
25 Bobby Bonilla DH 161 4215															3	1	1	2
50 Benny Agbayani RF 411 6010															4	0	2	3
10 Rey Ordonez SS 243 0211															2	0	0	0

	R/ER	1	2	3	4	5	6	7	8	9	10	11				
	R/ER	0/0	4/4	3/3	0/0	0/0	0/0	0/0	0/0	0/0			33	7	8	7
	H	0	4	4	0	0	0	0	0	0						
	E	0	0	0	0	0	0	0	0	0						
	LOB	0	1	2/3	0/3	0/3	0/3	2/5	1/6	0/6						

LH BENCH RH

Franco   Henderson   Pratt   Mora

SH Lopez

NYY PITCHERS	IP	R	ER	H	W	K	MISC.
Roger Clemens (13)	2⅔	7	7	8	2	3	17BF 10P 1HR 63S
Todd Erdos (64)	4	0	0	0	3	2	15BF
Dan Naulty (31)	2⅓	0	0	0	1	2	9BF

LH NYY BULLPEN RH

Stanton   Erdos Rocca Mendoza Naulty Grimsley

Pettit   Cone Hernandez 2

DL Irabu 15   Watson 15   Emerson 15

complete the trifecta. Win a game, stop a legendary streak from an all-time great pitcher, and keep the great Derek Jeter off base.

Starting in the second inning, the Mets absolutely destroyed Roger Clemens. Even the much-maligned Bobby Bonilla caused him pain as he delivered the two-run double that actually put the Mets on the board. But the biggest memory of this game would actually

Sunday
DATE June 6, 1999   STADIUM/CAP. Yankee Stadium   57,545   ATT. 56,294
GAME # Met 57 NYY 54   WEATHER Clear   START/FINISH 8:11 / 11:22   TIME 311

Mets   043 | 000 | 000   7
Yankees   000 | 010 | 010   2

SERIES Interleague Play
Subway Series
3 of 3
Season series
2-0 NYY

Mets fire Apodaca, Robson & Neiman. They hire Wallace, Brantley & Jackson.

©1996 Bob Carpenter Communications, Inc. All Rights Reserved

grow as the years went on because of its lasting impact. Mike Piazza delivered the knockout blow against Clemens by smoking a two-run home run in the third inning to make it 6–0. Piazza had even started the rally in the second inning against Roger when he ripped a double that initiated the four-run explosion. Mike would continue to have great success against Roger over the next year-plus, which would lead to a confrontation that would live in baseball history. Benny Agbayani officially ended Clemens's night with an RBI double. The great "Rocket" Roger Clemens walked off the mound to thunderous boos from Yankee fans and cheers from the Mets fans. Despite the impressive winning streak, this was his first year with the Yankees, and he was not having a good season. Remember, Roger had just won back-to-back Cy Young Awards in Toronto before being dealt during the off-season for the wildly popular David Wells. Despite Clemens's 5–0 record, he came into the game with a 4.11 ERA, which would balloon even higher after this ass-whupping. On the other side, Al Leiter pitched an incredibly strong game and the Mets left no doubt, winning a much-needed game against the Yankees. Clemens took the loss, Jeter went 0-for-4, and *voilà*, my dad had nailed it! In the moment it felt like a game that could turn the season around...and it did. This June night in the Bronx started with firings and ended with a team that was about go on a roll. As we departed Yankee Stadium that night, we knew good things were coming.

KEEPING SCORE: The Mets had played 55 games at the time the coaches were fired, and Bobby Valentine boldly remarked that if the team didn't improve over the next 55 games, he shouldn't be the manager anymore. The Mets went 40–15 in those games and were in first place by August. They stumbled late in the season but still went 70–38 after their lowest point and made the postseason for the first time since 1988.... The Mets and Yankees ended up splitting six games in 1999 as the Mets took two of three at Shea in July, including an unforgettable walk-off win against Mariano Rivera (*see* "The Matt Franco Game" on the next page).

THE MATT FRANCO GAME

METS 9 YANKEES 8

JULY 10, 1999, at SHEA STADIUM

IF I POLLED Met fans over the age of 30 and asked them to name the greatest Subway Series game they ever witnessed, I'm confident that nine out of 10 of them would proudly say the Matt Franco game. That's right, the pinch-hitter extraordinaire has a game named after him, and how could he not? A classic, back-and-forth slugfest between the Mets and Yankees on a picturesque Saturday afternoon came to be defined by its epic conclusion.

The Mets had beaten up Roger Clemens the night before for the second time in about a month and handed the Yankees a Game 1 loss. It was the first season that the Subway Series became a home-and-home affair. One month earlier the Mets had turned their season around after firing part of their coaching staff and salvaging the final game of the series in Yankee Stadium. That turned into a Mets hot streak, and so a month later the Mets were in a completely different spot, 11 games over .500 and tied for the wild-card in the National League. Yankee fans had secured bragging rights by winning the previous series, and to this point had won all three series played between the crosstown rivals. So, after winning the night before, the Mets came into this game looking to do something we had never seen—win a series against the Yankees. I think a part of why I downplay the Subway Series on the radio every year is that nothing to me can match the intensity of the early days. The crowds were louder, and probably because of my age, the bragging rights mattered more. At this point I was 15 years old, and the vast majority of my schoolmates were Yankees fans. Losing a series against them, which I had now become used to, would lead to constant mocking and a reminder that the Yankees were the kings of this town. Even winning a simple series in the regular season would go a long way as Mets fan. Despite the season series now being six games instead of

Yankees W-L 51-33 GB +3 Bos HOME 26-17 ROAD 25-16 VS DIV. 19-6
VISITOR
Mets W-L 49-38 GB 4 HOME 25-20 ROAD 24-18 VS DIV. 22-14
HOME

©1996 Bob Carpenter Communications, Inc. All Rights Reserved

three, winning on this Saturday afternoon ensured the three-game series win, which felt like a mini-championship. The problem is, I had learned early on, the dynasty Yankees were no easy team to beat.

There are so many crazy moments from this game, but looking back a few decades later there are three or four specific memories that I can still picture as clear as day. With the Mets trailing 6–4 in the bottom of the seventh inning, Mike Piazza came to the plate to face Ramiro Mendoza. To this point, the game had already featured multiple lead changes as the Yankees quickly blew an early 2–0 lead and the Mets promptly gave away a 4–2 lead. But here in the seventh inning the real memories started churning. Piazza hit a shot that, right off the bat, you knew was going into orbit, crushing a 2–1 pitch from Mendoza over the old picnic tent in distant left field. The moment the ball touched Mike's bat, I jumped into the air knowing the outcome. Piazza not only gave the Mets a 7-6 lead but had hit the longest home run I'd ever seen to this point in my life. It was almost as if Mike was letting out the aggression all Mets fans feel when facing the Yankees. The split crowd was a mix of roar and gasps as that ball cleared the picnic tents. The Mets were now six outs away from securing the series win.... But they were facing the dynastic New York Yankees. Nothing, even in victory, would ever be easy. The other vivid memory is Jorge Posada coming up to the plate the very next inning, batting from the right side and smoking a ball down the left-field line for a two-run home run. All the excitement from the Piazza jack had exited my body as Posada stole the game right back. Besides blowing the lead, it's also not enjoyable to hear your own ballpark rock in excitement for the other team. The crowd felt just about 50-50, but when either team did something great it felt as if everyone was behind the team that just got the big hit. So, in this moment, I was enduring the pain inside Yankee Stadium Queens. The Mets were now six outs away from losing, and the idea of facing Mariano Rivera in the ninth was quite daunting.

The other lasting memories from this classic would come in the bottom of the ninth inning. Two very strange things happened that set up a rare rally against Mo. First off, Rivera shockingly walked Rickey Henderson with one out and nobody on. What followed was equally as surprising. Bernie Williams misplayed a ball off the bat of Edgardo Alfonzo. It wasn't an error, but certainly a play Bernie should have made. After John Olerud grounded out and Piazza was intentionally walked, it set up the at-bat none of us will ever forget. Matt Franco vs. Mariano Rivera in an 8–7 game with the bases loaded and two out. I can see the entire pitch sequence in my head right now. Foul ball, swing and a miss...the count was 0–2. I'll admit this now, on the next pitch Matt Franco struck out on a cutter right down the middle that was ruled low. The crowd gasped as the pitch was called a ball, and on the very next pitch Matt hit a line drive to right, driving in the tying and winning runs. Jubilation at Shea, including me folding up my scorebook so I could promptly jump up and down next to my seat. Me and my father didn't want to leave Shea that day and kept soaking in an incredible win against the defending champions. As we drove home from Mets games, we had a simple routine. If the Mets won, we would listen to *Mets Extra*, but if they lost, my dad would put oldies music on. On this Saturday afternoon in 1999, we changed our habits. We decided to check in on John Sterling and listen to the Yankees postgame show. We wanted to drink Yankees tears...and boy did we drink up!

KEEPING SCORE: The winning pitcher was Pat Mahomes, who pitched a scoreless top of the ninth. The father of the future Kansas City Chiefs quarterback went 8–0 in 1999.... Rivera went 4–4 with 20 saves in 23 opportunities during the regular season against the Mets. His 3.53 ERA against them was more than a full run more than his career mark of 2.21 and the second-worst against any opponent (3.75 against the Los Angeles Angels).... It was the third (and final) time Franco and Rivera matched up, with Franco drawing a walk and grounding out the other two times.

THERE WILL BE A GAME 163

METS 2 PIRATES 1

OCTOBER 3, 1999, at SHEA STADIUM

THE 1999 pennant race had some striking similarities to the previous year's battle until it didn't. In 1998 the Mets lost their final five games of the regular season and missed out on the postseason by one game. It was quite a last-second collapse, and in 1999 the Mets appeared to be heading down the exact same road. When the Mets woke up on the morning of September 21, they were 92–58 and only one game behind the Braves for the NL East lead, plus they had a seemingly comfortable four-game lead over Cincinnati for the

Baseball scorecard:

VISITOR: Pirates — W-L 78-82 — GB 17½ — HOME 45-36 — ROAD 33-46 — VS DIV. 30-32

HOME: Mets — W-L 95-66 — GB 7 — HOME 48-32 — ROAD 47-34 — VS DIV. 27-23

WC- Clinch With card

	R	H	E	LOB
Pit	1	3	1	5
Met	2	9	0	12

WP Armando Benitez 4-3
LP Greg Hansell 1-3
SV ~~~~~

UMPIRES
H. rochbeck
2B
Nelson 3B • 1B Fletcher
HP
Freeming

Met DP/OPP 1 — DEFENSE — 0 E

Ricky — Darrel Hamilton — Roger Celano
Ray Ordonez — Edgardo Alfonzo
Robin Ventura — 4.66 Orel Hershiser — John Olerud
J. Lime — Mike Piazza — ejected in 3rd J. Jones — ejected by Renick

AL STANDINGS

x-NYY 98-63 / WC-Bos 5 / Tor 15 / BJ 20 / T9 30

x-Cle 97-64 / CWS 22 / Det 27 / KC 33 / Min 33½

x-Tex 95-66 / Oak 9 / Sea 16 / Ana 26

Bos 93-68 / Wild card winner

Pittsburgh Pirates	Ave	HR	H	1	2	3	4	5	6	7	8	9	10	11	AB 12	R 13	H 14	BI 15
28 Al Martin cf	260	171	1414												3	1	1	0
10 Abraham Nunez ss	277	24663	0217												3	0	0	0
37 Brent Brown RF / 13 Abrian Brown ph 1B	293 16658 / 274 4617														2 / 1	0 / 0	0 / 0	0 / 0
29 Kevin Young 1b	297	26 0105													4	0	2	1
30 Warren Morris 2b	299	15 173													3	0	0	0
16 Aramis Ramirez 3b	192	087													4	0	0	0
3 Chad Hermansen cf	246	181													3	0	0	0
17 Joe Oliver c	206	1217													3	0	0	0
34 Kris Benson P / 11 Dale Svevm Ph / 41 Jason Christiansen P / 57 Greg Hansell P / 54 Brad Clontz P															1 / 1	0 / 0	0 / 0	0 / 0

	1	2	3	4	5	6	7	8	9	10		
R/ER	1/1	010	0/0	0/0	0/0	0/0	0/0	0/0	0/0		28	
H	1	0	0	0	0	1	0	0	1			3
E	0	0	0	0	0	0	0	0	0			1
LOB	1	0/1	0/1	0/1	0/1	2/3	0/3	0/3	2/5			

BENCH: LH G. Ley / RH Whitmer, Osik, Meares, Laker, Brown E, Benjamin

Met PITCHERS	IP	R	ER	H	W	K	MISC.
(63)	13-12 4.46	5⅓	1	1	2	2	4	19BF
Dennis Cook (27)	⅓	0	0	0	1	1	2BF
Pat Mahomes (23)	⅓	0	0	0	0	1	1BF
Turk Wendell (99)	2⅔	0	0	1	0	2	9BF
Armando Benitez (49)	⅓	0	0	0	1	1	2BF

BULLPEN: LH Met RH
Rusch, Franco, McCloy / Rogers, Wendell, Leiter / Jones, Dotel, Yoshi, Reed
OL No one

wild-card spot. The Mets proceeded to completely crap the bed in Atlanta as Chipper Jones really cemented himself as a Mets killer. The collapse continued in Philadelphia and hit its crescendo when the Braves took two of three from the Mets at Shea Stadium. The series in Atlanta was when Chipper Jones whipped out his infamous "now Met fans can put their Yankee hats on" line that even further made him the evil villain that he was. The Mets had lost eight of

DATE Sunday October 3, 1999   STADIUM/CAP. Shea Stadium   53,777   ATT. 50,911

GAME # Pit 161 Met 162   WEATHER Sunny 73°   START/FINISH 1:42 / 4:49   TIME 307

NL STANDINGS   x- Clinch Division title

SERIES 3 of 3   Season Series 6-2 Met

Final Regular season Game of the year.
Mets celebrate, but if Reds win, 1 game playoff, if Reds lose Met win wild card
Pirates 1 00 000 000   1
Mets 000 100 001   2
1st base coach Joe Jones ejected.
Hershiser K's 2,000th career batter.
Mets force at least a 1 game Playoff

												AB	R	H	BI
New York Mets	Ave .279	HR 179	U 1535	1	2	3	4	5	6	7	8	9	10	11	12
24 Rickey Henderson LF														4	0	1	0

PITCHERS

PITCHERS	IP	R	ER	H	W	K	MISC.
Kris Benson (34)	7	1	0	7	2	3	3 IBB
Jason Christiansen (41)	1	0	0	0	1	0	4 BF
Greg Hansell (57)	⅓	1	1	2	1	0	4 BF
Brad Clontz (59)	0	0	0	0	0	0	IP 1WP

nine, which included a seven-game losing streak, to fall two games behind the Reds and Astros in the wild-card race. Since the Reds and Astros were simultaneously battling for the Central Division title, the Mets needed to tie or pass only one of those teams. So the final weekend of the season was set up like this: the Mets needed to find a way to get hot and sweep the lousy Pirates, while also hoping that *either* the Reds or Astros would lose two of three. If that happened, it would set up a tie for the wild-card spot.

After blowing an eighth-inning lead in the Friday night game, the Mets dramatically pulled out the needed win with Robin Ventura securing the walk-off hit. The following night Rick Reed was brilliant, and while that was happening, the Reds had supplied the choke we needed to bring destiny back into our hands. Cincinnati lost back-to-back games in Milwaukee, setting up an incredible Sunday. The Mets and Reds were now tied for the wild-card, and a simple win against Pittsburgh would at least ensure a 163rd game, either in the NLDS or as a one-game playoff with the Reds.

Walking into Shea that day, the buzz was palpable. Despite the previous year's choke, and how awful the Mets had played leading up to the Pittsburgh series, there was an odd confidence that they had figured things out and would take care of business in Game 162 against a sub .500 team. What made the confidence even weirder is that the aging Orel Hershiser was the man on the mound and he had been awful in his previous start against the Braves, when he got knocked out in the first inning. But here is the thing about Hershiser: he may have been 41 at the time and certainly dealing with diminished stuff, but we all knew he had balls. If the Pirates beat him around, it wouldn't have been because the moment was too big. He did allow a run in the first inning, but after that was utterly brilliant as he pitched into the sixth inning. Future Met Kris Benson was dealing on this Sunday afternoon, but thank God the Mets were able to scratch out an unearned run in the fourth inning to tie the game. While all of this was going on, the Brewers-Reds game had a huge "R" next to the game on the giant old Shea scoreboard. In the days before iPhones and iPads allowing us to watch other games, we needed to rely on the scoreboard to keep us posted. The rain in Milwaukee continued, so there was no way we would know the Mets' fate, win or lose, because the Brewers-Reds game was nowhere near starting. The anxiety of this 1–1 game continued to build and build. The confidence I once had started to fade the later the game went. In the bottom of the ninth inning of a tie game, Bobby Bonilla, who was in his second tour of duty with the Mets, but had a far different role than his first tenure, was sent up to pinch-hit. As he walked to the plate representing the winning run, I turned to my dad and said, "Could you imagine if it's this freakin' guy?" Bobby was being booed every single time he came to the plate, and when he grounded out meekly to start the ninth the boos rained down from Shea.

Shea Stadium was as loud as I had ever experienced at this point in my life, especially when Melvin Mora dropped in a one-out single off one-time Mets farmhand Greg Hansell. It rocked even louder when Edgardo Alfonzo went the other way with a single to put runners on first and third. The place was literally moving as John Olerud came up needing just a fly ball to move the Mets to a Game 163. What then followed was shocking at the time. The Pirates decided to intentionally walk Olerud to load the bases for Mike Piazza. So here was Piazza with the bases loaded and one out in a tie game, as the Mets are looking to keep the season going. Former Met Brad Clontz came into pitch, and what happened next was the greatest/ most anticlimactic thing you could ever write up. The very first pitch Clontz threw bounced onto the screen and the winning run scored. Piazza looked so damn dejected that he didn't get the chance to have an epic Mets moment, but bedlam was still occurring at Shea despite how the winning run scored. I was euphoric and so was the entire building as it rocked in celebration. As we left Shea that day, there was still uncertainty—the Reds-Brewers game had still not started, so the Mets were in a state of flux. If the Reds lost, the Mets would then head to Arizona to face the Diamondbacks in the NLDS. But if the Reds won, the Mets would go to Cincinnati to play a one-game playoff. Late at night, and honestly I forget how late it actually was, but my memory tells me it was like 1:00 AM, the Reds and Brewers finally played. My future radio station home WFAN decided to air the game so us Met fans could listen, and I went to bed with the sounds of Reds vs. Brewers baseball. I woke up to the news that the Reds had won, and the Mets would be in a one-game playoff for the wild-card. Even though they weren't officially in the playoffs, I walked out of Shea celebrating what felt like the first playoff berth of my sporting fandom life!

KEEPING SCORE: Kris Benson, who threw 120 pitches and got a no-decision for the Pirates that day, finished fourth in voting for Rookie of the Year that season and would join the Mets at the trade deadline in 2004.... Armando Benitez, who stranded the go-ahead run at second by striking out Aramis Ramirez to end the top of the ninth, received credit for the victory.

GOING TO THE "REAL" PLAYOFFS

METS 5 REDS 0
NATIONAL LEAGUE WILD CARD TIEBREAKER GAME
OCTOBER 4, 1999, at CINERGY FIELD (formerly Riverfront Stadium), CINCINNATI

A ONE-GAME playoff was freakin' magical. Growing up and learning baseball, the idea of a one- game playoff was a prominent event that made for remarkable baseball moments. One of the first history lessons I ever received was hearing about the best-of-three playoff between the Giants and Dodgers in 1951, that was capped off by Bobby Thomson's "Shot Heard 'Round the World." Who could then forget hearing endless stories about Bucky F—n' Dent sticking it to the Red Sox in 1978 to win the AL East? Nineteen ninety-nine was our turn, as the Mets and Reds were set to play one game for the National League wild-card spot. Even though the Dodgers and Giants playing for the NL pennant—and even the Yankees and Red Sox playing for the AL East division title—certainly seemed more prestigious than a game for the somewhat new wild-card spot, to me this was everything. After watching some bad baseball for the early part of my life, the Mets being just one win away from the

Mets W-L 96-66 GB 7 HOME 49-32 ROAD 47-34 VS DIV. 27-23										

VISITOR

Reds W-L 96-66 GB 1 HOME 45-36 ROAD 51-30 VS DIV. 38-25

HOME

WC - Wild Card Winner · FINAL · AL STANDINGS

Met	R 5	H 9	E 0	LOB 10	Cin DP/ OPP 2	DEFENSE	O E
Cin	0	2	0	5			

WP Al Leiter 13-12

LP Steve Parris 11-4

SV ∿∿∿∿∿

UMPIRES Hirschbeck 2B

Rapuano 3B · 1B Davis

HP Froemming

DEFENSE: Greg Vaughn, Jeffrey Hammonds, Dmitri Young, Barry Larkin, Pokey Reese, Aaron Boone, 336 Steve Parris, Sean Casey, C. Rojas, M. Wilson, Eddie Taubensee

AL STANDINGS:
- x-NYY 98-64 wc-Bos 4, Tor 14, Bal 20, TB 29
- x-Cle 97-65, Chw 21½, Det 27½, KC 32½, Min 33
- x-Tex 95-67, Oak 8, Sea 14, Ana 25
- Bos 94-68 Wild Card Winner

New York	Ave	HR	H												AB	R	H	BI
Mets	279	179	1544	1	2	3	4	5	6	7	8	9	10	11	12	13	14	15
24 Rickey Henderson LF 314 11e11 / 6 Melvin Mora LF (8) 161 061														5	2	2	1
13 Edgardo Alfonzo 2b 303 26e105														4	2	2	3
5 John Olerud 1b 297 19e96														5	0	2	0
31 Mike Piazza C 305 40e124														2	0	0	0
4 Robin Ventura 3b 301 32e119														3	0	1	1
18 Darryl Hamilton CF 315 9e45														4	0	1	0
19 Roger Cedeno RF 314 4e36														4	0	1	0
10 Rey Ordonez SS 258 1e60														3	1	0	0
22 Al Leiter P 14 0e5 / 12-12 2P 204 H 2e7 BB e9 SO 135 4.41														3	0	0	0
R/ER				2/2	0/0	1/1	0/0	1/1	1/1	0/0	0/0	0/0						
H				2	0	1	0	2	1	1	0	2			33	5	9	5
E				0	0	0	0	0	0	0	0	0						
LOB				0	0	3	0/3	3/6	1/7	2/4	0/9	1/10						

BENCH: LH Franco, Pratt, Mora, Dunston, Agbayani, Tora, SH Bonilla, Wilson, Kinkade, Lopez, Payton; RH Wilson; DL NO ONE

Cin	PITCHERS	IP	R	ER	H	W	K	MISC.
11-3 336	Steve Parris (58)	2⅔	3	3	3	3	1	1HR 1BBC
	Danny Neagle (15)	2⅓	1	1	2	3	2	1-3IRS 12BF 11K
	Danny Graves (32)	3	1	1	2	2	2	13BF
	Dennis Reyes (49)	1	0	0	2	0	0	4BF

BULLPEN: LH Reed, Haugle, Villone, White; Cin Gvenn, Williamson, Tonko, Hoensch, Belinda, Graves, Sullivan; DL Avery 15, Winchester 15, Wohlers 15

real postseason was as special as it gets. As the years would go by, the "one-game playoff" would lose its uniqueness in history. The previous season the Giants played the Cubs in a one-gamer, and we would see many more of them over the years until MLB created an artificial one-game playoff named "The Wild-Card Game" in 2012. But in 1999, this was a big freakin' deal.

DATE October 4, 1999 (Monday) STADIUM/CAP. Cinergy Field 52,953 ATT. 54,621 — Sell out & more

GAME # Met 163 Cin 163 WEATHER Rainy 56° START/FINISH 7:08 / 10:11 TIME 3:03

SERIES One Game Playoff for Wild Card Spot. Season Series 5-4 Cin

Mets 201/011/000 5
Reds 000/000/000 0

First ever 1 game playoff in Mets & Reds History. Mets Win Wild Card.

Met Pitchers: Al Leiter 12-12 4.41 (CG) IP 9 R 0 ER 0 H 2 W 4 K 7 — 328F 135P — CG Shutout

©1996 Bob Carpenter Communications, Inc. All Rights Reserved

Going to school on that Monday was probably the longest day I ever experienced. All I could think about was Al Leiter vs. Steve Parris at Riverfront Stadium, which would start in just a few short hours. Dancing in my head was what had just happened the previous weekend when the Mets won three straight from the Pirates and got a little bit of help to even force this playoff. This was far and away the most excited I had ever been to this point about a single game. As a sophomore at Lawrence High School, it's not that I ever really enjoyed school, but today was a day when staring at the clock in each class became an obsession. Could time move a little faster, please? Even history class, which was far and away my favorite subject became unbearable on this day. Who cares about Louis XIV when I have to figure out how to get Sean Casey out in a few hours! The periodic table meant nothing when a future Hall of Famer like Barry Larkin is in your way. Finally, the school day mercifully ended and the race home began. I set up my scorebook right away in anticipation of a baseball night I would never forget.

My confidence level going into the game was pretty decent too, as I really trusted big Al in a spot like this, considering the postseason experience he had accumulated with the Marlins. I settled in to watch this game in the den of my childhood home with my scorebook all set up and ready to roll. My stomach was churning from excitement and anticipation of what would potentially happen. My dad brought over a bottle of champagne, which of course I wouldn't drink at age 16, but we could at least use as our celebration prop in case the Mets actually pulled this off. Edgardo Alfonzo smoked a ball in the top of the first inning that set the tone for the next three hours. His two-run bomb off Parris gave the Mets a 2–0 lead, and from that moment on, there would be zero drama. Al Leiter was cooking, retiring 13 straight batters at one point, and wouldn't even allow a Reds base runner to get into scoring position until it was far too late. A 2–0 lead became 3–0, then 4–0 on a home run by Rickey Henderson, and then the initial hero, Alfonzo, put a capper on this game by ripping a RBI double in the sixth to make it 5–0. The rest of the game was a celebration as visions of a best-of-five series against Arizona started to permeate by brain. Al Leiter, who held the Reds to only two hits on the night, finished the job in the ninth, and as Alfonzo caught the soft liner off the bat of Dmitri Young to end it and pointed to the sky, I remember celebrating like the kid I was as the Mets secured their first playoff spot since before I could understand the sport. From the dregs of another collapse to four consecutive wins, the Mets were going to the National League Division Series! Though Randy Johnson, the most dominant left-hander of my generation awaited the Mets, that wasn't my concern on this Monday night in October. After spending my childhood watching the MLB playoffs as an independent observer, I was about to be right in the middle of the drama. It was playoff time, baby!

KEEPING SCORE: Maybe it was a good thing that the playoff game was played at Cincinnati and not New York. The Reds had swept a three-game series from the Mets at Shea Stadium in their only meeting of the season there from May 31 to June 2 during the eight-game losing streak that led to the firing of three coaches ("Stopping Streaks in the Bronx," p. 63).... Jeffrey Hammonds (second-inning single) and Pokey Reese (leadoff double in the ninth) had the only two hits allowed by Leiter.

LATE NIGHT BASEBALL

METS 8 DIAMONDBACKS 4
GAME 1, NATIONAL LEAGUE DIVISION SERIES
OCTOBER 5, 1999, at BANK ONE BALLPARK, PHOENIX

GROWING UP a diehard Mets fan who now had the obsession of scoring every damn game I could, there was one little bit of kryptonite that I had. When the Mets would go on a West Coast trip, I would still accept the challenge of staying up well past 1:00 AM to score the entire game. But it was not easy. In an era before DVRs, you legit had to stay up from the beginning until the game's conclusion to not miss a pitch. That was no easy task. While some nights I would accomplish the goal of making it through the entirety of a Mets-Dodgers game that began after 10:00 PM, there were more than a few occasions where I would pass out, pen in hand, in the midst of a commercial break during the late night game. That would create a major scoring crisis, because getting the information on how to fill out my scorecard from innings missed was quite the challenge in the late '90s. When the Mets secured their first playoff spot of my sports fandom after beating the Cincinnati Reds in the one-game playoff, the reward was a best-of-five series against the Arizona Diamondbacks. What I quickly found out would be an adventure I

DATE October 5.1999 STADIUM/CAP. Bank One Ballpark 48,500 ATT. 49,584

GAME # Met 1 Arz 1 WEATHER clear 85° START/FINISH 11:10 / 2:03 TIME 253

©1996 Bob Carpenter Communications, Inc. All Rights Reserved

never saw coming. Game 1 would begin at 11:10 PM Eastern Time. If I thought a 10:00 o'clock start was rough, get a load of this crap. Not only was it starting after 11:00, but playoff games are known for their longer commercial breaks, and if there were a lot of pitching changes we could be staring at a game that might not end until 2:00 AM. But, hey, this is the playoffs! This isn't some mid-May game in San Diego; this is what I've been waiting for and dreaming about my entire life. Playoff baseball...really, really, really late into the night playoff baseball!

In only their second year of existence, the Arizona Diamond-backs were the team that stood in our way, and they were led by the dominant Randy Johnson. Randy had become a star in Seattle, but a year earlier had been traded to the Astros at the trade deadline, before signing with Arizona during the off-season. I didn't realize it at the time, but Johnson had just finished a regular season that would be the first of four straight Cy Young Awards. As a Mets fan, though, I had no personal history with the Big Unit. I had watched him pitch really well as a key figure in the classic Mariners-Yankees ALDS from a few seasons earlier, and then be the loser in five consecutive post-season starts coming into our battle. Randy Johnson was something we didn't have—a true, put-the-fear-of-God-into-you ace. He was what felt like could be the difference in this series. The closest thing we had to an ace was Al Leiter, and he was just used a day earlier to secure the wild-card spot, when he pitched a shutout in the playoff against the Reds. Because of the way the regular season ended, not only wasn't Leiter available to match up with Randy, but neither was Rick Reed, who had pitched a few days earlier against the Pirates. So it was Masato Yoshii who was given the ball for this showdown in the desert. Yoshii had a solid rookie year in 1998 and went out and made just about every start in 1999, so he had turned into a dependable middle- to back-end-of-the-rotation arm. But could I trust him in a playoff game while staring down the great Randy Johnson?

I could not wait until 11:00 PM that night...and to kill time I had Game 1 of the Yankees against the Texas Rangers to serve as a dis-traction. It didn't help very much as the Yankees killed Texas in a non-drama filled blowout. Finally, 11:00 PM came around and it was go-time for my first-ever playoff game! Much like the night before, Edgardo Alfonzo got the Mets off to a great start with a shocking home run off of Randy Johnson. If that wasn't stunning enough, a few innings later, a lefty hitter took the Unit deep, which almost never happened. John Olerud touched him for a two-run home run, and the Mets had built a 3–0 lead on Arizona. Thrilled to get those runs against someone as good as Johnson, I also knew holding the D-Backs down with Yoshii wasn't going to last. Arizona kept fighting back and finally tied the game in the sixth when Luis Gonzalez took him yard. It was 4-4 late into the night, and I had no idea how the hell this thing would end. It was well after my normal bedtime, but I had no issues staying up on this night. Winning Game 1 with no off day ahead of time against the game's greatest pitcher would normally have felt like found money, but when you jump to numerous early leads, you cannot lose this freakin' game. Luckily Dennis Cook and Turk Wendell kept the game tied into the ninth inning.

Randy Johnson was *still* on the mound in something you would never see in today's game, but there he was in a 4-4 game. After singles by Robin Ventura and Rey Ordóñez, Johnson showed he was tiring when he walked Melvin Mora to the load the bases. Bobby Chouinard, a name that will live in Mets history forever because of what was about to transpire, came in to relieve Johnson. When Edgardo Alfonzo came up to the plate with two outs and the bases loaded in a tie game, it was very difficult to keep my composure. It was now about 1:45 AM and everyone other than my dad sitting next to me is sleeping as I'm trying to remain calm in this tension-filled moment. As soon as Fonzie worked the count to 3-1, I had calmed down. There was a confidence that a hitter as professional as Edgardo Alfonzo would take advantage of this moment. Whether it was drawing the go-ahead walk, or ripping a fat fastball, Fonzie was the guy I trusted most at the plate in a spot like this. Boy, did he prove my gut feeling right, as Alfonzo absolutely murdered the 3-1 pitch, and the only question was fair or foul. I stood up and tried to remain calm as we waited to see where the ball would land. Finally...we got the signal...GRAND SLAM! Edgardo Alfonzo had come through yet again in a monstrous spot. The Mets took an 8-4 lead, poor Randy Johnson was charged with seven of the eight runs, and we were on our way to a stunning Game 1 win. Armando Benitez calmly got the final three outs, and you couldn't have written a better script. This game had everything, and best of all, we were the victors. The game may have ended around 2:00 AM, but there was no shot I was going to be able to fall asleep anytime soon. As I lay in my bed that night, I couldn't even fathom the wild emotions of the last week. From choking away a playoff spot, to earning our right to a Game 163, to winning that game, to this. Defeating the most dominant lefty of my lifetime to win a playoff game. Wow...and who knew the fun was only beginning.

KEEPING SCORE: Buck Showalter was the Diamondbacks' manager in 1999, and in 2022 he became the first Mets manager to both manage for and against them in the postseason.... Chouinard didn't last much longer as a Diamondback. He was arrested that Christmas for assaulting his wife and pointing a gun at her and asked the team to release him a few months later. After being picked up by the Rockies, he was sentenced to a year in a Colorado jail that was to be spread out over several off-seasons.

HE JUMPS AND HE MISSED IT!

METS 4 DIAMONDBACKS 3 (10 INNINGS)
GAME 4, NATIONAL LEAGUE DIVISION SERIES
OCTOBER 9, 1999, at SHEA STADIUM

WALKING INTO Shea Stadium that Saturday afternoon in early October, there was a buzz in the air like no other. The Mets were now one win away from advancing to the NLCS after beating the Diamondbacks the day before 9–2. This was the true definition of a day game after night game, because the previous evening's contest ended after 11:00 o'clock, and here we were back at Big Shea just about 12 hours later for the potential clincher. I remember it being cloudy that day with a nice October chill in the air and raw anticipation of what possibly could happen. I barely slept the night before, but right now I was working on pure playoff adrenaline. Despite the last night's win and being one win away from advancing, there was some fear in the air. Yes, the Mets had success against Randy Johnson in the opener of the series, but he was a looming presence on this game and series. The Mets were facing Brian Anderson and had their own ace, Al Leiter, back on the mound, making his first start since the one-game playoff against Cincinnati. So the Mets clearly had the starting pitching edge going in, but the D-Backs would have a *major* advantage in a winner-take-all Game 5 if they could steal this game with the Big Unit ready to go on normal rest.

That was my worry as I, my father, and everyone in our section broke down the game and what could follow. The elder statesmen in this discussion made the Mike Scott/1986 comparison. When the Mets were battling the Astros 13 years earlier in that classic Game 6, the prospect of facing Mike Scott in Game 7 made the game feel like a must win for the Mets. Could the Mets beat Randy Johnson for a second time in this series while countering with Masato Yoshii? It didn't seem likely. So, much like 1986 with Mike Scott, Game 4 between the Mets and D-Backs felt like a game the Mets couldn't afford to lose.

The other major story that was causing us stress was **Mike Piazza's** injury situation. He was pretty quiet in the first two games in Arizona. A thumb injury that had been lingering for a few weeks reemerged, and Piazza was unable to play Games 3 and 4 at Shea Stadium. Besides feeling bad for ourselves as selfish fans, I also had compassion for big Mike. Piazza was the guy who had a chance for a heroic end to the regular season when he came up with the bases loaded only for the thing to end on a first-pitch wild pitch by Brad Clontz. Now here was big money Mike with huge expectations unable to be in the starting lineup for the Mets' first two home play-off games in 11 years. Todd Pratt had been a solid backup all season, but he was no Mike Piazza. It didn't matter much in Game 3 as the Mets won easily, but I had some concern that it could catch up to them in Game 4.

This baseball game we were about to watch was pound for pound as good as it gets. We also got our first taste of Armando Benitez coming up very small in a big spot. Bobby Valentine inserted him in the eighth inning nursing a one-run lead and looking for a four-out save. He promptly gave up the lead, allowing a two-run double to Jay Bell, and was about to make things worse when he gave up another hit to Matt Williams, but got his ass bailed out when Melvin Mora, who had just replaced Rickey Henderson in left field, threw a dart to the plate to nail Bell trying to score. It kept the game Arizona 3, Mets 2. But the damage had been done, and Benitez may have stuck a dagger in our hearts. Blowing an eighth-inning lead at home with Randy Johnson back in Arizona on the horizon? This was a problem. Luckily, a dropped fly ball by Tony Womack helped tie the game in the bottom of the inning, and to Armando's credit he did bounce back with a 1-2-3 ninth inning to keep the game tied. Shea Stadium was so tense at this point...could we possibly lose this game? Everything is a blur until you get to Matt Mantei vs. Todd Pratt in the 10th inning. Sometimes the most magical moments occur when you least expect them. When the bases are loaded in a tie game in the ninth, everyone stands up anticipating how the next pitch will likely be the moment of a game you will never forget. But then there are other times when the most incredible scenes come from absolutely nowhere. With one out in the 10th and Todd Pratt at the plate, we got the smack in the face brilliance no one in the building expected. Todd hit a fly ball to center field, and I figured Steve Finley would easily catch it. As he drifted back, I now thought there was a chance it could bounce off the wall. But when Finley jumped into the air, I was 90 percent sure he would grab it. As he came down, there was a quick moment of silence because we didn't know what had happened. Finally, Finley's dejected look told the story—he had jumped and missed it. Todd Pratt was now freaking out as he ran the bases. I remember looking down and seeing winning pitcher John Franco lose his mind as he danced toward home plate. The Mets had won the game and won the series, and I still couldn't believe Steve Finley, who was as good a defensive center fielder as anybody in the game somehow didn't make the play...but who gives an F!

"L.A. Woman" by The Doors, featuring the phrase "Mister Mojo Risin'," which somehow became the rally song of the team, blared over the PA system as hysteria ensued. Standing there in awe at Shea, my brain was having a tough time comprehending what the hell just happened. Did Todd Pratt, the backup to Mike Piazza just become a postseason legend? The Mets were going to the NLCS, and at the time the daunting opponent coming up was the last thing on my mind.

KEEPING SCORE: Leiter again came through like an ace, pitching into the eighth and leaving the game with a 2–1 lead and two runners on base before Benitez allowed them to score.... Pratt had been hitless in the series before his big home run. He went on to drive in three runs in the NLCS against Atlanta.

THE GRAND SLAM SINGLE

METS 4 BRAVES 3 (15 INNINGS)
GAME 5, NATIONAL LEAGUE CHAMPIONSHIP SERIES
OCTOBER 17, 1999, at SHEA STADIUM

THE METS beat the Braves, the Mets beat the Braves...a miracle had occurred a night earlier, the impossible had happened! The New York Mets won a freakin' baseball game against the Atlanta Braves. Going into Game 4 the previous evening, the Braves had gone 12–3 against the Mets in 1999. Want to go back further to the collapse of 1998? Okay, well, the Braves' record vs. the Mets balloons to 21–6 in their last 27 games. So winning a game against the Braves felt euphoric and like winning a World Series. The problem is we were still down 3–1 to the Braves in a best-of-seven NLCS. I had a very small goal in my head as I trudged into Shea Stadium on this Sunday afternoon and it was pretty simple. Keep the Atlanta Braves from partying and celebrating an NL championship at Shea Stadium. Just win another game and send this crap to the House of Horrors (also known as Turner Field), where eventually I would face my doom and be eliminated. This was my first year of watching the Mets in the playoffs, and after all the excitement of winning a one-game play-off and winning a tough four-game NLDS against Arizona, I think I could accept losing the NLCS to a better team, but please for the love of Casey Stengel, don't let them do it in Queens.

John Olerud hit a two-run home run in the first inning...but I sat at Shea waiting for the inevitable response from (likely) Chipper Jones and the Braves offense. That came in the fourth inning when Chipper Jones and Brian Jordan delivered back-to-back RBI hits to tie the game against Masato Yoshii, who was quickly chased from the game. Tied 2–2 in the fourth, it was the Mets bullpen vs. the legendary Greg Maddux. Yeah, that sure seemed like a fair fight. The game trudged on as the Mets pen did a spectacular job keeping the game close, especially former Mets nemesis Orel Hershisher, who got 10 outs of the pen.

This game was insane…every single inning it seemed like the Braves were poised to take the lead and eventually win the pennant, but the Mets escaped every damn time. This drunk baseball game had everything, including rookie Melvin Mora throwing out Keith Lockhart at the plate in the 13th inning after a Chipper Jones double to right field that could have given the Braves the lead. That moment figured to be the play that then set up the Mets to finally walk this shit off in the bottom of the 13th, especially with the heart of the order coming up. The problem was, that evil bastard John Rocker was finally inserted into the game, and we all knew we couldn't hit that square-headed prick even though he had allowed the game-winning hit to Olerud in Game 4. He easily set the Mets down 1-2-3 in the 13th inning. Was this game ever going to end? Luckily for us, it was a late-afternoon start of 4:11 PM, so the game lasting nearly six hours wasn't as nuts as if it had started at 8:00 PM. Finally, in the top of the 15th inning, which also happens to be the final inning I had room for in my scorebook, the Braves broke our hearts. With two outs, Lockhart ripped an RBI double into the gap in right-center field. The Braves had finally taken the lead and were three outs away from winning the National League pennant for the fifth time in eight completed seasons. There was one ounce of hope I could cling to: Rocker had already been used. So the Mets needed to scratch out a run against Kevin McGlinchy.

I will go to my grave saying Shawon Dunston put together the greatest at-bat I've ever seen. Dunston kept fouling off pitch after pitch and finally hit one through the hole at second base to begin the 15th with a single. After Matt Franco drew a walk and Edgardo Alfonzo laid down a sacrifice bunt, John Olerud was intentionally walked to bring up the cleanup hitter. *No*, it wasn't Mike Piazza. Mike was clearly banged up, and Bobby Valentine decided to pull him after he struck out to end the 13th inning, inserting Todd Pratt. This was *the* at-bat. Bases loaded, one out, down by a run. The rain at Shea Stadium was getting harder and harder. The little towel I had used to cover my book was now soaking wet. I wasn't sure my

VISITOR Braves	W-L 6-2	GB +2	HOME 3-1	ROAD 3-1	VS DIV. 3-1			
HOME Mets	W-L 4-4	GB 2	HOME 3-1	ROAD 1-3	VS DIV. 1-3			

book could take any more of it…nor could my stomach from watching this almost six-hour death march. When Pratt drew the walk to tie the game, I jumped high into the air. The Mets had come back to tie the game in the bottom of the 15th, which meant "Mr. Bases Loaded," Robin Ventura, would come up needing just a fly ball to win the game.

DATE _Sunday October 17, 1999_ STADIUM/CAP. _Shea Stadium_ 55,777 ATT. _55,723_

GAME # _All 9 Met 9_ WEATHER _cloudy 60's_ START/FINISH _4:11_ / _557_ TIME _5:46_

NL STANDINGS ☒ Longest Game in Postseason History ☒

DEFENSE — SERIES NLCS — Game 5

Wins in Series

All Met 3 1

Mets Force Game 6. Still Alive.

A classic.

Braves 000/200/000/000/001 3
Mets 200/000/000/000/002 4

Ventura hits Game Winning Grand Slam but never rounds base so gets only a Single

Yest. Conn's Star of the Game Yest.
All Robin 2 of 7 Game winning Met
Met 3 Ventura 21b 1RBI RBI. 1

New York Mets AVE HR H

©1996 Bob Carpenter Communications, Inc. All Rights Reserved

As the rain started pelting down on a warm October night, I did something I never do. I closed my scorebook and placed it into my bag before the conclusion of a game. As Robin Ventura strode to the plate to face McClinchy, my dad looked over at me. "You are shutting your scorebook?" he asked in an incredulous way. The rain had become worse and worse, and the towel I had used to keep my book dry was now soaking wet and could only take so much more water. It wasn't that I was confident Robin Ventura would end this game as much as it was my book had dealt with enough water! But I also knew something about this at-bat...good or bad, I would never forget it. Even if I didn't fill in the book in the car on the drive home, I could recite that entire AB more than two decades later. Ball one. Ball two...and then *boom!* A drive to right that sent the Mets back to Atlanta to force a Game 6. The cherry on top was that the ball went over the fence, and in a scene we may never see again, Robin Ventura was mobbed before he even got to second base, thus creating the infamous "Grand Slam Single." Thank goodness Robin ended the game right there. Not only because as a die-hard Mets fan the dream was alive...but it was the 15th inning in a 15-inning book with pouring rain falling down! What the heck would I have done if the game continued?

KEEPING SCORE: Seven Mets relievers (Hershiser, Turk Wendell, Dennis Cook, Pat Mahomes, John Franco, Armando Benitez, and Kenny Rogers) had kept the Braves off the board until Octavio Dotel, pitching in his third inning, allowed Lockhart's RBI double.... The Mets ended up using everyone on their 25-man roster except pitchers Rick Reed, who started Game 4, and Al Leiter, who would pitch Game 6.

IT CAN'T END LIKE THIS

BRAVES 10 METS 9 (11 INNINGS)
GAME 6, NATIONAL LEAGUE CHAMPIONSHIP SERIES
OCTOBER 19, 1999, at TURNER FIELD, ATLANTA

NO TEAM in the history of Major League Baseball had come back from a 3–0 deficit in any postseason series to this point in time. The New York Mets seemed like the unlikeliest team to break the streak. Dating back to the previous regular season, the Mets had a record of 6–21 against the Braves going into Game 4 of the 1999 NLDS, was that really going to be the team to rattle off four straight wins? But, as a naïve 16-year-old, the way the Mets had come back to win Game 5 made me believe in the impossible. Maybe, the 1999 Mets would be the team to obliterate logic and baseball history all in one fell swoop. The task at hand after winning back-to-back games at Shea was to simply win two games in Atlanta at Turner Field. The Mets' record at the aptly named House of Horrors was 1–13 over the past two seasons. So, yeah, winning consecutive games in that dump felt like a Herculean task.

To change the mojo, I began watching Game 6 on this Tuesday night in my parents' bedroom, which featured a very cool big-screen TV. It was straight out of the late 1990s, as it had a big fat base and was the complete opposite of the flatscreens we now love decades later. As a kid I thought it was the coolest thing and would sometimes make believe it was the Sharp TV screen at Shea Stadium as I would play pretend baseball in their room while watching it.

The first inning, though, made me rethink my mojo-changing decision as Al Leiter couldn't get a freakin' out. Al was clutch all season long, but with the season on the line and pitching on three days' rest, he had absolutely nothing. Al would reveal to me and my former radio partner Craig Carton on the air many years later that he had warmed up to pitch Game 5 in case the extra-inning affair had continued another inning. Looking back, that certainly is a fair excuse for why the normally clutch Al Leiter was so bad in this game, but in the moment I had no idea. Al was mercifully pulled for Pat Mahomes who somehow escaped what could have been an even worse first inning. Right from the get-go the Mets were down 5–0, and this game felt *finito*. At this point we changed the mojo again and returned to the den, where I had watched most Mets games throughout the season. Pat Mahomes (yes, the father of Patrick) did an excellent job keeping the score at 5–0, but the offense did nothing against Kevin Millwood, and this game felt like a slow death. But in true 1999 Mets fashion, they rallied to make it 5–3 in the sixth, keyed by a two-run single by Darryl Hamilton—and even after the Braves made it 7–3 in the bottom of the inning, the never-say-die Mets were at it again.

Besides the depressing conclusion, which we will certainly get to, there was a moment in this game that I think to this day ranks as one of the most spine-tingling moments in my life. It wasn't a play that won a game or even a series, but it was a home run that for my money was the single greatest thing Mike Piazza ever did as a Met, excluding the post-9/11 home run. John Smoltz was working out of

DATE October 19, 1999 Tuesday STADIUM/CAP. Turner Field 49,714 ATT. 52,335 _Largest crowd in stadium history_

GAME # Met 10 Atl 10 WEATHER Cloudy 60° START/FINISH 8:14 / TIME

NL STANDINGS

DEFENSE 10 A 2 E — Met DP/OPP 2

SERIES NLCS GAME 6

Wins in Series
Met 2
Atl 3

Braves win National League title

Mets	000	003	410	10	9
Braves	500	002	010	11	10

WOW NLCS M.V.P. Eddie Perez

A Great Run!

Rickey Henderson — Darryl Hamilton — Roger Cedeno
Ray Ordonez — Edgardo Alfonzo
Robin Ventura — 41 Al Leiter — John Olerud
N. Yost — Mike Piazza — G Hubba

Atlanta Braves	Ave .259	HR 6	H 11 RBI 81	1	2	3	4	5	6	7	8	9	10	11	12	13	14	15	AB	R	H	BI
27 Gerald Williams LF																						
24 Bret Boone 2b																						
10 Chipper Jones 3b																						
33 Brian Jordan RF																						
25 Andruw Jones CF																						
12 Eddie Perez C																						
19 Brian Hughes 1b																						
22 Walt Weiss SS																						

			R/ER	5/5	010	010	010	010	2|2	0|0	1|1	0|0	1|1	1|1
			H	2	0	1	0	0	2	0	3	0	2	1
			E	10	0	0	0	0	0	0	0	0	0
LH BENCH RH			LOB	0	0	1	0|1	0|1	2|3	0|3	1|4	1|5	1|6	3|9

Met PITCHERS	IP	R	ER	H	W	K	MISC.	LH Met BULLPEN RH
Al Leiter (22) 0-1 1.84		0	5	5	2	1	0	2UBF 25F 6BF
Pat Mahomes (23)	4	0	0	1	1	1	12BF
Turk Wendell (99)	1⅔	2	2	1	1	1	18F 1MBF
Dennis Cook (37)	⅓	0	0	1	0	0	2BF
Orel Hershiser (55)	1	0	0	0	0	0	11-2-7 5BF
John Franco (45)	1	1	1	2	0	1	5BF
Armando Benitez (49)	2	1	1	2	2	2	9BF

©1996 Bob Carpenter Communications, Inc. All Rights Reserved

the pen after having started Game 4 but clearly was not the same guy, as he had altered his delivery to throw sidearm. Smoltz labored through that seventh inning, and Bobby Cox allowed him to remain in the game to face Piazza with a man on and the score now 7–5. Mike swung and the ball exploded off his bat toward right-center field. As the ball cleared the fence, the emotion running though my body was like nothing I had ever experienced to this point. The Mets, who were down 5–0 in the House of Horrors, had miraculously rallied to tie the game on a majestic, opposite field, two-run home run by Piazza. After the shock and emotion of the moment wore off, the game settled into the worst/best/most agonizing experience I had ever witnessed as a baseball fan.

The Mets took the lead in the eighth on Melvin Mora's RBI single, but John Franco gave it back immediately in the bottom of the inning when Brian Hunter picked up an RBI single. In the 10th inning the Mets took the lead *again*—this time it was Todd Pratt delivering a tie-breaking sac fly. Todd had entered the game in the ninth inning after Bobby Valentine felt Piazza had been through enough psychically and pulled him from the game. Armando Benitez did a marvelous job keeping the game tied in the ninth as he navigated the top of the order, but when he began his second inning of work trying to hold a one-run lead and force a Game 7, Armando shoved it up our asses again. When he gave up the tying hit to Ozzie Guillen, I knew what our fate was. We didn't lose the game right then and there, but we kinda did. The Mets had now blown leads in the eighth and 10th innings with their two best relievers on the mound. They had squandered the leads with unlikely Braves coming through in those big spots. All the excitement from the comeback was leaving my body; entering it was depression. I knew we were fucked.

The bottom of the 11th is when the Mets lost the game, even if they really lost the game when they couldn't put the Braves away earlier. Kenny Rogers gave up a double to Gerald Williams to lead off the inning despite being ahead in the count 0–2. My God were we screwed now. Bret Boone laid down a sac bunt, so the Braves had the pennant-winning run on third base with one out. Bobby Valentine had no good choices now. The next three scheduled hitters with only one out were: Chipper Jones, Brian Jordan, and Andruw Jones. Obviously the easy part was walking Chipper, but at that point I would have taken my chances against Jordan. Instead Valentine also walked Jordan and set up bases loaded, one out, for Andruw Jones with zero margin for error. Valentine figured if they could somehow get Andruw out, the on-deck hitter would be pitcher Russ Springer, who would be forced to hit since Cox had no position players left on his bench. Valentine's other pitching option was to go to the young Octavio Dotel, who had pitched three innings the day before, but he stuck with Rogers. This sequence lives in my soul forever. Pitch one was low, pitch two was low, as well. A 2–0 count and nowhere to put Andruw Jones. Pitch three was a little tapper that just rolled foul, and thank God it did. If it remained fair, the game would have ended on an infield single. Pitch four was not even close, up and away. As I awaited the 3–1 delivery, all I was asking for was not to end this on a walk. *Let him hit the ball, and if he hits it out so be it. But this season cannot end on a damn walk.* The crowd chanted, "Andruw, Andruw!" from the top of their redneck lungs. Kenny nipped the outside corner to make the count full. All the while I remember everything the broadcasters were saying leading up to this fateful pitch. Joe Morgan was begging for the game to not end on a walk, and Bob Costas was talking about the wild ride the season had been for the Mets.

Kenny Rogers then did what we all feared. Ball four, series over, season over. Bob Costas screamed, "Bring on the Yankees!" as Gerald Williams marched toward home. I was speechless and quietly said good night to my dad as I stoically walked to my bedroom. I'm an emotional guy, so there have been a few occasions were an amazing win or incredible moment brought me tears of joy. On this night, it was different. I cried myself to sleep thinking about the journey, how close we were to doing the impossible and the amazing sadness of it all being over. I wrote "A Great Run" in my scorebook's notes section. It was a great run, but it had the saddest ending I could have ever imagined.

KEEPING SCORE: After using 23 players in Game 5, Bobby Valentine used every position player and every pitcher except Rick Reed, Masato Yoshii, and Dotel.... Gerald Williams ended up playing the final two seasons of his 11-year career with the Mets in 2004 and 2005.... The Braves went on to get swept by the Yankees in the 1999 World Series.

The

2000s

BAGELS AND BASEBALL

WHEN I READ the news months earlier that the Mets would open the 2000 season in Japan against the Cubs, I didn't think it was a big deal. I figured it would be like any other Opening Day that didn't begin at Shea Stadium, so even though we would lose one home game and the perfect home attendance would now be 80 instead of 81, I didn't think it was an earth-shattering development. What did alter my mood was when I saw the game times for the two contests to open the season. The scheduled first pitch for the highly anticipated 2000 season would be at 5:10 AM Eastern Time. I didn't mind waking up early, that didn't seem like too big a hindrance, but now I was going to have convince my mom that potentially having to show up to school a little bit late wasn't a big deal. Opening Day at Shea was already a national holiday in the Roberts household, so there was never an issue with skipping school for that one. But this one may be a tad more tricky since there was an unknown of when this game would end. If the game was clearly decided, then maybe it wouldn't be a big deal to miss the last inning or so. But what if the game was really close, or dare I say, an extra-inning affair? I was 16 years old and at the height of my Mets obsession, plus we were going into the most highly anticipated season of my lifetime! The Mets

Scorecard — Japan Series, Game 2 of 2

DATE: Thursday, March 30, 2000 — STADIUM/CAP. Tokyo Dome 55,000 — ATT. 55,000
GAME #: Met 2 Cub 2 — WEATHER: Dome — START/FINISH: 5:10 AM / 9:05 AM — TIME: 355

Met PITCHERS	IP	R	ER	H	W	K	MISC.
Rick Reed (35)	8	1	0	4	3	4	30 BF, 2 DP
John Franco (45)	1	0	0	1	1	2	5 BF
Turk Wendell (99)	2/3	0	0	0	2	0	4 BF
Dennis Cook (27)	1/3	0	0	0	1	1	2 BF
Armando Benitez (49)							

©1996 Bob Carpenter Communications, Inc. All Rights Reserved

had just a few months earlier lost a classic playoff series to Atlanta, and then during the off-season made a big trade for 20-game winner Mike Hampton (along with right fielder Derek Bell for Roger Cedeno, Octavio Dotel, and a minor league pitcher). They did lose John Olerud to the Seattle Mariners in free agency, but nonetheless the hype going into 2000 was off the charts.

Mets | W-L 0-1 | GB 1/2 | HOME 0-1 | ROAD 0-0 | VS DIV. 0-0
VISITOR
Cubs | W-L 1-0 | GB +1/2 | HOME 0-0 | ROAD 1-0 | VS DIV. 0-0
HOME
AL STANDINGS

	R	H	E	LOB	Cub DP/OPP	DEFENSE	E
Met	5	6	2	10			
Cub	1	5	0	10			

WP Dennis Cook 1-0
LP Danny Young 0-1 ☆ 1st ML. Loss
SV ~~~~~~~~

UMPIRES
Kulpa 2B
Marsh 3B • 1B Foster
HP
Hernandez

Defense: Henry, Rodriguez, Damon, Buford, Jenny, Josol, Jeff Huson, Eric Young, Shane Andrews, Kyle Farnsworth 0.00, Mack Grace, C. Rojas, M. Wilson, Joe Girardi

AL Standings:
Bal 0-0, 1B 0-0, Tor 0-0, Bos 0-0, NY 0-0
Min 0-0, Cle 0-0, KC 0-0, Det 0-0, Cws 0-0
Sea 0-0, Oak 0-0, Tex 0-0, Ana 0-0

New York Mets	Ave	HR	H	1	2	3	4	5	6	7	8	9	10	11	AB	R	H	BI
24 Rickey Henderson LF	.250														12	13	14	15

(Remaining scorecard cells contain handwritten play-by-play notations for each batter: Darryl Hamilton CF, Jay Payton, Edgardo Alfonzo 2B, Benny Agbayani, Armando Benitez P, Mike Piazza C, Robin Ventura 3B, Derek Bell RF, Todd Zeile 1B, Rey Ordonez SS, Rick Reed P, John Nunnally PH, Melvin Mora PH.)

R/ER	0	0	0	0	0	0	0	0	1	1	0	0	0	0	0	0	0	0	0	0	4	4
H	1	0	0	1	0	1	0	0	0	0	3
E	0	0	0	0	0	0	0	0	0	0	0
LOB	1	0	1	0	1	2	3	1	4	3	7	2	9	0	9	0	9	0	9	1	10

Cub PITCHERS	IP	R	ER	H	W	K	MISC.
Kyle Farnsworth (44)	5 2/3	1	1	3	4	4	1HBP 105P 28BF
Matt Karchner (52)	1 1/3	0	0	0	2	0	6BF
Mack Guthrie (30)	1/3	0	0	0	0	0	1BF
Brian Williams (51)	1	0	0	0	0	0	3BF
Felix Heredia (45)	2 1/3	0	0	0	0	0	7BF
Rick Aguilera (38)	1	0	0	0	0	1	11-2-3
Danny Young (35)	1	4	4	3	2	0	7BF 1HR

LH BENCH RH
Franco / Abbott
Nunnally / Pratt

DL
NO ONE

LH Cub BULLPEN RH

The season opener featured the aforementioned Mike Hampton, and it was a dud. Honestly I don't remember much about the game other than the fact Hampton couldn't find the strike zone, and we lost to the Chicago Cubs to begin the regular season. But the game that is etched in my memory was the second and final game of the Japan series. Rick Reed was on the mound to face future

Mets reliever Kyle Farnsworth. This game turned into everything I feared could cause some school arrival drama. A tight pitchers' duel between Reed and Farnsworth extended to each team's pen. Sometimes going back and looking at these games is a stark reminder of how different the game is now. I remember my father and grandfather bemoaning how different the sport was when I was a kid, and now I'm doing the same thing, but it's true! Rick Reed pitched eight innings, allowing only an unearned run in the bottom of the fifth inning due to an error by new first baseman Todd Zeile after the Mets scored in the top of the inning on a Rickey Henderson sac fly. It is now rare to see a pitcher go eight innings even in the middle of July let alone his first start in March.

The Mets pen kept it tied at 1–1 when Dennis Cook struck out Henry Rodriguez with the bases loaded in the 10th. As that was occurring, my mom was telling me time was up and it was time to go to school. What potentially could happen in the next few innings would certainly be more memorable than 11th grade Biology at 8:30 AM in late March 2000. How true is that statement? In the top of the 11th Benny Agbayani set the tone for what would be a very fun season to follow with a grand slam to dead center field. I can still picture the ball coming off his bat and Benny doing a little hop out of the batter's box, but I cannot tell you one freakin' thing I learned in Biology that year. Armando Benitez shut the door in the bottom of the 11th with two strikeouts, including Joe Girardi to end the game, and the Mets closed out the Japan series with a 5–1 win. While I'm no fan of neutral-site baseball games (or football games for that matter), I have to admit this a few decades later: if that game had been at Wrigley Field as Game 2 of the regular season, it would have been *far* less memorable. But when you factor in the oddity of waking up at 4:30 AM to watch baseball, the battle to miss the first few minutes of school and the outcome...you have an incredibly memorable moment. The Mets split the two games in Japan, Benny was a hero, and I came into school filling everyone in on what had just happened. I spent many a random morning at Lawrence High School, but walking in that morning a tad late was one of my favorites.

KEEPING SCORE: Their 5–3 loss on Opening Day marked the first time the Mets had lost consecutive season openers since they dropped their first eight from 1962 to 1969.... Former Met Rick Aguilera got the save in that game.... Agbayani's grand slam came against a lefty named Danny Young, making his major league debut after nine seasons in the minors. He made three more appearances for the Cubs in early April and never appeared in another major league game.

THE MOST MEMORABLE RAINOUT

[POSTPONED]

JUNE 11, 2000, at YANKEE STADIUM

THE FIRST TWO games of the 2000 Subway Series were very forgettable. I can cite almost everything that happened in 1997, 1998, and 1999. I also remember the latter part of the 2000 Subway Series and obviously the World Series like the back of my hand. But for some reason the first two games of the Yankee Stadium portion of the intercity rivalry have completely escaped my memory. Looking back, the Mets and Yankees split the first two games in blowout fashion, with the Mets winning on Friday night and the Yankees on Saturday afternoon. But the *Sunday Night Baseball* finale, which featured a very sexy pitching matchup of David Cone versus Mike Hampton is etched in my memory despite it never actually happening.

My father and I had excellent seats for the finale, field level about 12 rows off the field behind home plate. We would sit in these seats a couple times per season because my father was able to buy five games per season in an era when those seats were not crazy expensive. These days, those seats would qualify as legend seats and be well out of my price range. As we sat down for the rubber game of the series, the weather was very ominous as rain was in the forecast. David Cone was having an abysmal season, sporting an ERA over

6.00, but over the first three innings the Mets' bats could not touch him. In fact, Cone pitched three hitless innings and worked around two walks. The Yankees, on the other hand, touched up Hampton a bit to take an early 1–0 lead. I vividly remember Jay Payton making a sick catch in center field that actually saved Hampton from this game looking even worse. The rain started coming down profusely in the bottom of the third inning, and the game was finally stopped.

To this day I have a strategy with my scorebook during rain games. I have a mini towel that I use to cover the book and then I peek underneath to quickly write in what just happened in the game. The rain was so bad that my strategy was starting to backfire as the water filled up my towel. When the game stopped, my dad couldn't wait to hightail it back to the corridor in the bowels of Yankee Stadium to take cover. I did the same, and we stood in the runway waiting for the rain to stop. Whenever I have a moment where I miss the old Shea Stadium or the old Yankee Stadium, I think of this night to knock some sense into me. The worst thing about the old stadiums was a night like this. When it rained, there was legit nowhere to go! Thousands and thousands of people would stand next to each other, shoulder to shoulder, waiting. It was like standing in a crowded subway car, except in this case there was no endgame. This rain delay could take *hours*, who the hell knew? Finally, I decided to walk around the old stadium to kill some time. Again, not the most comfortable experience, as every part of the stadium was jam-packed. This was a night when it was a clear sellout and nobody was going to leave early because it was Mets-Yankees. The beer was also flowing, so not only was every single inch of Yankee Stadium packed, it also featured tons of drunk people talking trash about the two teams. I can't remember exactly how long I waited back there, but finally I said to my dad, "I don't care how wet I get, I can't take this anymore. I'm going back to the seat." He begrudgingly joined me back at the seat where the rain poured down on our heads. My dad even admitted after a few minutes that as uncomfortable as the rain might be, it was still a far better experience than standing in the sweaty, smelly, disgusting corridors of Yankee Stadium.

Nets W-L 34-27 GB 5 HOME 19-11 ROAD 15-16 VS DIV. 3-6
VISITOR
Yankees W-L 43-24 GB +1 Bos HOME 16-11 ROAD 17-13 VS DIV. 8-7
HOME
AL STANDINGS

Met	R	H	E	LOB
NYY				
WP				
LP				
SV				

Met — Game Postponed in 3rd inning. Due to Rain.

NYY DP/OPP DEFENSE

UMPIRES Hernandez?
2B
Foster 3B • 1B Marsh
HP
Kulpa

Shane Spencer — Bernie Williams — Paul O'Neil

Derek Jeter — Clay Bellinger

Scott Brosius — (6.19 Derek Cone) — Tino Martinez

C. Reyes — M. Wilson

Chris Turner

AL STANDINGS:
① NYY 43-24 / Bos 1 / Tor 3½ / Bal 3½ / TB 12
② Cws 47-24 / Cle 2 / KC 5 / Min 10 / Det 14½
③ Oak 41-28 / Sea 1½ / Ana 1½ / Tex 3½
④ Cle 41-25 / Bos 1 / KC 2 / KC/Ana 3

New York Mets Ave 265 HR 79 H 553

	Player	Pos	Ave	HR	H	1	2	3	4	5	6	7	8	9	10	11	AB 12	R 13	H 14	BI 15
11	Jason Tyner	lf	286	0	3	⓪/4-3	③ DP /L4													
16	Derek Bell	rf	295	8	31	⓵/6/3						R								
13	Edgardo Alfonzo	2b	347	12	47	④/5/1 k						A	O							
31	Mike Piazza	DH	367	16	53	⓪/7/3							T	U						
4	Robin Ventura	3b	231	12	34	//BB							N	T						
9	Todd Zeile	1b	266	16	43	②/7/9														
44	Jay Payton	cf	265	6	24	⓪/7/3														
7	Todd Pratt	c				4-3 ⓪/7/BB														
20	Kurt Abbott	ss	215	2	3	⓪/7/K														

Mike Hampton 6-5 3.49 GS 13 GRO
IP 83⅔ H 92 BB 47 SO 53

	R/ER	1	2	3											
	R/ER	010	010	0/0											
	H	0	0	0											
	E	0	0	0											
	LOB	0	1	0/1											

LH BENCH RH
Franco Agbayani
Hosey Mora
McEwing

DL
Hamilton 15 Ochoa 15

NYY PITCHERS

		IP	R	ER	H	W	K	MISC.
1-6 6.49 David Cone	36	3	0	0	0	2	4	10BF
		5	T	A	T	S		
		0	o	n	-	+		
		C	0	v	n	+		

LH NYY BULLPEN RH
Stanton Erdos
Watson Nelson
Grimsley
Rivera

Staff Clemens
Pettitte Hernandez
Mendoza

DL
De Los Santos 15

©1996 Bob Carpenter Communications, Inc. All Rights Reserved

Because of how the first few innings went, I started to root to just can the game. Down 1–0 with Cone dealing, I preferred just raining the game out and moving on. I also wasn't sure how a rainout would be handled...would they make this game up on a common off day late in the season? Would they move the game to Shea Stadium? I wasn't sure, but I was very curious to see how it would play out. Finally, about a half hour later, the decision to get rained

DATE _June 11, 2000_ (Sunday) STADIUM/CAP. _Yankee Stadium_ ATT. _____

GAME # Met 62 NYY 58 WEATHER _Overcast Muggy_ START/FINISH _8:09_ / _Never_ TIME _Finished_

NL STANDINGS

SERIES — Subway Series, Interleague Play, 3 of 3 season series

1-1 tie — Ventura puts on Rain Delay theater.
Mets 0 0 0 — Rain out.
Yankees 0 1

Game Postponed!! Will be made up on history Day. Night Yankee Sked Day Night Double Header on 7/8/00

Ernie's Star of the Game — NO Star

New York Yankees	Ave	HR	H	1	2	3	4	5	6	7	8	9	10	11	AB	R	H	BI
2 Derek Jeter SS	.341								R									
51 Bernie Williams CF	.336				K				A	O								
21 Paul O'Neil RF	.299							A	O									
20 Jorge Posada DH	.326							I	U									
Tino Martinez 1b	.279				K			N	T									
47 Shane Spencer LF	.257		BB															
18 Scott Brosius 3b	.248																	
26 Chris Turner C	.300																	
35 Clay Bellinger 2b	.219																	

	R/ER	0:0	1:1										
	H	2	2										
	E	0	0										
	LOB	2	2/4										

BENCH — Knoblauch, Leyritz, SU, Jose, Delgado

Met PITCHERS	IP	R	ER	H	W	K	MISC.
Mike Hampton	2⅔	1	1	4	1	3	12 BF / 47 P

STATS Don't Count

©1996 Bob Carpenter Communications, Inc. All Rights Reserved

on paid off in a way I least expected. I started to hear a buzz coming out of the few hundred people that were also sitting in their seats and getting rained on. I glanced up to see a man donning a Mike Piazza jersey heading toward where home plate would be on the puddled-up tarpaulin. We quickly realized it was Robin Ventura dressed as Mike, also sporting a fake mustache and fake sideburns.

The crowd began to roar as the fake Piazza strode to the plate and began imitating all of Mike's mannerisms. Robin then swung his bat and to a damn T started running to first base exactly like Mike would. He turned first and headed toward second as he dove in headfirst with a huge splash occurring as he got there. The crowd was now roaring its approval as we laughed hysterically watching it unfold. We could also see the entire Mets dugout had come back from the locker room to watch what was going on. Fake Piazza then took a lead off second and started racing around third base, he dove headfirst into home again making a huge splash. We were now on our feet exploding in approval. A soaked Ventura then stood up and waved to the crowd.

Besides getting to enjoy this shocking moment, we also knew he wasn't going to pull that act if the game was going to restart. So the handwriting was on the wall that this game was being banged. I was so happy that we went to our seat, because if we were stuck back in the Yankee Stadium corridor, we would have missed this awesome moment. And you could mock it all you want now, but that moment was freakin' awesome! How many times have you sat at a rain delay looking at that soaked tarpaulin, thinking, *Damn, wouldn't it be fun to run around on that big old Slip 'n Slide?* Robin Ventura, while imitating Mike Piazza, did it! He rewarded us loonies for sticking out a long rain delay by getting to see his comedy show. If that wasn't fun enough, when the game was canned, it was announced that the following month history would be made. The Mets and Yankees would play a two-stadium, one-day double-header. Little did I know, but both of those games would live in history for all the wrong reasons.

KEEPING SCORE: Ventura would make Yankee Stadium his home two years later, after the Mets traded him to the Yankees in a deal for David Justice, who the Mets then flipped to the Oakland A's for lefty reliever Mark Guthrie.... Hampton's next start, three days later at Chicago's Wrigley Field, was also impacted by rain. He came out after the first inning in a game the Mets would go on to win 10–8.

THE 10-RUN INNING

METS 11 BRAVES 8

JUNE 30, 2000, at SHEA STADIUM

AS A TEENAGER I absolutely loved Fireworks Night at Shea Stadium, and it had nothing to do with fireworks. I'm the same way today, but even as a kid I wanted to get out of the stadium I was in as fast as possible. If you waited even a few minutes to enjoy a win, you were stuck arm to arm with people slowly walking out down the endless corridors and then likely to sit in traffic getting out of the lot. Fireworks Nights were awesome because everybody would stay for the show, and we would very easily walk out of Shea without a hitch. A year earlier in 1999, the Mets played the Braves also on a Fireworks Night and got absolutely pummeled, 16–0. Since my father and I both have a rule of never leaving early, we were the oddities walking out of Shea after the game concluded with everyone staying in their seat in anticipation of fireworks. Even as a teenager I was like an old man. I was a hell of a lot more concerned with departing a stadium and getting home at a reasonable hour than watching a fireworks display. Losing by 16 runs sucked, but walking out of Shea casually and in no rush was sort of nice. Unfortunately, one year later, against the exact same opponent, we were witnessing the same outcome. The Braves were blowing out the Mets on Fireworks Night by a score of 8–1 in the eighth inning...and then something magical happened.

After the epic 1999 NLCS, we had to wait until late June for the Mets to get another crack at the hated Atlanta Braves. The night before it finally happened, and as expected, we lost *again*. Despite the shocking wins a year earlier in Games 4 and 5 of the NLCS, the Braves still absolutely owned us, and it was continuing on this night. We couldn't even blame the usual culprit Chipper Jones because he was not in the lineup. The third baseman filling in for him...Bobby Bonilla. Yeah, you can't make this shit up. What's so nuts about that

©1996 Bob Carpenter Communications, Inc. All Rights Reserved

infamous 10-run eighth inning against the Braves is that it really seemed to manifest from nothing. The Mets had scratched out one run in the inning to make it 8–2, but there two outs and only one guy on base. The Mets then got six base runners in a row on with a mix of singles and walks. When Derek Bell drew the third consecutive bases-loaded walk to make it 8–6 with Edgardo Alfonzo coming up,

Friday

DATE June 30, 2000   STADIUM/CAP. Shea Stadium   55,777   Sell out 52,831 ATT.

GAME # All 75 Met 77   WEATHER clear 70's   START/FINISH 7:11 / 10:36   TIME 325

NL STANDINGS

SERIES   2 of 4

Season Series
1 to All

Piazza's RBI's in 4th extends streak of consec. games w/ RBC to 19.

Braves 103 | 000 | 000 | 13 0 8
Mets 000 | 000 | 110X | 11

WOW   Mets trailed 8 to 1 in 7th before beginning incredible comeback.

New York Mets	Ave	HR	H
Mets	271	101	707

©1996 Bob Carpenter Communications, Inc. All Rights Reserved

that was legit the first time in the inning where I thought to myself, *Holy crap, we might actually come back.* Alfonzo was the most clutch hitter on the Mets—we all witnessed it a year earlier as he came through multiple times during each round of the Mets' deep playoff run. I trusted Fonzie more than any other Met, and here he was one hit away from miraculously tying this game up. Edgardo fell behind

Terry Mulholland 1–2 before he stroked the game-tying single to left field. Shea Stadium was rocking as the tying runs scored and the Mets had somehow come back from 8–1 down in the eighth to tie this up. What added to the magic of this comeback was that a crowd of more than 50,000 was rocking Shea Stadium to a October-like decibel level. Without Fireworks Night, this doesn't happen! Let's be honest, if there was no postgame fireworks show, half of that crowd would have hit the exits two innings prior. If not then, they would have fled after Brian Jordan hit the three-run home run in the top of the eighth that turned a 5–1 game into 8–1. Thank God for those dopey fireworks, because that forced each and every person to be in their seat to witness a moment they would never forget.

Mike Piazza was now up in a tie game, and there was zero doubt in my mind that big Mike would break this tie. I say this with no ill will, but Piazza had a habit of basically hijacking Edgardo Alfonzo's big moments. Obviously that wasn't a malicious thing, but it was damn true. So I knew Mike would make this about him by getting the game-winning hit, which would make the clutchness of Fonzie coming through down 1–2 in the count forgettable. Piazza ripped the first pitch he saw from Terry Mulholland over the left-field fence, and Shea was now delirious. Ten runs in the eighth, with nine of them coming with two outs...the Mets had pulled off the most shocking comeback you could imagine against the most unlikely opponent. Armando Benitez made it a little nerve-racking in the ninth, but got the final three outs to secure the victory. What an insane win, with memorable moments. And the best part, you ask? We didn't have to rush to leave the building because everyone waited to see their fireworks. The eighth inning supplied enough of those for me!

KEEPING SCORE: Benitez was credited with the victory by the official scorer because the pitcher of record when the Mets took the lead, Eric Cammack (who gave up the three-run homer to Jordan), had been ineffective.... The 10-run inning was the second in Mets history, the first was a far less dramatic rally from 5–2 down in the sixth inning to beat the Cincinnati Reds at Shea in June 1979.

DOC RETURNS

YANKEES 4 METS 2 (FIRST GAME)
JULY 8, 2000, at SHEA STADIUM

IT HAS BEEN many years since the passing of George Steinbrenner, and as time has gone by the legend of him has only grown. From his will to win to the crazy spending and over-the-top demands of winning at all costs, there is one other attribute of The Boss that he owned. His desire to, and obsession with, sticking it to the crosstown Mets. One could only imagine what George Steinbrenner would do in modern times with an owner like Steve Cohen sharing the city. But in the late '90s, besides winning and spending, there was one other thing George took to legendary proportions...screwing with the little brother Mets.

It started with him collecting former 1986 Mets like they were freakin' trading cards. I don't deny that George did a lot of good by giving men well-deserved second chances, but one has to wonder... are those second chances given if they didn't play for the 1986 Mets? First, it was Darryl Strawberry in 1995, and then in 1996 after serving a full one-year suspension, Dwight "Doc" Gooden did the impossible and joined the Yankees. The night he pitched a no-hitter I sat there with incredibly mixed feelings. I loved Doc as a kid growing up, but seeing him do something no Mets pitcher had ever done at this point for the Yankees was painful. Doc then floated around MLB for a while, pitching for the Indians and then in 2000 starting the season with the Astros before quickly joining his hometown Tampa Bay Devil Rays. As soon as he was released in May 2000, the rumors began to percolate on another Doc-Yankees marriage. It didn't take long for George to scoop him up in mid-June despite Doc struggling through the 2000 season. The Mets and Yankees were scheduled to hook up in the second portion of the 2000 Subway Series a few weeks later, which would include a unique two-stadium, single-day doubleheader. As we creeped closer and closer to the big series and as Doc pitched a couple games in rookie ball, something was becoming obvious in my head. George Steinbrenner, ever the showman, was going to have Doc Gooden return as a Yankee against the Mets at Shea Stadium.

Oh, well, wouldn't you know. On the historic day when the Mets and Yankees would play a two-stadium doubleheader, Dwight Gooden would return to Shea for the first time since departing the

DATE July 8, 2000 (Saturday) STADIUM/CAP. Shea Stadium 55,777 ATT. 54,165

GAME # N44 81 Mal 84 WEATHER sunny 76° START/FINISH 1:21 / 4:37 TIME 3:16

NL STANDINGS

SERIES Subway Series
Interleague Play Round 2
2 of 4
Game 1 of historic Day/Night 2 stadium Doubleheader.
Season Series
2-1 N44

Yankees 200 001 010 4
Mets 010 010 000 2

Valentine ejected arguing interference call in 1st inn.

Tino Martinez 24 HR 3RBI — 3 of 4, Go ahead HR in 6th

New York Mets AVE .270 HR 111 H 769

		AB	R	H	BI
	1 2 3 4 5 6 7 8 9 10 11	12	13	14	15

PITCHERS

PITCHERS	IP	R	ER	H	W	K	MISC.
Doc Gooden (17)	2-3 6.86	5	2	2	6	1	1	22 BF
Jason Grimsley (38)	1⅔	0	0	0	0	1	6 BF
Jeff Nelson (43)	1⅓	0	0	0	0	1	4 BF
Mariano Rivera (42)	1	0	0	0	0	1	11 2-3

©1996 Bob Carpenter Communications, Inc. All Rights Reserved

Mets six years earlier. Doc would pitch Game 1 at Shea, and Roger Clemens would start the nightcap at Yankee Stadium. The former dueling aces of 1986 would now team up 14 years later to take on the Mets. I was completely sick over this. Forget winning or losing the game, the idea of seeing Doc pitch for the Yankees at Shea Stadium was an image that would be like seeing a sex video of an ex-girlfriend in your bedroom. I knew immediately how I would react—cheers, it had to be cheers. Doc Gooden was a legendary Met, who unfortunately had personal demons that affected his tenure and essentially ended it. While I wanted Mets ownership to give him a second chance and bring him back, I also understood why they didn't. I also wasn't sure how much Gooden even had left. But still, he was without question going to get a standing ovation from me at the beginning of the game.

The game began in the oddest way you could imagine. Chuck Knoblauch blooped a single and was thrown out trying to stretch it to a double. What stunned all of us in the crowd was that Knoblauch was awarded second base, thanks to the insistence of Yankees first-base coach Lee Mazzilli (another 1986 Met), because obstruction was called on the first basemen Todd Zeile for interfering with the base runner. In the days before I could whip out my iPad to see the play, we were all stunned and confused on why that call was made. Of course, the freakin' Yankees would take advantage of it, led by the Captain of being a pain in my ass, Derek Jeter, driving in the first run of the game with a double and scoring three batters later on a single by Tino Martinez. So as Doc took the mound to a very nice ovation, he had already been given a 2–0 lead. While Doc received just about all cheers, I do think the enthusiasm for him was tempered by the Mets trailing by two runs. Here is what I remember most about this game after Doc received his warm ovation: the Mets just couldn't pound him, despite that being the expectation. Remember, Gooden was released by the freakin' Tampa Bay Devil Rays and had an ERA of just about 7.00 coming into this game. There was zero excuse for the Mets bats not to explode. But they didn't. Mike Piazza made a couple of meek outs, and even though they rallied to tie the game at 2–2 in the fifth inning on a double by Derek Bell, it never felt like enough. They also couldn't hit the Yankees pen at all, as Jason Grimsley, Jeff Nelson, and Mariano Rivera shut the Mets' bats down after the Yankees regained the lead in the sixth on a Tino Martinez home run off Bobby Jones. We lost 4–2. What a freakin' buzzkill... they couldn't hit Doc, they couldn't hit the Yankees bullpen, and now a cloud hung over us as we began the trek to Yankee Stadium for Game 2 that night.

KEEPING SCORE: The split-stadium doubleheader was the first of its kind since Labor Day 1903 when the Giants and Dodgers played a morning game in Brooklyn and an afternoon game in Manhattan.... Gooden went 4–2 after joining the Yankees and made two postseason appearances in 2000 (none in the World Series), his last year in the majors.

CLEMENS BEANS PIAZZA IN THE HEAD

YANKEES 4 METS 2 (SECOND GAME)

JULY 8, 2000, at YANKEE STADIUM

I WAS LUCKY as hell that my dad would take me to these awesome Mets games throughout my years growing up. After sitting in our seats at Shea for the afternoon game between the Mets and Yankees, there was no doubt when this historic two-stadium doubleheader was announced that we would also be going to Yankee Stadium for the nightcap. The night game in the Bronx was the makeup game for the rainout from a month earlier, which was best remembered as the day Robin Ventura imitated Mike Piazza and used the tarp as an adult Slip 'n Slide (*see* "The Most Memorable Rainout," p. 107). So we were able to use our same tickets from that game for the makeup affair, which happened to be awesome seats right behind home plate. What I didn't understand was our plan for getting to Game 2. We kept our car parked at Shea and then proceeded to take the convoluted train ride from Shea to Yankee Stadium, which is not as easy as the "Subway Series" nickname would imply. We needed to take the

Mets W-L 47-37 GB 3 HOME 28-17 ROAD 19-20 VS DIV. 10-12
VISITOR
Yankees W-L 44-37 GB +1 Tor HOME 19-17 ROAD 24-26 VS DIV. 14-13
HOME

Met	R 2	H 7	E 0	LOB 7
N4Y	4	5	1	2

WP Roger Clemens 6-6
LP Glendon Rusch 5-7
SV Mariano Rivera 21

UMPIRES
DeMuth 2B
cook 3B • 1B Carlson
HP Elkings

DEFENSE — Shane Spencer, Bernie Williams, Paul O'Neill, Derek Jeter, Chuck Knoblauch, Scott Brosius, Roger Clemens, Tino Martinez, C. Rojas, M. Watson, Chris Turner

New York	Ave	HR	H	1	2	3	4	5	6	7	8	9	10	11	AB 12	R 13	H 14	BI 15
Mets	269	111	775															
Lenny Harris LF 175 1613															3	1	0	0
Derek Bell RF 313 12452															4	0	3	1
Edgardo Alfonzo 2b 320 13857															4	0	2	1
Mike Piazza DH 314 24672															0	0	0	0
Matt Franco PC 230 045															2	0	1	0
Benny Agbayani PH 295 7229															1	0	0	0
Robin Ventura 3b 238 1653															4	0	0	0
Todd Zeile 1b 310 18251															4	0	0	0
Jay Payton CF 256 3027															4	0	0	0
Todd Pratt C 277 6216															4	0	0	0
Melvin Mora SS 290 5225															3	1	1	0
Mark Johnson PH 198 166															1	0	0	0

Glendon Rusch 6-6 4.38 63 14 6R1
JV 53⅓H 99 88 17 50 71

	R/ER	0/0	0/0	0/0	0/0	2/2	0/0	0/0	0/0	0/0
	H	1	0	0	2	3	0	0	1	0
	E	0	0	0	0	0	0	0	0	0
LOB		0	1	0/1	2/3	2/5	0/5	0/5	1/6	1/7

LH BENCH RH
Franco McEwing
Johnson Agbayani
SH Leub
OL
Hamilton 15 Abbott 15 Ochoa 60

N4Y PITCHERS	IP	R	ER	H	W	K	MISC.
5-6 4.38 (8) Roger Clemens	7⅓	2	2	7	1	4	30BF 1HP
Mike Stanton (29)	2/3	0	0	0	0	1	2BF
Mariano Rivera (4)	1	0	0	0	0	0	4BF

LH N4Y BULLPEN RH
Stanton, Daymon, Choate, Entrom, Nelson, stuff, Grimsley, Cone, Gooden, Hernandez
OL Watson 15 De Los Santos 60, Mendoza 15

7 Train into Manhattan before switching over to the 4 to ride up to the Bronx. A car ride would have been much easier, but I'm guessing my dad didn't want to deal with the parking situation in the Bronx. Either way, I'm not complaining! Okay, maybe all these years later, I just know I would have done it slightly differently.

Roger Clemens was on the mound for the Yankees as the Mets tried to win a game in this expanded four-game series after losing the first two contests. The Mets had sort of become Clemens's daddy over the years. Since becoming a Yankee in 1999, he had pitched 13⅔ innings and allowed 20 earned runs in three starts, all losses, against the Mets. Mike Piazza had inflicted a lot of the damage on the Rocket during the course of those three beatdowns (5-for-8 with three home runs and eight RBIs). On this night in the Bronx, Roger would finally do something about his shortcomings. Leading off the top of the second inning as the designated hitter, Mike strode to the plate to take on his buddy. Clemens poured in a fast ball for strike one. The second pitch from Roger came way up and way in as it drilled Piazza in the noggin. Being as close as we were, we could hear the *pop* as the baseball hit Mike's helmet. He went down in a heap, and we jumped out of our seats as Mike laid motionless in the batter's box. The crowd at Yankee Stadium, which was mostly Yankee fans began buzzing and booing. While Yankee fans were certainly not rooting for the Mets or for Mike, they also knew what Clemens was. They had all witnessed it firsthand being on the other side. Clemens was a head-hunting piece of shit, and every single Yankees fan in that building that night knew what they had just seen. A dominant starting pitcher, who for some reason was having recent struggles against a particular team and *major* struggles against another premier player, took his anger out by pitching dangerously up and in and showing no care in the world. Derek Jeter knew what it was like to be buzzed and drilled by Clemens, and as he stood there at shortstop that night, I'm sure he had some minor flashbacks. My anger was tempered by my concern for Mike, who still lay on the ground. He would eventually get up but obviously had to leave the game.

As the contest went on, my anger began to boil. When the Mets scored two runs in the fifth inning on consecutive two-out RBI singles by Derek Bell and Edgardo Alfonzo to take a 2–0 lead, it was Matt Franco, taking over Piazza's spot in the order, who came up with two runners on base and made the final out that inning. For some reason, that sequence pissed me off. Mike should have been up, and based on his recent history, he would likely have done damage against Clemens in that spot. Glendon Rusch gave it all back in the bottom of the fifth, capped off by a three-run homer by Chuck Knoblauch, and the Mets trailed 4–2. I vividly remember Todd Pratt hitting a ball in the ninth off Mariano that I thought for a second was going to get out for a game-tying two-run homer, but to no avail. The Mets didn't do much against Clemens that night, which really pissed me off. Due to the DH, the Mets had no ability to retaliate by beaning Clemens. But they could have responded with their bats, which they did not. The Mets lost the game and got swept in this historic two-stadium double dip. The train ride from the Bronx through Manhattan and back to Queens seemed endless, but on the train, there was one discussion at hand: Roger "The Douche" Clemens. As the train began to empty, the only remaining people on board were depressed Mets fans, who proceeded to get angrier and angrier. Instead of thinking about two losses and a limp offense, our minds boiled thinking about what Clemens had done to Mike. Otherwise I'd be beyond depressed by losing another game to the Yankees, but our attention was completely distracted with thoughts of revenge against Clemens.

KEEPING SCORE: That one bad inning doomed Rusch, who pitched a complete game with 10 strikeouts and no walks.... The Mets were able to salvage the final game of the weekend series back at Shea the next afternoon, as Todd Zeile homered and Mike Hampton combined with Armando Benitez on a 2–0 shutout over Andy Pettitte.

THE BITTERSWEET CLINCH

METS 6 BRAVES 2

SEPTEMBER 27, 2000, at SHEA STADIUM

IT'S FUNNY how quickly your expectations can change. Just a few years earlier in 1997, I thought being between four and seven games out of the wild-card race was a real pennant race! In 1999 I acted like forcing a 163rd game was equivalent to winning a World Series. But in the year 2000, my bar had been raised considerably. The Mets were looking to make the postseason for the second straight year and finally knock off the team to beat in the National League, the Atlanta Braves. After coming so close to pulling off the greatest comeback in

VISITOR Braves W-L 99-63 GB +5 Met HOME 50-28 ROAD 44-35 VS DIV. 37-22

HOME Mets W-L 89-68 GB 5 HOME 50-26 ROAD 39-42 VS DIV. 22-23

AL STANDINGS

	R	H	E	LOB	Met DP/OPP	DEFENSE		E
Atl	2	6	0	6				
Met	6	7	1	7				

WP Rick Reed 11-5
LP Kevin Millwood 10-13
SV ∿∿∿∿∿∿

UMPIRES Walke
2B
Scott 3B • 1B Hudson
HP
C.bucston

Atlanta	Ave	HR	H			1	2	3	4	5	6	7	8	9	10	11	AB	R	H	BI
Braves	.273	174	145														12	13	14	15

	R/ER	H	E	LOB
	41			
	010	1	0	
	010	1	0	213
	010	1	0	.14
	010	0	0	014
	010	0	0	014
	010	0	0	014
	010	0	124	015
	1/1	2	0	116

Met	PITCHERS	IP	R	ER	H	W	K	MISC.
10-5 4.24	Rick Reed	8	1	1	4	1	7	30EF 1HR
	Armando Benitez	1	1	1	2	0	3	4BF 1HR

LH BENCH RH
LH Met BULLPEN RH

©1996 Bob Carpenter Communications, Inc. All Rights Reserved

sports history the previous season, the expectation was winning this division from them and showing we had officially arrived. The first five months of the regular season featured a tight race between the Mets and Braves—in fact we were in first place as late as September 1, but it was going to come down to beating the Braves head to head. The Mets went to Atlanta in mid-September trailing by three games in the division, and as always came up very short. They lost the first

Wednesday

DATE September 27, 2000   STADIUM/CAP. Shea Stadium   55,777   ATT. 50,841

GAME # All 158 Met 158   WEATHER clear   START/FINISH 7:11 / 9:46   TIME 235

NL STANDINGS

SERIES   2 of 3
Season Series
7-4 Atl

★ Mets clinch N.L. Wild Card ★
1st ever Met team to make playoffs in back 2 back years.

Braves 1 0 0 | 0 0 0 | 0 0 1   2
Mets   0 0 0 | 1 3 1 | 1 0 X   6

Bell homers in 5th after banging up his knee on great catch.

Plays of the Game

	AB	R	H	BI

New York   Ave   HR   R
Mets   263   194   1399

		1	2	3	4	5	6	7	8	9	10	11	12	13	14	15
6	Timo Perez																
16	Derek Bell																
19	Darryl Hamilton																
13	Edgardo Alfonzo																
31	Mike Piazza																
4	Robin Ventura																
9	Todd Zeile																
44	Jay Payton																
17	Mike Bordick																

	R/ER	0|0	0|0	0|0	1|1	3|3	1|1	1|1	0|0							
	H	0	0	0	1	3	2	2	1								
	E	0	0	0	0	0	0	0	0								
	LOB	0	0	0	3	0|3	2|5	1|6	1|7								

LH	BENCH	RH	

PITCHERS	IP	R	ER	H	W	K	MISC.
Kevin Millwood	5⅓	5	5	6	3	4	1HR, 25 BF
Scott Kamieniecki	1⅔	1	1	2	2	0	8BF
Kevin McGlinchy	1	0	0	1	0	1	4BF

LH   AH   BULLPEN   RH

©1996 Bob Carpenter Communications, Inc. All Rights Reserved

two games of the series, and any hope of winning the NL East had pretty much vanished. When the Braves came to Shea for the final week of the regular season, it was all over except making things official. The Braves' magic number was 2 going into the opener of the series, so all they had to do was beat us at Shea and they would celebrate officially winning the NL East on our field. They did it in a drama-free game, 7–1, and like the arrogant pricks they were, they barely celebrated. Winning a division title was old hat for them, so they casually shook hands as they were officially crowned NL East champions for the sixth consecutive time. The following night at Shea, we had our chance to celebrate, if we wanted.

The Mets were one win away from a great accomplishment, even though it felt sort of depressing. If the Mets beat the Braves on this night, they would make the postseason in back-to-back seasons for the first time in franchise history, and trust me, I was pumped about that! The problem was, it felt like a disappointment. The Mets had dominated baseball through August, and I really thought we were going to take the NL East. But in September they were average and allowed Atlanta to take back control of the division. So as nearly 50,000 fans descended on Shea Stadium for a possible clincher, the thoughts in my head were that it should have been more. Other than wanting to clinch on his particular night, there really wasn't pressure on the Mets. They had a five-game lead with five games remaining, so all they needed was either a win in their final five games or a Dodgers loss in their final five games to make this clinch official. Since 1999 had been so damn awkward in terms of "clinching," I did want to see it on the field tonight.

Rick Reed allowed an early home run to Andruw Jones, but then pitched a hell of a game after that. Mr. Clutch, Edgardo Alfonzo, supplied the power with a two-run home run off Kevin Milwood during a three-run fifth inning, and the Mets had a 6–2 lead in the ninth with Armando Benitez on the mound. The crowd was roaring as Benitez was one strike away—we had not witnessed a home clinch of a playoff spot since 1988, and the year before there was a wild celebration on clinching extending the season, but not knowing where we were going. When Keith Lockhart struck out to end the game, it became official. The Mets followed the Braves' lead in casually shaking hands in lieu of a wild on-field party. The PA system announced the Mets as wild-card winners and marked the fact that this was the first time the franchise would qualify for the postseason in back-to-back seasons. I was excited but also muted in my celebration too. I wanted that NL East, and to know the Braves had clinched a night earlier, it felt odd, if not pathetic, to celebrate second place the following night. I felt good that night and excited about the prospects ahead, but I also didn't feel confident we would ever beat the Braves when it mattered most. As the regular season was winding down, I felt like the 2000 Mets in some ways were better than the previous incarnation. Specifically, going into the postseason with Mike Hampton in the rotation forming a potent 1-2 punch with Al Leiter felt like our strength. But I sensed the '99 team had more magic on their side. They had so many wins during the regular season that you could picture on a world championship highlight video. Other than the 10-run inning against the Braves on the last day of June (*see* "The 10-Run Inning," p. 112), the 2000 Mets didn't have as many magical moments as the team from a year earlier. I know that really means nothing, but that's what was going through my mind as we prepared for another postseason excursion. It would be Mets-Giants in the NLDS and Braves-Cardinals on the other side, if we could get past the Giants, would we finally be able to beat the freakin' Braves? I wasn't so sure.

KEEPING SCORE: The Mets would win their next four games to end the season on a five-game winning streak.... Their 94–68 record put them one game behind the Braves in the final standings.... The Mets went 6–7 against the Braves, their third of eight consecutive seasons losing the season series to Atlanta between 1998 and 2005.

STRIKE THREE LOOKING TO BONDS

METS 5 GIANTS 4 (10 INNINGS)
GAME 2, NATIONAL LEAGUE DIVISION SERIES
OCTOBER 5, 2000, at PACIFIC BELL PARK, SAN FRANCISCO

IF I'M MAKING the Mount Rushmore of greatest Mets baseball games I've ever witnessed, this one in 2000 has a very strong case. Think of the circumstances around this contest. The Mets had lost Game 1 of the 2000 National League Division Series the previous afternoon when they couldn't hit Livan Hernandez. So they were already trailing 1–0 in a best-of-five series going into a game they really needed if they were going to win the series. Unlike a year earlier, the lords of baseball did not relegate the Mets first-round series to 11:00 PM start times. In 1999 when facing the Arizona Diamondbacks, the first two games of the NLDS started at that absurd start time, but a year later against another western team, the start time for the second game was a much more reasonable 8:00 PM on the East Coast, which gave us a classic twilight sun field at Pac Bell Park. This game and this series is why to this day I refuse to call the Giants home stadium anything other than Pac Bell. Once a stadium or arena has a classic series or game, it's tough to abide by all the absurd name changes. As the Mets entered Game 2 of this series, it felt like a must win. Sure, teams have come back from 0–2 down, but losing with Mike Hampton in Game 1 and then potentially losing with Al Leiter in Game 2 would feel like a death sentence. Bottom line was this: they needed to win this freakin' game, and little did I know memories would be created in this game that will live deep in my soul for the rest of time.

Timo Perez officially became an everyday player on this day, because a day earlier Derek Bell would play his last game as a Met as he left early with an ankle injury. Bell had an insane April and then was mediocre the rest of the way, becoming a forgotten footnote in Mets history. Timo Perez had only played a handful of games but

Baseball scorecard for Mets vs. Giants.

was now pushed into a pivotal role as he was leading off Game 2 and essentially replacing Bell as an everyday player. He delivered a huge second-inning hit off Shawn Estes with the bases loaded to give the Mets an early lead. They would nurse a 2–1 lead all the way into the ninth before Edgardo Alfonzo *seemingly* put this game away with a two-run home run to make it 4–1.

DATE October 5, 2000 Thursday STADIUM/CAP. Pac Bell Park 40,800 ATT. 40,430

GAME # Met 2 SF 2 WEATHER Sunny 60's START/FINISH 8:15 / 11:56 TIME 3:41

NL STANDINGS

DEFENSE

SERIES Division Series Game 2

Estes leaves with twisted ankle.

Mets 020|000|002/1 5 10inn
Giants 010|000|003/0 4

©1996 Bob Carpenter Communications, Inc. All Rights Reserved

I had no issue with what Bobby Valentine did next, he allowed Al Leiter to start the ninth but was pulled after he allowed a lead-off double to Barry Bonds. Armando Benitez was the closer and had been very good throughout the regular season, so I was completely on board with him getting the ball now to close it out. To this point Armando had our trust, but this would be the game where he'd lose it. Up by three runs with one out and the tying run at the plate, he allowed a fly ball to J.T. Snow down the right-field line. As the ball traveled through the air, I prayed it would go foul—if not, it was either going to be a two-run double or a game-tying long ball. As my stomach dropped and I leaned my head to the right, hoping that 3,000 miles away my neck bend would somehow make a difference, I heard a loud *smash*. That sound was the ball hitting the foul pole and my worst fear coming true. Snow put his arm up in the air in celebration, as he had tied the game in the ninth with a three-run homer. I was stunned. From a victory to a tie game in the span of what felt like seconds. Pac Bell Park was exploding in excitement as Snow rounded the bases. Where I will give Armando a fraction of credit is that he calmly got the next two outs to keep the game tied and move it to the 10th. For some reason, Felix Rodriguez was still in the game for the Giants after allowing the Alfonzo home run the previous inning. Out of nowhere with two outs and nobody on, pinch-hitter Darryl Hamilton doubled and Jay Payton delivered the go-ahead hit to put the Mets back on top. Again, we were three outs away from victory.

Bobby V. allowed Benitez to start the 10th, which I didn't agree with. At this point I would have gone right to John Franco to try and get a save like it was the old days. After Benitez promptly allowed a leadoff hit to Armando Rios, Franco was summoned, and he got two outs on a sac bunt and a fielder's choice with Rios being thrown out at third, taking the tying run out of scoring position. It set up the most memorable moment from this game, and I'd argue the biggest moment of John Franco's illustrious career. Barry Bonds at the plate with the tying run on base facing longtime closer John Franco. I pictured Bonds erasing years of postseason demons and parking one in McCovey Cove in right field. The 3–2 pitch Franco delivered was an off-speed pitch that was probably a tad inside and high. But my opinion meant nothing, all that mattered was what home plate umpire Gary Cederstrom would think. He signaled strike three, and I jumped out of my chair back on Long Island with as much enthusiasm as one could have. The Mets had somehow blown a ninth-inning lead and then responded immediately to take it back. Franco's jumping in the air was very similar to the reaction of me and millions of Met fans across the country. Somehow we had survived, and the series was tied at one game apiece. I was emotionally wiped out after this instant classic as the series headed back to New York.

KEEPING SCORE: Before allowing the double to Bonds in the ninth, Leiter had allowed four hits while striking out six and walking three.... Payton had been 0-for-7 in the series before his big hit but had driven in the Mets' only run in their Game 1 loss with a sacrifice fly.

BENNY THE LEGEND

METS 3 GIANTS 2 (13 INNINGS)
GAME 3, NATIONAL LEAGUE DIVISION SERIES
OCTOBER 7, 2000, at SHEA STADIUM

WHEN YOU SIT down at a baseball stadium, whether it's for a regular season contest or a postseason game, you have no idea how long you are going to be there. When I go to basketball games, I joke with my wife that I usually can guess and be correct within 15 minutes of when I'll get home and walk through the door. Baseball is a completely different animal. You could sit in your seat and be done with a neat and tightly played game in less than two and a half hours, or your ass may get very sore from sitting in the same position for nearly five. On a late Saturday afternoon in October with a huge swing in a best-of-five series on the line, we were about to experience the latter.

In the 10 minutes before first pitch of a huge Game 3 of the 2000 NLDS between the Mets and Giants, something very unusual was happening at the old Shea Stadium. The ballpark was rocking with a sound you would never hear in Queens...the sound of people doing the tomahawk chop with that annoying *Ooooo* rhythmic sound.

Our arms were flying through the air as we all sounded constipated doing the chop and making the sound that goes with it. Our arch-nemesis and our kryptonite, the Atlanta Braves, had just shockingly been eliminated in three straight games by the St. Louis Cardinals. Despite being much more competitive against Atlanta in the 2000 regular season (6–7), the overall results were the same, we came up short. Chipper Jones still put the fear of God into all of us, so

Baseball scorecard — Division Series Game 3, October 7, 2000, Shea Stadium. Giants 000 200 000 000 0 — 2; Mets 000 001 010 000 1 — 3 (13 innings).

while it was the fantasy to knock off the Braves, let's be honest…it likely wasn't happening. The Braves were better than us, so let the Cardinals do our dirty work, I don't care! Just get me to the World Series—by any means necessary. It was still a surreal moment as we all in unison mocked the Braves by doing their chant. The final score had flashed up just before first pitch of this pivotal Game 3, and we were all celebrating, even though our future was still in doubt. But there is no question we all thought the same thing: while we still had work to do in defeating the Giants, the road to the Fall Classic just got paved a little easier.

With the Giants leading by a score of 2–1 in the eighth inning, Dusty Baker went to his closer, looking to get a four-out save and take a 2–1 lead in this best-of-five series. Robb Nen was one of the elite closers in baseball, but he was staring down our most clutch player, Edgardo Alfonzo. The runner on first was Lenny Harris, who promptly stole second base and put the tying run in scoring position. As beloved as Fonzie was, I still don't think he gets enough credit for how many damn times he would come up with a huge hit. It isn't anyone's fault, but some of his biggest clutch hits have become footnotes because of another moment that takes the shine. There is no Piazza home run to cap the 10-run inning against the Braves without Edgardo, and this Game 3 known for Benny Agbayani's walk-off doesn't happen without Fonzie too. Because with two outs in the eighth inning against an elite MLB closer, Alfonzo smoked an RBI double to left field that tied the game.

The Mets and Giants were now involved in a classic that started to go deep into the October night. Meanwhile, a few miles away the Yankees were getting beat up by the Oakland Athletics, who were on the verge of forcing a winner-take-all Game 5 back in Oakland. I don't know if this is true, but let's go with it because it sounds cool: I have heard the Yankees-Athletics game was so boring that most of the crowd had popped on the Mets game via their Walkman or transistor radios and were reacting to the action of the Mets-Giants extra-inning affair. Legend goes that when Benny Agbayani hit the walk off home run, a buzz occurred at Yankee Stadium. Like most walk-off home runs, Benny's came out of nowhere. It was the 13th inning, and the Mets had had a few opportunities to win the game in the previous extra frames, but it was the bomb out of nowhere that did the trick. As soon as the ball flew of Benny's bat against rookie lefty Aaron Fultz, we all knew where it was going. Twice in 1999 the Mets had postseason walk-offs, and here we were again watching the Mets celebrate a classic playoff win.

Benny was a lovable Met, so his being the guy who hit it was really cool, because it meant his name would live in Mets history forever. There was only one bad moment as we celebrated this Game 3 win—the song choice. While "L.A. Woman" and its "Mister Mojo Risin'" refrain had been the cool rally cry from a season earlier, in 2000 some brainiac decided to roll with "Who Let the Dogs Out." Even that couldn't dampen my mood. The Mets had taken a 2–1 lead; Benny was a hero; and the damn Wicked Witch of the South, known as the Braves, was dead.

KEEPING SCORE: The Mets bullpen combined for seven scoreless innings with 11 strikeouts in relief of Rick Reed, with Rick White picking up the victory by pitching the 12th and 13th innings.... Agbayani never hit a regular season walk-off home run during his major league career.

THE BOBBY JONES ONE-HITTER

METS 4 GIANTS 0
GAME 4, NATIONAL LEAGUE DIVISION SERIES
OCTOBER 8, 2000, at SHEA STADIUM

THE METS' turnaround began in 1997 when this franchise went from the darkness of the early '90s into a future that would see pennant races and eventually back-to-back postseason berths. But when you look at their 2000 roster, you saw a lot of guys who really didn't experience much of the bad times from the pre-1997 days. Obviously, John Franco had been a Met for a long time, so he knew full well what it looked like, and Edgardo Alfonzo was a young rookie back in 1995, but those examples were few and far between. The core of the 2000 Mets was built on trades and free agency—a rotation led by Al Leiter and Mike Hampton and a lineup whose core besides

Alfonzo was Mike Piazza, Robin Ventura, and Todd Zeile. So most of the players didn't have the full Mets experience of being on some pitiful teams that really sucked. But the starting pitcher for Game 4, with the Mets one win away from another NLCS, knew damn well what the full Mets experience looked like.

Bobby Jones was our top pitching prospect when he was called up in August 1993. As you probably recall, 1993 was one of the

DATE Sunday October 8, 2000 STADIUM/CAP. Shea Stadium 55,777 ATT. 52,888 Sell out

GAME # SF 4 Met 4 WEATHER Sunny high 40's START/FINISH 4:11 / 6:59 TIME 248

NL STANDINGS

SERIES Division Series Game 4

Mets advance to N.L.CS. Win Series. Will face Stl in NLCS

Giants	000	000	00	0
Mets	200	020	00 X	4

Jones pitches 4 perfect innings.

DEFENSE — Marvin Benard (CF), Ellis Burks (RF), Rich Aurilia, Jeff Kent, Bill Mueller, Mark Gardner (P), J.T. Snow, C. Rejas, Doug Mirabelli, M. Wilson

New York Mets	Avc	HR	H	1	2	3	4	5	6	7	8	9	10	11	AB	R	H	BI
Timo Perez RF	308														4	1	1	0
Edgardo Alfonzo 2b	296														4	0	1	2
Mike Piazza c	273														3	1	0	0
Robin Ventura 3b	093														2	1	1	2
Benny Agbayani lf / Joe McEwing															4	0	2	0
Jay Payton cf	154														4	0	1	0
Todd Zeile 1b	091														3	0	0	0
Mike Bordick ss	222														3	0	0	0
Bobby J. Jones P	000														4	1	0	0
				R/ER	2|2	0|0	0|0	0|0	2|2	0|0	0|0	0|0			31	4	6	4
				H	1	0	0	1	2	1	0	1						
				E	0	0	0	0	0	0								
				LOB	0	0	0	2										

PITCHERS	IP	R	ER	H	W	K	MISC.
Mark Gardner	4⅓	4	4	4	2	5	
Doug Henry	1⅔	0	0	1	2	0	
Alan Cabine	1	0	0	0	0	0	
Miguel Del Toro	1	0	0	1	0	2	

LH BENCH RH LH SF BULLPEN RH

single worst seasons a professional sports team ever had. A bunch of high-priced veterans who collectively not only weren't very good, but actually managed to lose 103 games and be dubbed "the worst team money could buy." Young Bobby Jones was one of the bright spots on this shit-stained season. Jones would become a very dependable starter during these bad times and would actually go on and start three Opening Days, which at the time trailed only the legendary Tom Seaver and Doc Gooden for most in Mets history. After watching Jones pitch for just about eight seasons, one thing became abundantly clear about him: when he didn't have it, it would be very, very bad. But on the days when his balloon curveball fell in for strikes and he was on his game, Bobby could dominate. In 2000, Jones was the clear fourth starter on this team behind Leiter, Hampton, and Rick Reed. In fact, the 2000 regular season was the worst season of Bobby Jones's career. He actually spent time trying to find himself in the minor leagues early in the regular season and finished with an ERA over 5.00. Glendon Rusch probably deserved to make the Game 4 start over Jones but was deemed more valuable as a lefty long reliever out of the pen. When Jones was scheduled to start Game 4 against Mark Gardner, the thought in my head was we were going to need to score some runs to close this series out.

It was only fitting then that the man who got called up in 1993 and had seen so much bad baseball, was able to finally contribute to the Mets when they finally became good. Jones didn't contribute much in 1999 and, as I mentioned, really struggled in 2000. But on this day in October, at the most opportune time, Robert Joseph Jones decided to throw the best game of his life. He set the Giants down 1-2-3 in the first, 1-2-3 in the second, 1-2-3 in the third.

"Holy shit, Dad, is Bobby Freakin' Jones gonna be the guy, and in the playoffs of all places?"

Another 1-2-3 in the fourth. The Mets had taken an early 2-0 lead in the first when Robin Ventura hit a two-run home run. Jones took the mound with a perfect game to start the fifth inning, and here was what was nuts: Jones wasn't getting lucky or anything. It seemed like all contact was weak contact. Jeff Kent led off the fifth inning, and I had a bad feeling about it. Kent was a former Met who managed to morph into an MVP-type player, so it was no surprise when he was the one bastard who managed to get a hit off the god of the mound that day, Bobby Jones. The great Dusty Baker made a huge mistake that inning. Jones was human and issued a few walks, so the Giants, down by two runs, had the bases loaded with two outs against Jones. Dusty decided to stick with his pitcher, Mark Gardner, instead of sending up a pinch-hitter...the result was predictable as Gardner popped out. Those three base runners against Bobby Jones in the fifth inning would be their only base runners of the entire game. The Mets chased Gardner in the bottom of the inning as Alfonzo added some insurance with a two-run double, and the party was on. The Mets were on the verge of advancing to the NLCS, but we all wanted to see Bobby Jones finish the job. And boy did he ever. Jones came out for the ninth and within a blink of an eye did indeed finish the job. Barry Bonds hit a fly ball to Jay Payton in center field that ended it and allowed the wild celebration to commence. Bobby Jones had pitched not only the game of his life, but you could argue one of the best-pitched games in Mets history. Only three base runners, and he twirled eight 1-2-3 innings en route to a complete-game, one-hit shutout. As we were celebrating the Mets advancing and Jones's incredible outing, I started to think how close he was to making this even more remarkable. The guy was a Jeff Kent double away from pitching a postseason no-hitter. I mean, that's some crazy crap! Bobby would make two more starts as a Met, but I wish this would have been his last Mets start. Unfortunately, as much as I want to remember Bobby for this one game, there is one other moment he was a part of that edges it. More on that later.

KEEPING SCORE: The Mets held Bonds to just three hits in 17 at-bats (.176) in the four games.... It was Jones's first shutout in three years and the only one-hitter of his career.... The Mets had another Bobby Jones on their pitching staff in 2000, left-hander Robert Mitchell Jones, whom they acquired from the Colorado Rockies for Masato Yoshii.... Al Leiter had held the Giants to just two hits and a walk over eight innings with John Franco completing the 2–0 shutout two months earlier on August 13. Kent got one of the two San Francisco hits on that occasion.

WINNING THE 2000 PENNANT

METS 7 CARDINALS 0
GAME 5, NATIONAL LEAGUE CHAMPIONSHIP SERIES
OCTOBER 16, 2000, at SHEA STADIUM

ON THE RADIO several times I've talked about enjoying blowouts and dreading close games. As much as we will remember each and every big moment from a tension-filled game, the blowouts are fun. Knowing you are about to win not only takes the stress out of the game, it allows you to look around and enjoy the moment. When I think of a game that perfectly defines that sentiment—a game that featured little to no drama, and yet was incredibly memorable—I think of the party that was the Mets clinching the NL pennant in 2000.

I went into the 2000 NLCS with a bit of confidence, and it wasn't necessarily anything against the 95-win Cardinals. The Mets had just defeated the San Francisco Giants in four games in advancing to their second consecutive NLCS. The Cardinals had done the Mets' dirty work by eliminating the Braves in three straight games. Impressively for them, they had done it with Mark McGwire limited because of a knee injury. Big Mac was nearing the end of his career, and the only thing slowing him down was a knee injury that caused him to miss two months, which limited him to exclusively pinch-hitting duties after he returned in September. McGwire still managed to hit 32 home runs despite appearing in only 89 games, but the threat he posed was limited since he would only bat once per game. When I think back to the Cardinals' upset over the Braves, the most memorable thing about that series was actually a negative for St. Louis. Rick Ankiel had melted down in the series and couldn't manage to throw strikes. Ankiel would go on and successfully transition into a position player years later, but at this moment he was the talk of baseball for all the wrong reasons. Despite Ankiel's struggles, the Cardinals still managed to eliminate the Braves.

Cardinals W-L 4-3 GB 2 HOME 2-2 ROAD 2-1 VS DIV. 0-0
VISITOR
Mets W-L 6-2 GB +2 HOME 3-1 ROAD 3-1 VS DIV. 0-0
HOME

AL STANDINGS

[A handwritten baseball scorecard for a St. Louis Cardinals vs. New York Mets game follows, showing lineups, defensive positions, inning-by-inning scoring, and pitching lines.]

WP Mike Hampton 2-1
LP Pat Hentgen 0-1
SV

UMPIRES
Rapuano
Freeming 2B Scott
Tschida 3B 1B Rippley
HP
DeMuth

St. Louis Cardinals			1	2	3	4	5	6	7	8	9	10	11	AB	R	H	BI

©1996 Bob Carpenter Communications, Inc. All Rights Reserved

I had a quiet confidence going into this series, and the Mets supported my faith by winning the first two games in St. Louis. After dropping Game 3, the Mets bats exploded against Darryl Kile on short rest and made up for the fact that Bobby Jones came crashing down to earth after his marvelous one-hitter against the Giants. The Mets were now one win away from winning their first pennant since 1986. As a fan, the anxiety I had for Game 5 was over whether my

DATE October 16, 2000   STADIUM/CAP. Shea Stadium   55,777   ATT. 55,695

GAME # StL 8 Met 9   WEATHER Rain   50's   START/FINISH 8:22 /   TIME

NL STANDINGS

SERIES NLCS   Game 5
StL Series Met
1   3
Payton hit in back in 5th r7/4 brakes out.

Cardinals 000/000/000 0 7
Mets   300/300/10X   9

Piazza sets NLCS record with 8 runs scored.
Mets win N.L. Pennant
NLCS M.V.P. Mike Hampton
Evans Star of the Game

New York Mets	Ave .230	HR 7	H 63	1	2	3	4	5	6	7	8	9	10	11	AB 12	R 13	H 14	BI 15
Timo Perez															5	2	2	0
Edgardo Alfonzo 2b															4	1	2	1
Mike Piazza c															4	2	1	0
Robin Ventura 3b															3	1	1	1
Todd Zeile 1b															4	0	1	3
Benny Agbayani lf															2	0	1	0
Jay Payton cf / Joe McEwing															4	0	1	0
Mike Bordick ss															4	1	1	0
Mike Hampton p															3	0	0	0

LH BENCH RH
Franco   Trammell
Harris   Pratt
Hamilton Abbott

PITCHERS	IP	R	ER	H	W	K	MISC.
Pat Hentgen	3⅔	6	6	7	5	2	23BF
Mike Timlin	⅓	0	0	1	0	6	2BF
Britt Reames	2	0	0	2	1	0	9BF
Rick Ankiel	⅔	1	1	0	2	1	4BF 2WP
Mike James	⅓	0	0	0	0	0	1BF
Dave Veres	1	0	0	1	0	0	4BF 5BF

favorite team would do something live right in front of me that I had dreamt about since I was a young kid—win the NL pennant. If the Mets had lost Game 5, I still had confidence that they could manage winning one game in St. Louis to win the series anyway, but I really wanted to see the Mets celebrate in person.

Mike Hampton was on the mound looking to have his defining Mets moment as he took on the former Cy Young Award winner

Pat Hentgen. Right from the get-go, any drama the game had would morph into one giant party. The Mets jumped all over Hentgen in the first inning, taking advantage of numerous Cardinals defensive miscues to go up 3–0. Hampton was in complete control and never even allowed the Cardinals to put a runner in scoring position. This was why he was here! When the Mets had dealt for Hampton during the off-season in exchange for Roger Cedeno and Octavio Dotel, we fantasized about moments like this. Shea Stadium was rocking in anticipation of the inevitable. As Hampton collected out after out, the place got louder and louder. If three runs weren't enough of a reason to be confident, Todd Zeile broke the game even more wide open in the fourth inning with a bases-loaded double to knock out Hentgen, staking Hampton to a 6–0 lead.

Never in my life as a Mets fan did one game no longer feel like a game, but one giant frat party. I will never forget the surreal moment in the bottom of the eighth inning when we rowdy Mets fans almost incited a full-blown brawl. Tony La Russa had brought in his closer Dave Veres with the Cardinals down 7–0. The crowd started singing "Na Na Hey Hey Kiss Him Goodbye" to the Cardinals as the Mets were now only three outs away from eliminating them. I joined in...this was awesome! All of a sudden Veres uncorked a pitch that went right off the helmet of Jay Payton. Jay immediately got up and started power-walking to the mound to confront Veres, who did not back down. The benches very quickly emptied and no punches were thrown, but Payton was livid. I can still see the image of Payton being held back as blood poured down his eye. I have no way to prove it, but all these years later I'd like to think the Met fans so annoyed Veres with the singing of "Na Na Hey Hey Kiss Him Goodbye" that he decided to take his aggression out on Payton by drilling him. Since he couldn't plunk 50,000 people, Payton served as the next best thing.

Once order was restored and the inning ended, Mike Hampton was allowed to finish the job, much like Bobby Jones did a week earlier in eliminating the Giants at Shea. Hampton pitched a 1-2-3 ninth that ended with fly ball to center field, and instead of Payton, who was removed from the game an inning earlier, it was Timo Perez who jumped in the air prior to squeezing the final out. Once he did, the party that had been going on in Queens for the previous three hours hit a fever pitch. The New York Mets were the 2000 National League champions! I stood on my seat with my arm thrusting through the air. I turned back behind me to see Mets owner Fred Wilpon in his box celebrating, and we made eye contact as we exchanged fist pumps. Little did I know that my dislike for the Wilpons would grow, but in this moment I loved him. Even at 17 years old, I was in touch with my emotions as a few tears rained down my cheeks. I had watched a lot of bad baseball over the years and dealt with some brutal defeats, but here we were accomplishing something I'd only dreamt about. My father and I stayed at Shea as long after the game as I could recall. We wanted to fully appreciate the moment and, boy, did we ever. The Mets were champions of the National League!

KEEPING SCORE: For you Mets history buffs, the Mets clinched the 2000 pennant on the 31st anniversary of them winning the 1969 World Series against the Baltimore Orioles.... Rick Wilkins, the player who hit the final fly ball to Payton, spent a week with the Mets in May 1998, starting three games behind the plate before being cut the day the Mets acquired Mike Piazza from the Marlins.

ONE OF THOSE GAMES
YOU WILL NEVER GET OVER

YANKEES 4 METS 3 (12 INNINGS)
GAME 1, WORLD SERIES
OCTOBER 21, 2000, at YANKEE STADIUM

IT HAS BEEN 20-plus years, but there are certain losses that you will never, ever get over. This qualifies. It was Game 1 of the 2000 World Series, and my father and sister were sitting in left field, while I was by myself in the lower bowl in the right-field corner. Tickets were very expensive and tough to acquire for the first Subway Series in 44 years, so that's what led to the awkward seating arrangement. This was obviously my first World Series experience and having to face the Yankees was the last thing I wanted for a couple of reasons. The Yankees had won three straight championships, and while Ric Flair's legendary "You have to beat the man to be the man" line sounds great on paper, it ain't true in baseball! If the Mariners had not allowed Roger Clemens to punk them in Game 4, or they hadn't blown a four-run lead in Game 6, then that line would have been complete bullshit, because the Mets would get a chance to play the Mariners for the title. Look at how the Mets even got here. We all knew the Braves had owned the Mets, but luckily the St. Louis Cardinals upset them in the Division Series. Did I feel bad that the Mets didn't beat "the man" to win the NL pennant? No shot! So bring on the worse team. The other issue was the fans of the New York Yankees. In high school it felt like 85 percent of the baseball fans in the school were Yankees fans, and that's despite being on Long Island. Again, the Yankees were in the midst of a dynasty, so I fully understood the roaring popularity they had. That aspect of the series made things even worse. When the Mets would lose to the Braves, I didn't have to rub shoulders with Braves fans day in and day out. The Yankees are a completely different story. But the one positive was being in the building. If the Mets were facing the Mariners, or basically any other American League team, I wouldn't have been lucky enough to attend a game I'd been dreaming about since I learned what a baseball was...Game 1 of the World Series.

I sat next to two Mets fans that night in the right-field corner of the old Yankee Stadium, and the infamous lawyer Johnnie Cochran sat a few rows in front of me. This was such a hot ticket

DATE October 21, 2000 — Saturday — STADIUM/CAP. Yankee Stadium — ATT. 55,913

GAME # Met 10 NYY 12 — WEATHER clear 60's — START/FINISH 8:13 / 1:04 — TIME 451 ★

AL STANDINGS ★ Longest World Series game ever.

©1996 Bob Carpenter Communications, Inc. All Rights Reserved

that a household name like Johnnie Cochran couldn't do better than the right-field corner! So here I am at age 17, by myself at Yankee Stadium for the biggest game of my life with the oversized Bob Carpenter scorebook on my lap.

The Timo Perez non-run in the sixth inning (when he should have scored on Todd Zeile's double) is what gets most of the attention from this classic Game 1, but that night my angle told me a completely different story. I didn't notice that Timo wasn't running, but what I did notice was Derek Jeter making a crazy running play on the relay and then a tremendous throw to nail Perez at the plate. And even though the Yankees took the lead on a David Justice two-run double in the bottom of the inning, Bubba Trammell delivered a monster pinch-hit in the seventh to tie it, and we had a freakin' lead with six outs to go after another clutch hit by Edgardo Alfonzo. I've given John Franco crap over the years, but here is the truth: with a one-run lead, he got through the heart of the Yankees order in the eighth after giving up a leadoff single to Jeter and handed the ball to Armando Benitez with a chance to take Game 1 and alter everything about this Series. Franco went into the belly of the beast and got the job done—it's been forgotten because of what happened next, but Johnny did his job in the biggest moment of his baseball life.

The Paul O'Neill at-bat still haunts me to this day. Armando is a strike away from being an out away! Every foul ball caused physical pain for me, and when he walked him, I knew what the inevitable outcome would be. Sure enough, the Yankees went on to load the bases, and Chuck Knoblauch brought home O'Neill with a sac fly. The extra innings of this game were like a slow death deep into the Bronx night. The Mets had no base runners and no chance to take the lead, but the Yankees threatened every single inning, and somehow the Mets would escape with the score remaining tied. The insides of my stomach couldn't take very much more of what I was witnessing. The prime example of the Mets' escape act was in the 10th when O'Neill of all people grounded into a double play with the bases loaded against Glendon Rusch. The end of this marathon game still resonates in my nightmares. One out away from the 13th, when the Mets would have finally gotten to the soft spot of the Yankees pen with the heart of the order coming up. But on the first pitch from Turk Wendell, former Met Jose Vizcaino crushed our dreams with a bases-loaded hit to left field. As soon as I saw Tino Martinez touch home, I was on a wild sprint to get the hell out of the Bronx. To this day, I'm very quick to get out of stadiums or arenas when the game is over, but nothing will ever match the speed I had on this October night.

My dad had great foresight and gave me the key to the car where I would meet him and my sister after the game. I ran as fast as I could out of the building and then through the streets of the Bronx to our car and sat there for at least 20 minutes waiting for them. I was stewing...I was angry, pissed, sad, frustrated, and I also knew what losing that game meant. I replayed the O'Neill at-bat in my head over and over. Sometimes you experience something in life and you know you will never forget that moment and the feeling you have during it. That sick feeling still resides deep in my soul more than two decades later.

KEEPING SCORE: Al Leiter was in line to pick up the victory until the Yankees tied the game in the ninth, allowing five hits and two runs in seven innings while striking out seven.... Bubba Trammell, another would-be hero, also drove in an insurance run with a sac fly in Game 3.

ROGER CLEMENS THREW A BAT

YANKEES 6 METS 5
GAME 2, WORLD SERIES
OCTOBER 22, 2000, at YANKEE STADIUM

AS PAINFUL AS Game 1 of the 2000 Subway World Series was, and it was as bad as it gets, the beauty of baseball is that a lot of times you get right to the ballpark the next day. Less than 24 hours later, my father and I made another trek to the Bronx for Game 2. Unlike the previous night, when we were separated in where we sat, we would be together in the upper deck of the old Yankee Stadium along the left-field line. The Mets were down 0–1 in the Series, similar to how

Mets — VISITOR — W-L 7-3 — GB 1 — HOME 4-1 — ROAD 3-2 — VS DIV. 0-0

Yankees — HOME — W-L 8-4 — GB +1 — HOME 4-2 — ROAD 4-2 — VS DIV. 0-0

NL STANDINGS

| Met | R 5 | H 7 | E 3 | LOB 4 |
| NYY | 6 | 12 | 1 | 12 |

WP Roger Clemens 2-2
LP Mike Hampton 2-2
SV

UMPIRES
2B
3B • 1B Kellogg
HP

DEFENSE

NYY DP/OPP 0 1PB — I E

New York Mets AVE .237 HR 7 H 83

PITCHERS

	IP	R	ER	H	W	K	MISC.
Roger Clemens	8	0	0	2	0	9	
Jeff Nelson	0	2	2	3	0	0	
Mariano Rivera	1	3	3	2	0	1	

©1996 Bob Carpenter Communications, Inc. All Rights Reserved

they were down 0–1 in the Division Series against the Giants, and I knew that as bad as Game 1 was, if the Mets could even up this series, my entire mood would change.

Mike Hampton, fresh off of his stupendous pitching in the pennant-clinching game, was on the mound set to face old Mets nemesis Roger Clemens. The last time we saw Roger against the Mets, he was beaning Mike Piazza in the head. What elevated the situation is that

Handwritten baseball scorecard:

DATE October 22, 2000 Sunday STADIUM/CAP. Yankee Stadium ATT. 56,059

GAME # Met 11 NYY 13 WEATHER Clear + Cold START/FINISH 8:05 / TIME

AL STANDINGS

World Series Game 2

Mets   000 000 005   5
Yankees 210 010 11X   6

Clemens throws bat at Piazza, benches empty. The feud continues.

Ferris Star of the Game: Roger 2P 8 R 0 / Clemens H2 K9

New York Yankees Ave. 264 HR 7 H 110

	AB	R	H	BI
Chuck Knoblauch DH	4	0	0	0
Derek Jeter SS	5	1	3	0
David Justice LF / Clay Bellinger LF	3	1	0	0
Bernie Williams CF	3	1	0	0
Tino Martinez 1b	5	1	3	2
Jorge Posada C	3	1	2	1
Paul O'Neill RF				
Scott Brosius 3b				
Jose Vizcaino 2b				

Mets PITCHERS	IP	R	ER	H	W	K
Mike Hampton	6	4	4	8	5	4
Glendon Rusch	1/3	1	1	2	0	0
Rick White	1 1/3	1	1	1	1	1
Dennis Cook	1/3	0	0	1	0	0

Piazza accused Roger of doing it on purpose. So the Clemens-Piazza feud was at a fever pitch as they were set to face each other for the first time since the incident. A lot of Mets fans made the accusation that Clemens was afraid to face the Mets at Shea, where he could potentially face real retaliation. Sure, Roger was an option to start Game 1, where he would then be lined up to pitch in either Game 4 on short rest or Game 5, both games set for Shea. But Joe Torre opted for him to start Game 2, where he would then be lined up to pitch a potential Game 6 also at Yankee Stadium. Was Roger ducking Shea? Probably so, but at this point I didn't care as much about plunking him as I did about kicking his ass like the Mets had done many times before during the regular season.

I admit that it's possible my memory is playing tricks on me, but here is what I think I remember from Clemens's first inning prior to facing Mike Piazza. First you had "Rocket Man" blaring from the PA system and you had Bob Sheppard doing something I don't recall him ever doing. "And pitching for the Yankees...Rocket Roger Clemens." Usually he just said the name, not adding a nickname like "Rocket." Was this a request by Roger? Was this a Sheppard ad-lib? Was this something my brain is telling me that happened that never actually happened? I don't know the answer. But I admit, I was as fired up as Roger was for this confrontation and the anticipation of not only that, but the pressures of Game 2 of the World Series.

Piazza came up to face Clemens in the top of the first inning with two outs and nobody on. Strike one, strike two, both with fastballs on the inside corner, then Mike laid off a splitter. The entire crowd was standing! With the count 1–2, Piazza fouled off an inside fastball that shattered his bat, sending the barrel in comeback fashion to Clemens (which you've probably seen and replayed numerous times). Luckily, my eyes were fixated on Clemens as he fielded the piece of broken bat and threw it in Piazza's direction. I have shown great restraint over the years when I'm at games, mostly keeping my emotions bottled inside. Especially on the road, I try not to say too much, as I am a visitor in someone else's ballpark and even though I was still technically a kid, you never know who you might piss off with a comment. When Clemens threw the bat, I snapped. At the top of my lungs I yelled—and I apologize for the language, but I want to be as accurate as I can with what transpired in this moment—"You fuckin' piece of shit! Fuck you, you shithead!" I wasn't very creative with my cursing, but it's what came out of my mouth. I'll never forget Yankees fans looking at me and not confronting me, but actually agreeing with me. In this moment there was nobody at Yankee

Stadium who was going to passionately defend the bat-throwing, head-hunting douche. At this moment I was as angry as I'd ever been at a sporting event. Piazza would meekly ground out and the inning was over.

My anger would turn to panic, as Mike Hampton allowed two runs in the first inning on run-scoring hits by Tino Martinez and Jorge Posada, and the Yankees continued all the momentum they had gained from coming back to win Game 1, putting the Mets on their heels trailing early against Roger Clemens. As Clemens continued mowing down Mets hitters and the Yankees kept adding on runs, I started thinking about that first inning and how Piazza should have charged the mound and set up an all-out brawl. Why didn't he do it? Sure, Piazza would have been ejected from the game, but there is a very good chance Roger would have been thrown out as well. I love Piazza, but I sure as hell would trade Piazza for Clemens, especially as I watched Roger thoroughly dominate the Mets lineup, something he rarely did when facing us. Clemens had dominated in his last postseason start, blowing away the Mariners in striking out 15 in a complete-game win. Clemens was essentially doing the same thing; it's as if the bat throw gave him some extra juice. Finally, down 6–0 in the ninth inning the Mets were done facing Roger as Jeff Nelson came into the game. In the true definition of too little too late, the Mets scored five runs. Piazza hit a two-run home run, then Jay Payton did the impossible when he tagged the immortal Mariano Rivera for an opposite-field, three-run homer that cut it to 6–5. It was tough to be too excited when Payton went yard, because there were still two outs and nobody on with the game coming down to backup shortstop Kurt Abbott. I'll give Kurt this—he made it very quick as he struck out on three pitches. As I walked out of Yankee Stadium that night I boiled in my hatred for Clemens and also tried to think about how this Series wasn't over despite it feeling that way. The '86 Mets had come back from 0–2 (against Clemens's team), was my rationale, but I knew the cold, hard truth. This wasn't the 1986 Mets, and the Yankees in the midst of a dynasty were certainly not ready to collapse like the '86 Red Sox.

KEEPING SCORE: It might have been a good night for the Yankees, but not for Mariano Rivera. Payton's home run was the second and last one he gave up in 96 postseason appearances (the first was a walk-off by Cleveland's Sandy Alomar Jr. to win Game 4 of the 1997 ALDS).... It was also the first of only two times he allowed more than one run (the second was when he took the loss in Game 2 of the 2001 World Series to Arizona).

WINNING A WORLD SERIES GAME

METS 4 YANKEES 2
GAME 3, WORLD SERIES
OCTOBER 24, 2000, at SHEA STADIUM

THE DAYS BETWEEN the Yankees going up 2–0 and Game 3 finally happening felt like an eternity. The first two games took place on a Saturday and Sunday, which meant the scheduled off day would take place on Monday and the Series would resume on Tuesday night. That gave me two consecutive school days to face the noise of being down 0–2 in the World Series against big brother. Despite growing up on Long Island, which is usually considered Mets country, Lawrence High School in the year 2000 was nowhere near being Mets country. Maybe I'm exaggerating the numbers a couple of decades later, but it seemed like we Met fans were outnumbered about 5–1 walking the halls. What was there to say other than just verbally assaulting Roger Clemens? The Mets blew Game 1 because Armando Benitez couldn't hold a ninth-inning lead, and our ace got thoroughly outpitched by their ace in Game 2. I had a small pebble of hope during the off day between Games 2 and 3 of the Series, and that kernel of hope was from what happened in an entirely different sport. The night before, the Jets completed the now famous "Miracle at the Meadowlands," as they came back on the hated Miami Dolphins

©1996 Bob Carpenter Communications, Inc. All Rights Reserved

after trailing 30–7 very late in the third quarter. That insane over-time victory meant the Mets maybe weren't dead yet despite being halfway to elimination.

The Yankees only won 87 games during the 2000 regular season and had a September to forget as they crumbled down the stretch. Despite all that, they defeated the Athletics in the Divison Series, and took down the Mariners in six games in the ALCS. After taking

Tuesday
DATE October 24, 2000   STADIUM/CAP. Shea Stadium   55,777   ATT. 55,299
GAME # NYY 14 Met 12   WEATHER clear   50's   START/FINISH 8:37 / 12:16   TIME 3:39

NL STANDINGS

(Scorecard — Bob Carpenter Communications, Inc. All Rights Reserved, ©1996)

World Series Game 3
Yankees 001 | 100 | 000 2
Mets   010 | 001 | 02X 4
Yankees 14 game World Series winning streak ends.

New York Mets

6 Tino Perez RF
13 Edgardo Alfonzo 2b
31 Mike Piazza c
4 Robin Ventura 3b
9 Todd Zeile 1b
50 Benny Agbayani LF
47 Joe McEwing PH/LF
44 Jay Payton CF
17 Mike Bordick SS
35 Rick Reed P
Mike Stanton P
Mike Hampton P
Armando Benitez P

the first two games of the World Series, the 87 wins felt like the distant past and the dynastic Yankees were back. Coming into Game 3, they had not lost a World Series game since Game 2 of the 1996 Series. That meant the Yankees had won 14 consecutive World Series games. NSYNC sang the anthem that night, and I laughed as they were met with a mixed reaction...I guess the Mets and Yankees fans weren't looking for a boy band to initiate us into Game 3. The Mets had just tied up the game 2–2 in the sixth inning and were poised to take the lead with the bases loaded and nobody out. Orlando "El Duque" Hernandez had created a reputation as someone who would find ways to make the pitch when he needed to, and he certainly did as he managed to escape that bases-loaded jam. The Yankees fans were loud as El Duque struck out Jay Payton and Mike Bordick, and then got Darryl Hamilton to ground out to keep the game tied. The crowds seemed louder at Shea for Game 3 than they had been for the previous two games in the Bronx, but that may have been because of how split the crowd was. Benny Agbayani broke the tie in the eighth when he ripped an RBI double to score Todd Zeile from first base, which put the Mets three outs away from winning a game in this Series. The problem was Armando Benitez had broken all trust he once had with Mets fans after the debacle that was Game 1. He somehow managed to record the three outs needed to secure Game 3 and make the series 2–1 Yankees.

That ninth inning scared the crap out of me. He allowed a lead-off single to Chuck Knoblach to bring the tying run to the plate, and when David Justice came up with two outs, I had visions of him parking one off the scoreboard in right. Instead Armando got him to pop up to second base to end the game. I had no jubilation or any kind of celebratory attitude as we departed Shea that night. The feeling I had was relief. Relief from avoiding the constant mocking we as Mets fans would face in school after another terrible defeat, and relief that we weren't facing the daunting prospect of being down 0–3. Did I think we were alive in this series? Eh, it was a sorta feeling. I think I needed to see the Mets win again and tie this series to really believe again; the losses in the first two games really wiped all the confidence I had right out of me. This was the dynastic New York Yankees we were facing, not that home-field advantage was much of a thing, but it certainly didn't help that instead of 50,000 crazy Mets fans rooting our team on, we were forced to defend our own stadium against a very loud and boisterous enemy. This Subway Series, which was supposed to be such an exciting time because I was witnessing my favorite team battling for a championship was anything but. I hated the Series, I hated the pressure, and I really hated the enemy and their fans. I would do no trash talking in school on that victory Wednesday. There would be no bragging about Rick Reed's solid performance, or Johnny Franco earning the win, or Benny Agbayani's clutch double. I kept quiet and humble...and it's probably because deep down I knew the truth. Our end was near.

KEEPING SCORE: It was El Duque's first loss of the 2000 postseason after picking up three victories in the first two rounds. He gave up a solo home run to Robin Ventura to open the scoring in the second.... Reed struck out eight in six innings, including a big K of Jose Vizcaino with runners on second and third to end the top of the fourth.

FIRST-PITCH DOOM

YANKEES 3 METS 2
GAME 4, WORLD SERIES
OCTOBER 25, 2000, at SHEA STADIUM

HOW OFTEN can a baseball game be defined by the very first pitch? The answer to this rhetorical question is never, except if we are talking about the one example in the history of Major League Baseball where it did. As we entered Game 4 of the 2000 World Series, the Mets finally won a game and now trailed two games to one, so there was finally a glimmer of hope. The pitching matchup made us all think we were going to see a lot of runs scored. Despite the dominance of Bobby Jones in the Division Series clincher, Bobby was Bobby. He had pitched to a 5.00-plus ERA during the regular season and came crashing back down to earth when he got beat around by the Cardinals in Game 4 of the NLCS. Lefty Denny Neagle was a trade-deadline acquisition by the Yankees, and he had pitched very poorly after being acquired, losing both games he started in the

Yankees	W-L 9-5	GB +1	HOME 5-2	ROAD 4-3	VS DIV. 0-0			
VISITOR								
Mets	W-L 8-4	GB 1	HOME 5-1	ROAD 3-3	VS DIV. 0-0			
HOME							AL STANDINGS	

NY4 R 3 H 8 E 0 LOB 9
Met 2 6 1 6

WP David Cone 1-0
LP Bobby J. Jones 1-1
SV Mariano Rivera

UMPIRES
Reliford Crawford Kellogg
2B
Montague 3B • 1B McClelland
HP
Welke

DEFENSE
Met DP/OPP

Benny Agbayani   Jay Payton   Timo Perez
Mike Bordick   Rey Ordoñez   Edgardo Alfonzo
Robin Ventura   8:15 Bobby J. Jones   Todd Zeile
J. Randolph
MIKE PIAZZA
L. Mazzilli

WORLD Series
Met 1
NY4 3
G1 NY4 3 G2 Met 5
    NY4 4   NY4 6
G3 NY4 3
    Met 4
ALCS
Sea 2
NY4 4
Division Series
2A 3
Cws 0
Division Series
NY4 3
OAC 2

New York Yankees	AVG	HR	H	1	2	3	4	5	6	7	8	9	10	11	12	13	14	15
	.269	8	130												AB	R	H	BI
2 Derek Jeter SS .315 .267																		
14 L.J. Sojo 2B .220 .047																		
28 David Justice LF .222 3012																		
35 Clay Bellinger LF 1.000 .051																		
51 Bernie Williams CF .274 .124																		
24 Tino Martinez 1B .379 .117																		
21 Paul O'Neil RF .314 .047																		
20 Jorge Posada C .204 .045																		
18 Scott Brosius 3B .209 .113																		
12 Denny Neagle P .000 .000																		
36 David Cone P																		
33 Jose Canseco Ph .000 .000																		
43 Jeff Nelson P																		
31 Mike Stanton P 2.0 1.28																		
42 Mariano Rivera P																		

	1	2	3	4	5	6	7	8	9	10	11	12	13	14	15
R/ER	4/1	1/1	1/1	0/0	0/0	0/0	0/0	0/0	0/0						
H	1	1	1	1	0	2	1	1	0						
E	0	0	0	0	0	0	0	0	1/0						
LOB	0	1	0/1	2/3	2/4	2/6	2/7	0/7	2/9						

LH BENCH RH
Polonia
Turner
Hill
Knoblauch
Vizcaino

Met PITCHERS	IP	R	ER	H	W	K	MISC.
1-0 4.15 Bobby J. Jones	5	3	3	4	3	3	1HR 22BF
Glendon Rusch	2	0	0	3	0	2	9BF
John Franco	1	0	0	1	0	1	3BF
Armando Benitez	1	0	0	0	1	0	5BF

LH Met BULLPEN RH
Wendell
White
Cook
Reed
Leiter
Hampton

ALCS, the only two games the Yankees had lost in the series. So it seemed this game was set up to be a slugfest.

My scorebook was all set up as the first pitch was set to be thrown at 8:31 PM, and we were about to witness a brand-new leadoff hitter for the Yankees. Since we were playing with no DH, the regular Yankees leadoff man, Chuck Knoblauch, wasn't in the lineup. In Game 3 the night before, World Series Game 1 hero and former

DATE Wednesday October 25, 2000   STADIUM/CAP. Shea Stadium   55,777   ATT. 55,290

GAME # N44 15 Met 13   WEATHER clear 50's   START/FINISH 8:31 / _____ TIME _____

NL STANDINGS

DEFENSE

SERIES World Series Game 4

Yankees 1 1 1 | 000 | 000 3
Mets   0 0 2 | 000 | 000 2

New York Mets	Ave .238	HR 10	H 99	1	2	3	4	5	6	7	8	9	10	11	AB	R	H	BI

PITCHERS	IP	R	ER	H	W	K	MISC.
Denny Neagle (15) 0-2 4.50	4⅔	3	3	4	2	3	300F
David Cone (36)	⅓	0	0	0	0	0	10F
Jeff Nelson (43)	1⅓	0	0	1	1	1	50F
Mike Stanton (29)	⅔	0	0	0	0	2	20F
Mariano Rivera (42)	2	0	0	1	0	2	75F

Met Jose Vizcaino was given the honor, but tonight that spot in the order was given to Derek Jeter. Jeter batted mostly second throughout the 2000 regular season and postseason, but leading off wasn't completely uncommon for him either. What had become a normal tradition was light bulbs flashing from everyone attempting to take a picture of the opening pitch. This had become normal throughout this Sseries, and it certainly wasn't about to change for this pivotal

Game 4. Derek Jeter was already a full-blown Mets killer and had been the subject of many a debate between me and Yankees fans at school. I knew Jeter was very good, but I would compare his numbers to other elite shortstops and rightfully explain how his numbers came up small against the likes of Alex Rodriguez and Nomar Garciaparra. The retort was always that Jeter was a winner and you couldn't measure his greatness just in pure stats. My days of debating Jeter's greatness were now nearing their conclusion because I could no longer fight it. Bobby Jones was now on the mound staring down his sign from Mike Piazza. Somehow they had come up with the brilliant game plan of throwing Jeter a batting practice fastball right down the middle. Maybe he'd take the pitch, they assumed. Jones rocked into his delivery and threw his first pitch as Shea Stadium lit up with flashbulbs from all directions. Jeter swung and launched one to left-center field. "Oh, shit," came out of my mouth as the ball soared through the air. It landed about five rows deep into the bleachers, and the Yankees fans wasted no time making noise and taking over our building yet again. It was 1–0 Yankees, and even though we were facing the mediocre Neagle, it still felt like 7–0. The Mets ended the Yankees' World Series winning streak hours earlier, and the Yankees wasted no time punching back.

Jeter punished us again in the third inning when he delivered a leadoff triple that set up the Yankees' third run and gave them a 3–0 lead. The only ounce of offense the Mets could muster came in the bottom of the third inning when Mike Piazza hit a two-run bomb off Neagle to make it 3–2. We would never put a runner in scoring position after that as the offense fizzled against Neagle and the Yankees pen. In the bottom of the fifth with two out and nobody on, Joe Torre stuck it to Neagle by pulling him one out away from qualifying for a win. While angering Neagle, he also stuck it to us as Mets fans because he summoned a former popular Met, David Cone, to come in and face Mike Piazza. At the time, I genuinely thought Torre wanted to cause us pain by bringing in the former Met, but the truth is it was a sound strategy by Joe. Piazza had taken Neagle deep earlier, so why risk it again? Instead he brought in the righty to face

Mike and it worked out for them. Piazza hit a lazy infield popup that ended the inning.

The rest of this game felt like a slow death march, especially when the great Mariano Rivera came into the game looking for the six-out save. He officially did it when he struck out his old nemesis from 1999, Matt Franco, to end the game. The Yankees had taken command of the Series and were now one win away from their third straight championship. This loss was on the Mets offense, as they only managed two runs, but I couldn't get the first pitch of the game out of my head. For all the good Bobby Jones had accomplished throughout his Mets career and his mesmerizing NLDS performance against the Giants, the thought of him lobbing in a cookie to Derek Jeter to open Game 4 superseded everything. It turned out to be Jones's final outing as a Met, and I hate myself for feeling this way, but I mostly remember Bobby these days for that first-pitch mistake. Even if he bounced a curveball, I doubt the results would have been different, but that first pitch felt like the air coming out of the balloon of hope we once had. The Mets were down 3–1, and now all we could hope for is not facing the indignation of watching the Yankees celebrate a title in our building.

KEEPING SCORE: Jeter's blast marked only the sixth time the first batter homered in a World Series game and the first time since Rickey Henderson did it 11 years earlier for the Oakland A's against their Bay area neighbors, the San Francisco Giants.... Jose Canseco made his only appearance of the World Series as a pinch-hitter for Cone, and Glendon Rusch struck him out with two on to end the top of the sixth.

LOSING THE 2000 WORLD SERIES

YANKEES 4 METS 2
GAME 5, WORLD SERIES
OCTOBER 26, 2000, at SHEA STADIUM

ENTERING SHEA STADIUM for Game 5 of the 2000 World Series, I had the same emotions that I experienced a year earlier with the Braves. When the Mets went down 3–0 to Atlanta, my attitude was simply "don't let this happen here." While I was still holding out hope for the miracle comeback, I just wanted the Mets to avoid at all costs the embarrassment of the Braves celebrating an NL pennant in my park. Luckily for me, the Mets accomplished that tiny goal before eventually succumbing to the mighty Braves in Atlanta. After losing Game 4 to the Yankees when Derek Jeter set the tone with a first-pitch home run and now facing a daunting 3–1 hole, I had the exact same attitude. Get this crap back to Yankee Stadium where we'll get another crack at the douche Roger Clemens. But there was one other major reason why getting this back to the Bronx was so paramount—unlike the Braves series from a year earlier, I was sitting shoulder to shoulder with Yankees fans in my building. Can you imagine Yankees fans celebrating not just a win but a freakin' world championship in our home ballpark? This was a nightmare that only added to the pressure of Game 5 of the World Series.

My dad and I sat in our seats a good hour and a half before first pitch on this very comfortable, 61-degree Thursday night. We noticed something as the building started to fill up that made me very uneasy...there were a lot more Yankees fans converging on Shea than the previous two nights. The Yankees fans always represented themselves quite well in these Subway Series, but something about this night felt different. Maybe it was being one win away from a third straight championship, maybe it was Mets fans trying to avoid the embarrassment, but all I knew was that this environment was going to feel a little bit different than Games 3 and 4 did.

The always trustworthy Al Leiter was on the mound in a rematch of Game 1 as he faced Andy Pettitte. In a marathon at-bat leading off the second inning, Bernie Williams hit a ball down the left-field line. I leaned to my left hoping that was going to cause the ball to hook foul. My body language didn't work, and Shea Stadium exploded with Yankees fans as they took the early 1–0 lead. **But the bottom of the second saw a mini-miracle. A two-on, two-out rally seemed**

Thursday
DATE October 26, 2000   STADIUM/CAP. Shea Stadium   55,777   ATT. _____

GAME # NYY 16 Met 14   WEATHER clear   START/FINISH 1:28 / _____   TIME _____

NL STANDINGS

World Series	NYY DP/OPP 0	SERIES
Met 1		World Series
NYY 3	DEFENSE	NYY Series Met

SERIES World Series Game 5

Yankees 010 001 002 4
Mets 020 000 000 2

Yankees win 3rd straight World Championship

Series MVP
Derek Jeter

New York Mets	Ave 274	HR 11	H 105	1	2	3	4	5	6	7	8	9	10	11	12 AB	13 R	14 H	15 BI
50 Benny Agbayani lf															4	0	1	1
13 Edgardo Alfonzo 2b	288		4410												5	0	1	0
31 Mike Piazza c	292		407												5	0	2	0
9 Todd Zeile 1b	320		169												3	0	0	0
4 Robin Ventura 3b	182		207												4	0	0	0
33 Bubba Trammell rf	200		043												3	1	1	0
44 Jay Payton cf	208		227												4	1	2	0
20 Kurt Abbott ss	100		000												3	0	1	0
22 Al Leiter p	000		000												2	0	0	0
15 Darryl Hamilton ph	350		000												1	0	0	0

	R/ER	H	E	LOB

PITCHERS	IP	R	ER	H	W	K	MISC.
Andy Pettitte	7	2	0	8	3	5	32 BF 1 PO
Mike Stanton	1	0	0	0	0	1	3 BF
Mariano Rivera	1	0	0	0	1	1	4 BF

©1996 Bob Carpenter Communications, Inc. All Rights Reserved

destined for failure with the light-hitting Leiter up, but he laid down a perfect drag bunt, and a bobble by Pettitte allowed him to reach first and tie the game. Then Benny Agbayani followed with a little infield single to take the lead. *Holy crap*, I thought. We responded immediately to the Bernie home run and now I started counting the outs until Game 6. Yes, in the third inning, 17-year-old Evan was naïve enough to start counting freakin' outs. We needed more runs, but weren't getting any against the stingy Andy Pettitte. But so far Al Leiter was making this 2–1 lead hold up. But then in the top of the sixth inning, just 11 outs away from Game 6, Derek Jeter came to the plate. Season ticket holders in our section had become like family, and one of the guys, a man named Larry, would always stand up when Jeter came up and scream *"Pretty boy!... Heyyyyy, pretty boy!"* I always found this funny, but not on this night and certainly not in this moment. Jeter, the pretty boy himself, who kicked us in the balls a night earlier, drove a 2–0 pitch over the left-field fence to tie the game. Sitting next to Larry was a female Yankees fan, who for some godforsaken reason was invited to each and every Subway Series game, began screaming at the top of her lungs. Her scream of excitement was like nails on a chalkboard.

The game was tied 2–2, and the Mets offense was showing zero signs of life. We trudged along into the ninth inning with the game still tied and Al Leiter still on the mound. He struck out the first two hitters as his pitch count continued to balloon. Al then lost Jorge Posada by issuing a walk and allowed a single to Scott Brosius. John Franco was warming in the bullpen as Luis Sojo came to the plate with two on and two out. Al was at 141 pitches, and I was totally with Bobby Valentine on this...let Al finish the job. On the very first pitch, Luis hit a slow roller up the middle that got past a diving Kurt Abbott and into center field. To make matters worse, the throw from center field hit the base runner and allowed a second run to score. My heart dropped and the lady next to me was enjoying her foreplay as she moaned loudly. The Yankees had taken a 4–2 lead and were now three outs away from a threepeat. John Franco now entered the game to face a guy who tortured him his entire career, Glenallen Hill. Luckily, Hill just missed connecting solidly with Franco's 3–2 pitch and flied out to left to end this most painful top of the ninth. Mariano Rivera jogged in to a standing ovation from the Yankees fans who had now taken over our building en masse.

Our final shot against Mariano flew by very quickly. We were given a gift from the GOAT closer when he walked Benny Agbayani on four pitches with one out to at least bring the tying run to the plate with Edgardo Alfonzo and Mike Piazza to follow. As I sat in my seat, all I could think about was 1986. While I didn't experience it, I heard the stories my entire life and was somehow praying to the baseball gods that the stories I heard as a child would now happen in real life. Alfonzo hit a soft fly ball to right, and we were down to our final out. Mike Piazza was our last hope. Could this at-bat be the at-bat I tell my future kids about? Could this be my Mookie Wilson moment? Mike took strike one right down the middle. The second pitch was blasted. As that ball flew through the air toward center field, I couldn't believe what I was watching. My 1986 right before my eyes! The greatest closer in history vs. the greatest hitting catcher of our generation...was he about to do it? I noticed that Bernie Williams calmly stopped in front of the warning track. My stomach dropped...Bernie made the catch. I quickly put my book away and couldn't wait to leave. I didn't want to see any of this, not Mariano jumping up and down, not Jeter pumping his fist, nothing. And I didn't. I looked away, but unfortunately, I couldn't close my ears. That woman sitting next to us started screaming at the top of her lungs—a sound that haunts me to this day. The sound of pleasure she was expressing rang in my ears as I tried to promptly leave Shea as fast as possible. Yankees fans remained in the building to celebrate, so it was just us Mets fans hightailing it out. As we left the building, we found it impossible to get to our cars because of the many police barricades that were set up. I would like to apologize to the NYPD for what my dad and I did in this moment. I appreciate all the hard work our local heroes do to protect us, but in this moment we were angry and thought all the barricades were set up so that the Yankees fan mayor could leave in an easy and convenient way. So we proceeded kick a lot of the barricades down. I'm not proud of this moment, but we were angry, bitter, sad Mets fans.

I have a lot of awful memories from that game, but nothing will ever be as harmful as that sound. That scream from that lady still haunts my dreams two decades later.

KEEPING SCORE: Leiter, who was in line for a victory in Game 1, put up a 2.87 ERA for the Series with 16 strikeouts in 15⅔ innings…. Todd Zeile was the top Mets batter with eight hits and a .400 average.

BACK IN NEW YORK
FOR BASEBALL

BRAVES 5 METS 4 (11 INNINGS)
SEPTEMBER 23, 2001, at SHEA STADIUM

IF I WAS making a list of monumental Mets games I have missed scoring over the past 30-plus years, the return of baseball to New York City post-9/11 would clearly top the list. A few months earlier, I had left my home on Long Island to take a job in Washington, D.C., working for the newly launched XM Satellite Radio. For the first few months, I lived in a dorm at American University and then got my first apartment in Silver Spring, Maryland, where I lived for the next few years. The scheduled launch date for XM Satellite Radio and for my channel was originally supposed to be the same week as 9/11. Like all of us, that day still brings back horrendous and vivid memories. I woke up that morning to the news of an "accident." As I drove to a class I was taking at the local community college, I heard the reporter on TV announce it to the shock of me and everyone listening that a second plane hit the towers. It was very difficult in the moment to fully understand the ramifications of what was happening. Despite the horror of what was happening, I decided to still attend my class, and I'm glad I did. The professor was an older lady, and I will never forget what she said as she began the class. "I've been around for a very long time and I've seen it all…but I've never felt the sadness of what I feel right now." It took her putting in perspective what was happening to really make it sink in.

Braves | VISITOR | W-L 79-69 | GB +½ Phi | HOME 34-38 | ROAD 45-31 | VS DIV. 33-29

Mets | HOME | W-L 76-73 | GB 3½ | HOME 42-32 | ROAD 34-41 | VS DIV. 38-25

AL STANDINGS

	R	H	E	O	LOB
Atl	5	8	0		5
Met	4	10	0		7

WP John Smoltz 3-3
LP Jerrod Riggan 3-3
SV ~~~~~~

Met DP/OPP 2   IOA   DEFENSE   O   E

UMPIRES
Ball 2B
Foster 3B • 1B Kulpa
HP
Hirschbeck

©1996 Bob Carpenter Communications, Inc. All Rights Reserved

The launch was pushed back, as we all sat in horror watching the attack on our country. On Friday, September 21, when baseball returned to New York City, I too was coming home. I spent my evening on Amtrak riding the train from Union Station in D.C. back home to New York City. While I didn't score the game, I listened to it in its entirety in a very old-school way—on my portable transistor

Sunday
DATE September 23, 2001   STADIUM/CAP. Shea Stadium   55,777   ATT. 41,168

GAME # All 149 Met 150   WEATHER Sunny 73°   START/FINISH 1:13 / 4:58   TIME 3:45

NL STANDINGS

DEFENSE   SERIES 3 of 3   Season Series 8-7 Met

Braves 0 0 0 | 0 0 0 | 1 0 3 | 0 1   5
Mets   0 1 1 | 0 0 0 | 0 2 0 | 0 0   4

Alfonzo extends hit streak to 16.

©1996 Bob Carpenter Communications, Inc. All Rights Reserved

radio. I fought back tears listening to the voice of my childhood, Bob Murphy, describe the atmosphere around the emotional return of baseball after 9/11. As I was getting closer to home was when I heard Murph call Mike Piazza's dramatic home run in the eighth inning against Steve Karsay that gave the Mets the lead. While I wish I was at Shea for that night, there was no better person to describe everything going on than the great Bob Murphy and Gary Cohen. That weekend my family and I visited the site of Ground Zero, and all these years later I can still sense the smell hitting me as we got closer. That night the Mets played the Braves and defeated them for the second straight time. Very quietly the 2001 Mets were making a late push. When the baseball stopped on 9/11, the Mets were playing better, but still sat two games under .500 and trailed the Braves by eight games in the NL East. Upon returning, the Mets swept the Pirates in Pittsburgh and won the first two games back home against the Braves. All of a sudden, the Mets were only 3½ games back of Atlanta going into the finale of this three-game series. With three more games in Atlanta the following weekend, the Mets were legit in a race if they could finish off the sweep and cut the Braves lead to 2½.

The Mets got off to another strong start as Jay Payton gave them an early 1–0 lead with an RBI single in the second inning. And it was quickly 2–0 when Joe McEwing hit a solo home run an inning later off Tom Glavine. Al Leiter was cooking on the mound as the Mets were creeping closer and closer to a sweep of their longtime nemesis. It seemed like the sweep was really going to happen when the Mets added two insurance runs in the bottom of the eighth inning to make it 4–1. The Mets were now three outs away from a sweep and cutting the NL East lead to a measly 2½ games. We could make a long list of Armando Benitez blown saves that caused us pain as Mets fans, with the 2000 World Series being the clear leader in the clubhouse. While that will always top the list, what was about to happen was very, very close. The Mets were on this emotional run as they are doing their best to distract us from the horror of the real world around us, and Armando Benitez decided this was the time to stick it up all of our collective asses. Up by three runs and one out away from victory, Benitez allowed what felt at the time to be a harmless two-run home run to Brian Jordan that made it a 4–3 game. Despite that, the Mets were still just one out away from victory. Future Nationals manager Dave Martinez worked a walk, and Andruw Jones delivered a single. The Braves were now set up with two on and two out for the pinch-hitter B.J. Surhoff. Can Armando just get a freakin' out and end this? Nope...Surhoff tied the game with an RBI single, and the vultures were out for Benitez as he was pulled from the game. I'm not one to boo, but if there was ever a moment where I had a major urge to let it out, it was in this moment. The game remained tied until the 11ᵗʰ inning when Brian Jordan did it again, hitting a leadoff home run off Jerrod Riggan. The Mets had blown the game, and I left Shea fuming. What's crazy is the Mets kept winning and again were back on the Braves' doorstep going into the following weekend series in Atlanta. Armando did it again, when the Mets blew a 5–1 ninth-inning lead in Atlanta on Saturday that was capped off by a walk-off grand slam by Jordan—this time off John Franco. The Mets gave us some hope and a little bit of a tease late in 2001, but the tag-team combo of Brian Jordan and Armando Benitez made sure it would lead to nothing.

KEEPING SCORE: Jordan had five home runs and 19 RBIs in 19 games against the Mets that season. In 111 career games against them between 1992 and 2006, he batted .287 with 19 homers and 83 RBIs.... After the 2001 season, Riggan was traded to the Cleveland Indians in an ill-fated deal for Roberto Alomar.

WE HATED HIM IN ATLANTA, WE HATE HIM IN NEW YORK

CUBS 15 METS 2

MARCH 31, 2003, at SHEA STADIUM

AFTER FINISHING above .500 and being in some form of a pennant race every season between 1997 and 2001, the Mets of 2002 were a disaster. They had acquired Mo Vaughn and Roberto Alomar and brought back old Mets Jeremy Burnitz and Roger Cedeno as they tried to retool. The results were very bad as Alomar looked completely washed up and the team finished 11 games under .500. During the off-season the Mets remained aggressive by signing a longtime rival whom we had hated for a decade. The Mets brought in 37-year-old left-hander Tom Glavine to join the top of the rotation and create a formidable 1-2 punch with fellow 37-year-old lefty

DATE Monday March 31, 2003   STADIUM/CAP. Shea Stadium   Queens, NY   ATT. 53,586

GAME # Cub 1 Met 1   WEATHER Sunny + Cold 39°   START/FINISH 1:13 / 4:42   TIME 329

NL STANDINGS

SERIES Opening Day ★
1 of 3
1st Meeting of the Season.

Cubs 401 | 014 | 500 15
Mets 020 | 000 | 000   2

©1996 Bob Carpenter Communications, Inc. All Rights Reserved

Al Leiter. To go along with losing Edgardo Alfonzo and replacing Bobby Valentine with Art Howe, the 2003 Mets had almost zero resemblance to the team that had won the pennant only three seasons earlier.

I was not a huge fan of signing Glavine away from the Atlanta Braves for numerous reasons, some logical, some irrational. First off, fuck him, he was an Atlanta Brave. The Mets and Braves had been the bitterest of rivals for the last half-decade and now all of a sudden I have root for this guy? But even the rational side of me didn't love this move. Despite getting solid seasons out of Mo Vaughn and Mike Piazza and a very good season from Edgardo Alfonzo, the Mets finished with a losing record in 2002. They also made a decision that I hated at the time, and that was to let Fonzie walk to the Giants. It almost felt as if they had decided to keep Roberto Alomar over Alfonzo, and even though history would tell us it turned out to be a wise decision to let Fonzie walk, he was a career Met who was still only 28 years old. Now they were adding a 37-year-old who, despite coming off a very solid season, was clearly closer to the end. Did they really think this team was going to improve by 10-plus games and compete for the playoffs? In the years before the Madoff scandal made the Mets a cheap organization, I did appreciate the spending, but I didn't think it was wise in this case.

On Opening Day 2003, Shea Stadium had your normal pomp and circumstance. Everyone was cheered during the introductions, the good luck wreath was presented to new manager Art Howe, and we were all freezing our asses off. It was a bright sunny day, but it was also frigid. My memories tell me this was the coldest Opening Day I had ever experienced as temperatures hovered in the mid-to-high 30s. At the time I was still living in Maryland, but nothing was going to stop my Opening Day streak, so I drove up to New York the night before ready for the ballgame. Tom Glavine got the opening day nod over Al Leiter, because fuck loyalty, let's just reward the ancient mercenary who probably didn't even want to come here, but felt a loyalty to the players' association to take the highest contract offer. Opening Day is largely a symbolic day, and I didn't love handing the ball to this dude right out of the gate.

We all know now how Tom Glavine's five-year Mets tenure would end, but his beginning wasn't much better. On this frigid cold day, where we are begging to be optimistic, Glavine beat the positivity out of us very early. He allowed the first four base runners to reach, and the Mets trailed 3–0 just four batters into the game.

That New York groan was out early as we were all disgusted with Tom's first impression. When the Mets cut the deficit to 4–2 against Kerry Wood in the second inning on an RBI double by Burnitz and a grounder by Rey Sanchez, there was some hope that Glavine would settle in and keep this game close as he had done many times in his career. But this Tom Glavine was a cheap facsimile of the Hall of Famer from Atlanta, so as soon as the Mets scored those two runs, Glavine gave it right back in the top of the third. When he was finally chased from the game in the fourth inning after walking Sammy Sosa, the vultures were out in full swing. Glavine was loudly booed as he causally walked off the mound at Shea Stadium looking as if he didn't give two shits about what happened. The game became a bloodbath as the pen allowed it to get completely out of hand. When it was all said and done, the Mets had lost the opener at Shea by a final score of 15–2. Glavine had allowed five runs and four walks in just 3⅔ innings as he made the worst possible first impression. He was never a beloved New York Met, even during his good times in his Mets career, when to his credit he went out and made every single start. I'm convinced that, along with being a hated Brave, the horrific first impression he made left a lasting impression that was tough to come back from. While many Opening Days aren't very memorable, this one in 2003 was, and for all the wrong reasons.

KEEPING SCORE: Wood, who would lead the majors in strikeouts in 2003, fanned five in five innings in the opener.... The Cubs went on to win their first division title in 14 seasons before losing the NLCS to the Florida Marlins.... Meanwhile, the Mets finished in last place in the NL East with a 66–95 record, their worst season since 1993.

MEET THE NEW METS, SAME AS THE OLD METS

REDS 7 METS 6

APRIL 4, 2005, at GREAT AMERICAN BALL PARK, CINCINNATI

OMAR MINAYA was the new GM, Willie Randolph was the new manager, Pedro Martinez was the most dominant pitcher of our time, Carlos Beltrán was coming off the greatest postseason run we had seen in decades...we present to you the new New York Mets. The off-season of 2004–2005 was like the Christmas that never ended for us as Mets fans. Despite the legit concerns around the durability and future of Pedro Martinez, signing Pedro fresh off his world championship with the Red Sox felt surreal. At the time I sorta believed the theory that in order to get other guys to follow you needed the credibility of bringing in Pedro. The big fish, though, was Carlos Beltrán, who had just completed one of the most torrid postseasons you'll ever see as he led the Astros to the seventh game of the NLCS before falling short against the Cardinals. Beltrán was 28 and in the prime of his career and a true star in the game. I was excited about Willie Randolph getting the opportunity to manage, as he'd clearly paid his dues as a longtime coach on Joe Torre's staff, and the idea of his being a Yankee wasn't a big turnoff for me. Willie was a New York guy, and if he could manage, I didn't care that his baseball ties were mostly with the Yankees rather than the one year he spent on our team in 1992. There were two clear holes the Mets had going into 2005 that needed to be rectified if they were going to be a contender. The closer was still Braden Looper, and after striking out on the big target of acquiring Carlos Delgado, they settled for the light-hitting Doug Mientkiewicz. There were two positives about Mientkiewicz that I personally liked: he was an elite defensive first baseman, and I enjoyed spelling his name, which I would now do nightly when I filled out my scorecard.

Mets
VISITOR
Reds
HOME

W-L 0-0 GB — HOME 0-0 ROAD 0-0 VS DIV. 0-0
W-L 0-0 GB — HOME 0-0 ROAD 0-0 VS DIV. 0-0

AL STANDINGS

	R	H	E	LOB		
Met	6	14	0	8		
Cin	7	8	0	2		

WP Danny Graves 1-0
LP Braden Looper 0-1
SV ~~~~~~

UMPIRES
Everitt
2B
Timmons 3B • 1B Meriwether
HP
McClelland

Cin DP/OPP   DEFENSE   E

Alex Dunn   Ken Griffey Jr.   Austin Kearns

Rich Aurilia   D'Angelo Jimenez

Joe Randa   0.00 Paul Wilson   Sean Casey

M. Acta   J. Manuel

Jason LaRue

① NY 1-0
TB ½
Bal ½
Tor ½
Bos 1

② Det 0-0
Min 0-0
CWS 0-0
KC 0-0
Cle 0-0

③ Sea 0-0
Tex 0-0
Oak 0-0
LAA 0-0

New York Mets   Avg .000   HR 0   R/G 0

			1	2	3	4	5	6	7	8	9	10	11	AB 12	R 13	H 14	BI 15
7	Jose Reyes	SS .000 .000															
25	Kaz Matsui	2b .000 .000															
15	Carlos Beltran	cf .000 .000															
31	Mike Piazza	c .000 .000															
30	Cliff Floyd	lf .000 .000															
16	Doug Mientkiewicz	1b .000 .000															
5	David Wright	3b .000 .000															
57	Eric Valent	rf .000 .000															
45	Pedro Martinez	p .000 .000															

	1	2	3	4	5	6	7	8	9
R/ER	1|1	0|0	2|2	0|0	0|0	0|0	3|3	0|0	0|0
H	1	0	2	1	0	2	5	0	
E	0	0	0	0	0	0	0	0	0
LOB	0	1	1|2	1|3	1|4	2|6	1|7	1|8	0|8

LH BENCH RH
Robinson   Castro
Diaz
Cairo
Woodward

Cin PITCHERS	IP	R	ER	H	W	K	
39-53 4.54 Paul Wilson (40)	6	3	3	8	2	2	27BF 2HP
David Weathers (35)	⅔	2	2	3	0	0	4BF
Kent Mercker (30)	⅓	1	1	2	0	0	3BF 1HR
Ryan Wagner (38)	1	0	0	1	0	1	4BF
Danny Graves (32)	1	0	0	0	0	0	3BF

LH Cin BULLPEN RH

Back in 2005, I was hosting a nightly talk show on Maxim Radio. Luckily for me, the show started at 7:00 PM, so Opening Day, which started at 2:00 PM would not need to be on any kind of DVR delay. My producer at the time was also a big Mets fan, so we decided to do a liquid lunch and watch the game from a bar near our studios in Manhattan. You can picture if you so choose: a 21-year-old me, with

DATE April 4, 2005 (Monday) STADIUM/CAP. Great American Ball Park Cincinnati, OH ATT. 42,794

GAME # Met 1 Cin 1 WEATHER Sunny 68° START/FINISH 2:08 / 4:52 TIME 2:44

NL STANDINGS

Mets 102 | 000 | 300 6
Reds 300 | 000 | 103 7

SERIES Opening Day '04 Season Series (1 of 6) 3-3 Tie

DEFENSE — Cliff Floyd, Carlos Beltran, Eric Valent, Jose Reyes, Kaz Matsui, David Wright, Pedro Martinez (0.00), Doug Mientkiewicz, Mike Piazza, Whisler

Cincinnati Reds				Ave 000	HR 0	R/G 0	1	2	3	4	5	6	7	8	9	10	11	12	13	14	15
3	D'Angelo	Jimenez	2b																		
30	Ken	Griffey Jr.	cf																		
21	Sean	Casey	1b																		
28	Austin	Kearns	rf																		
44	Adam	Dunn	lf																		
16	Joe	Randa	3b																		
33	Rich	Aurilia	ss																		
	Jason	LaRue	c																		

		IP	R	ER	H	W	K
Met PITCHERS							
Pedro Martinez (45)	112-76.3 2.75	6	3	3	3	2	12
Manny Aybar (36)		1	1	1	2	0	2
Dae-Sung Koo (17)		1	0	0	0	0	2
Braden Looper (40)		0	3	3	3	0	0

LH BENCH RH

©1996 Bob Carpenter Communications, Inc. All Rights Reserved

his scorebook in hand sitting at a New York City bar while stuffing my face with bar food and Blue Moon beer. I never really enjoyed watching games at bars because of all the things that could potentially happen to my precious scorebook. Ketchup stains, beer drips, I mean the list goes on and on. But I wanted this momentous occasion to be social, and I thought the atmosphere would be cool to watch

Opening Day surrounded by Mets fans on a weekday afternoon in New York City. I've mentioned this before, but a lot of Opening Days, whether on the road or at home, seem to run together where you sorta forget what happened. This Opening Day in Cincinnati was certainly not an example of that.

Pedro Martinez was a pitcher I had long admired, especially in his days with Montreal, where he blossomed into a true megastar. I held out hope that the Mets would deal for Pedro once it became clear the Expos were shopping him around the league. Unfortunately, the Red Sox won the Pedro derby, and he took his star to an even higher level in Boston, where he became the Sandy Koufax of our generation. Despite the age and concerns around him, it was still super surreal to see Pedro don the Mets road grays with No. 45 on his back. Kaz Matsui, whom the Mets had signed one season earlier, was beginning his second season after coming over from Japan. But this time he was shifted to second base after a season of proving to the world he was a subpar defensive shortstop. Matsui made the bar erupt when he hit a solo home run in the first inning to give the Mets a quick 1–0 lead. Matsui had done the same thing one year earlier when he went deep on the first pitch of the 2004 season. The only redeeming quality of Matsui's MLB career was his uncanny knack of hitting season-beginning homers. Shockingly, in Pedro Martinez's first inning as a Met, he promptly gave up a three-run bomb to Adam Dunn, and the Mets' lead quickly evaporated. Luckily, we then got to witness vintage Pedro for the next five innings as he carved up the Reds lineup to keep the game tied after the Mets evened it up in the third inning. Pedro ended up living up to the hype as he struck out 12 Reds and held them to just those three runs in the first inning.

Even though things would change quickly over the next few months, Beltrán also made a great first impression! He hit the home run to tie the game in the third and gave the Mets the lead with an RBI single in the seventh inning. Cliff Floyd hit a two-run homer later in the seventh, and it was all set up for a feel-good Opening Day win as the Mets had a comfortable 6–4 lead entering he bottom of the ninth inning. In what felt like a 30-second meltdown, Braden Looper proceeded to flush the entire game down the toilet. He allowed a game-tying bomb to Adam Dunn and then Joe Randa finished off the meltdown with a walk-off jack of his own. I quickly picked up my scorebook and flew out of that bar as quickly as I could, absolutely disgusted. Luckily, I had paid the bar tab an inning earlier, so no, I was not walking out on my bill! I cursed Braden Looper for the next few hours as I got ready for my radio show that night. For all the good feelings of the off-season, to then watch the game end that way was freakin' disgusting. When you think about all the Mets closers throughout history, they all seem to have that one big "shit the bed" moment that jumps out above the rest. For Braden Looper, Opening Day 2005 was the moment you knew what we already should have known...he was not long for our world.

KEEPING SCORE: The home runs by Matsui and Beltrán were both given up by former Met Paul Wilson, who was beginning what would be his last major league season.... Matsui missed Opening Day of the 2006 season with a knee injury but homered in his first plate appearance for the third straight season upon his return in late April.... Joe Randa had been a Met for a week in December 1998. The Mets had acquired the third baseman from the Detroit Tigers for pitcher Willie Blair but then flipped him to the Kansas City Royals, where he had his best seasons, for a minor league outfielder who never reached the majors named Juan LeBron.

A CLASSIC REGULAR SEASON GAME

METS 5 ANGELS 3 (10 INNINGS)
JUNE 11, 2005, at SHEA STADIUM

IN THE SPRING of 2005, along with hosting a nightly talk show on Maxim Radio, I was now doing overnights at WFAN. My DVR had become my best friend in this era of Mets baseball because the only way I'd be able to continue my obsession of never missing a pitch and scoring nearly every damn game was the greatest invention of the 20th century—the DVR. It was quite the challenge because my show hours were not only from 7:00–10:00 PM, but my route home to Long Island City, Queens, would involve taking the 7 Train. So every night when I hit Grand Central Station, I would see hordes of Mets fans getting off the train. I would try to literally cover my ears to not accidentally hear what they could be saying about the game. I also would jump to conclusions—if the trains didn't feature Mets fans deboarding, that to me was a hint that the game happened to be a very long one. My favorite memory of my unhealthy DVRing-the-Mets obsession was the night I ran into Mets pitcher Victor Zambrano in my building's elevator. I awkwardly told Victor that I recorded the Mets game and didn't want to know what happened. Much like when he was struggling on the mound, Victor looked at me as if he had no idea what I was saying. Thankfully, while Victor always disappointed us on the mound or in the MRI tube, he came through that night, as he gave me no indication of what happened in the Mets game.

This experience made me appreciate more than ever going to games. The only games I would be able to attend were weekend games that didn't conflict with work. Occasionally I'd sneak in a weekday afternoon game before my nighttime radio show, but I was mostly held to Saturday and Sunday games at Shea. On this Saturday night in June, the Mets were hosting the Los Angeles Angels of Anaheim in an interleague showdown. It was raining at Shea, so we had to wait out a rain delay that lasted about an hour and a half. Spoiled Evan back in the day wouldn't care too much about delays or rain-outs, because I knew whenever the game was made up I'd likely be in attendance. But in 2005, every Met game I went to was very special, and I couldn't risk a game being banged and not being able to see the makeup affair. Luckily, Mets-Angels began at a little after 8:30, and little did I know I was about to watch a game that I would remember decades after it was played. The pitching matchup of Jarrod Washburn and Kris Benson wasn't sexy at all, but both guys pitched well.

	W-L	GB		HOME	ROAD	VS DIV.
VISITOR Angels	35-25	+2½ Tex		15-11	20-14	11-6
HOME Mets	31-30	4	HOME	21-14	10-16	15-15

AL STANDINGS

	R	H	E	LOB
LAA	3	8	O	5
Met	5	9	1	7

10 inn

WP Brandon Looper 2-1
LP Brendan Donnelly 4-2
SV ∼∼∼∼∼

UMPIRES
Culbreth
2B
Hudson 3B • 1B Cooper
HP
Young

Met DP/OPP

DEFENSE

Cliff Floyd — Carlos Beltran — Mike Cameron
Jose Reyes — Kaz Matsui
David Wright — 4.02 Kris Benson — Chris Woodward
R. Roenicke — A. Griffin
Mike Piazza

AL STANDINGS
- Bal 36-24
- Bos 4
- Tor 5½
- NYY 7
- TB 16½
- CWS 44-19
- Min 5½
- Cle 11½
- Det 13
- KC 22
- LAA 35-25
- Tex 2½
- Sea 8½
- Oak 11
- Min 35-24
- Tex 3
- Bos 3½
- Tor 5

Los Angeles Angels of Anaheim	Ave	HR	R/G	1	2	3	4	5	6	7	8	9	10	11	12	13	14	15
17 Darin Erstad	1b	.290														AB	R	H	BI

R/ER — 0|0 1|1 0|0 0|0 1|1 0|0 0|0 0|0 0|0 1|0
H — 0 2 0 0 1 0 0 0 0
E — 0 0 0 0 0 0 0 0 0 1E3
LOB — 0 0 0 0 0 0 1 0|1 2|3 2|5

LH BENCH RH
Kotchman Rivera
Quinlan
Figgins
DL: Salmon GO, Molina GO
Izturis 15

Met PITCHERS	IP	R	ER	H	W	K		LH Met BULLPEN RH
Kris Benson	7	2	2	4	0	2		
Aaron Heilman	2	0	0	2	0	2		
Brandon Looper	1	1	0	2	0	0		

©1996 Bob Carpenter Communications, Inc. All Rights Reserved

Carlos Beltrán made a home run–saving catch in the seventh inning against Angels catcher Bengie Molina that kept the score close. The Mets trailed 2–1 most of the game with their only run coming when Washburn walked Benson with the bases loaded and entered the bottom of the ninth inning down by the same score facing one of the elite closers in the game, future Met Francisco "K-Rod" Rodriguez.

Saturday

DATE June 11, 2005 STADIUM/CAP. Shea Stadium Flushing, NY ATT. 33,889

GAME # LAA 61 Met 62 WEATHER Overcast 76° START/FINISH 8:34 / 11:51 TIME 317

NL STANDINGS Rain Delay of 124 to start game

LAA DP/OPP DEFENSE E | SERIES Interleague 2 of 3 | Play ☆

Season Series 1-0 LAA

10'inn

	1	2	3
Angels	0 1 0	0 1 0	0 0 0	1	3
Mets	0 1 0	0 0 0	0 0 1	3	5

New York Mets	Avg 263	HR 64	R/G 4.43	1	2	3	4	5	6	7	8	9	10	11	12	13	14	15
													AB	R	H	BI

R/ER · H · E · LOB

LAA	PITCHERS	IP	R	ER	H	W	K
	70-52 4.05		6⅓	1	1	6	2	3
Jarrod Washburn								
Scott Shields	1⅔	0	0	0	0	1		
Francisco Rodriguez	1	1	1	1	0	3		
Brendan Donnelly	1	3	3	2	1	2		

©1996 Bob Carpenter Communications, Inc. All Rights Reserved

I then witnessed something I'd never seen. With one out and nobody on, pinch-hitter Marlon Anderson drove a ball to the gap in right-center field, and old friend Steve Finley (the man who failed to successfully jump and catch the Todd Pratt walk-off in the 1999 NLDS) kicked the ball in his attempt to cut the ball off in the alley. Anderson rounded the bases and was ruled safe on a bang-bang play at the plate. I remember Molina screaming in protest and Anderson lying in pain near the plate, and all the while the crowd was going absolutely nuts. Marlon got up and received a standing ovation as he walked back into the Mets dugout. In the thousands of baseball games I've watched, I don't think I ever remember seeing a game being tied in the ninth inning like that.

Braden Looper did his best to stick it up our ass by allowing the lead run to score in the 10th on a two-out single by Darin Erstad. This set up an epic Shea Stadium moment and my best memory from the 2005 season. Carlos Beltrán and Mike Piazza had both just struck out with two runners on base in the 10th inning down one run. So it left the game in the hands of Cliff Floyd. On a 3–2 pitch from Brendan Donnelly with the runners going and Shea Stadium standing in anticipation, Floyd hit a ball that off the bat we all knew was gone. He ripped one of his trademark screaming line drives over the right-field fence to win the game. As Cliff rounded the bases, my appreciation for being in the building and seeing a flat-out great game like this went through my mind. In the past, I would take moments like this for granted. This clutch moment and that Cliff swing stuck with me, because one year later when he came to the plate in the seventh game of the NLCS against the Cardinals, I envisioned that swing and that result happening again. It did not, but on this June night in 2005 it did, and it was spectacular.

KEEPING SCORE: Through 2023, Anderson remains the only Mets pinch-hitter to hit an inside-the-park home run.... The Angels, who were making their first trip to Shea Stadium to face the Mets (they had faced the Yankees there in 1974, 1975, and 1998), would go on to win the AL West that season before losing in the ALCS to the eventual World Series–champion Chicago White Sox.

DIVISION CLINCHER AND I'M FREE

METS 4 MARLINS 0
SEPTEMBER 18, 2006, at SHEA STADIUM

THE 2006 regular season turned into one giant coronation of a really good baseball team. It became quite obvious in the months earlier that the Mets would not only cruise to their first divisional championship that I was old enough to be aware of (I was five in 1988), but they would enter the postseason as the clear team to beat in the National League. I spent 2006 watching every second of every Mets game, but it came with quite a few challenges. I did a nighttime show on Sirius Radio that coincided with every single weeknight game the Mets played, and twice a week I would also host an overnight WFAN show. During the days when I didn't work at FAN, it was easy. I'd go home after work and right around 11:00 PM, I would watch the Mets game from start to finish on DVR. On those nights when I worked a double, I had to essentially watch a Mets game while doing a Maxim Radio talk show. Which suffered more... my ability to host a radio show, or my concentration on the Mets? The answer is very easy to guess. As August started creeping closer to September, a reality started to hit me. During the postseason I would be forced to watch every single game on DVR, which felt like an impossible burden. There is no way in my mind I could go to work for a job I started to dislike and potentially miss the one thing I've waited my whole life for—a Mets championship run. I wasn't being cocky, but I was being hopeful when it became obvious I needed to make a very important life-altering decision. I knew that I needed to pick between these two important things. Having a full-time job at Sirius or enjoying the New York Mets in October.

Having very little to no dating life and working two jobs led me to a very nice place financially. I actually had the ability to quit my full-time gig at Sirius and enjoy a semi-retirement for a few months before I would need to find myself another job to pay the bills.

150
V/G Marlins W-L 74-75 GB 16½ H 40-35 R 34-40 W 14-16 C 21-15 E 30-35 IL 9-9
149
H/G Mets W-L 90-58 GB +13½ Phi H 47-26 R 43-32 W 23-10 C 23-17 E 35-22 IL 6-9

AL · STANDINGS

	R	H	E	LOB
FL~	0	4	2	4
Met	4	8	0	5

WP Steve Trachsel 15-7
LP Brian Moehler 7-9
SV ~~~~~~~~~~

START 7:11
FINISH 9:40
TIME 229

DATE Monday 9/18/06
ATT. 46,729
WX 73° clear

Met DP/OPP 1

DEFENSE O E

Cliff Floyd
Carlos Beltran
Shawn Green
Jose Reyes
Jose Valentin
David Wright
4.11 Steve Trachsel
Carlos Delgado
B. Meechem
Paul Lo Duca
P. Hill

© NYY 90-59 #4
Bos 87
Tor 11
Det 26
TB 37

② Det 81 co -
Min 1
cws 5
clc 13½
kc 31½

③ oak 96-62 #7
LAA 7
Tex 11
Sea 15½

④ KCA 91-61
cws 4
Bos 7½
LAA 8½

Florida
Marlins Ave 265 HR 167 R/G 4.77

	1	2	3	4	5	6	7	8	9	10	11	AB 12	R 13	H 14	BI 15
3 Hanley Ramirez ss 290 13.52												4	0	0	0
c Leo Uggla 2b 294 36.69												4	0	0	0
24 Miguel Cabrera 3b 340 29.110															
14 Josh Willingham LF 278 26.73															
17 Mike Jacobs 1b 255 17.75															
12 Cody Ross RF 253 12.43															
4 Alfredo Amezaga CF 267 3.16															
30 Miguel Olivo c 21½ 15.54															

R/ER 0|0 0|0 0|0 0|0 0|0 0|0 0|0 0|0 0|0
H 0 0 0 1 0 0 2 1 0
E 0 0 0 0 0 0 0 0 0
LOB 1 0|1 0|1 1|2 0|2 0|2 2|4 0|4 0|4

LH BENCH RH

Met PITCHERS IP R ER H W K
133-142 4.29 Steve Trachsel ㉔ 6⅓ 0 0 3 1 3 23ßß
Guillermo Mota ㉚ 7 ⅔ 0 0 0 0 0 2ß
Aaron Heilman ⑭ 8 1 0 0 1 0 1 3ㄴ
Billy Wagner ⑬ 9 1 0 0 0 0 0 3ßß

LH Met BULLPEN RH

©1996 Bob Carpenter Communications, Inc. All Rights Reserved

Working two overnights a week at WFAN was nice and all, but it certainly wasn't going to be something I could live off of long-term. I have told people over the years that I quit a full-time job for the Mets, and it's damn true, but I also knew my time at that job wasn't going to last forever. So why would I let a job that would be a footnote in my life supersede a sports memory that I might cherish for the rest of time? If I had truly loved what I was doing on Maxim Radio, would I have quit it for the Mets? Probably not, but I honestly don't know. The job being something I no longer had passion for helped makes things easier, that's for sure. So on Monday, September 11, 2006, I penned a resignation letter to my boss at Sirius in which I explained that I no longer enjoyed doing the show anymore and it was best for me to move on. I decided to leave out any mention of the New York Mets in my letter, and I sorta regret that to this day. They should have known the truth...it wasn't 100 percent on them, it was the 2006 New York Mets that made me do it.

The Mets went to Pittsburgh a few days later and stubbed their toe a bit, which caused them to not be able to pop the champagne and officially clinch the NL East. Much like in 1986 where a sweep in Philadelphia caused the clinch to be at Shea, the same was seeming to come true for the '06 Mets. On Monday, September 18, one week after I gave my two weeks' notice, the Mets sat with a magic number of 1 as they were scheduled to host the then Florida Marlins at Shea Stadium. With one foot out the door, I politely asked for an off day and it was granted—my dad and I would be at Shea on this Monday night just like old times. I was a bit nervous, though...it's one thing to ask for an off day with only five shows left in my Sirius career, but if God forbid the Mets lost, would I have the balls to ask for another? "Don't worry about it," my dad said. "It ends *tonight*."

With Steve Trachsel toeing the rubber on this picturesque evening, the Mets left little doubt. Trachsel was in full control as he hurled shutout baseball into the seventh inning, and second baseman José Valentín, who had been one of the biggest surprises of 2006, hit a pair of home runs to give the Mets a 3–0 lead. Now up 4–0 entering the ninth inning, the party was about to begin. To this point in my Mets fan lifetime, I had only seen the Mets make the playoffs twice, as a wild-card team in 1999 after winning a one-game playoff and then again the following season in 2000, when we had lost the race for the division against Atlanta. This party was about to be a first for me—a celebration of a division championship. Left fielder Cliff Floyd, who had seen the real bad a few years earlier, was the man who caught the final out, and the Mets officially won the 2006 National League East. It was a very cool moment, which seemed so different from the celebrations in 1999 and 2000. We knew there was more to this mission than just the division title, but it was nevertheless a very important accomplishment. As I celebrated that night, I'm not sure what I was most excited about—the

Mets winning the East, or me freeing myself from a job that was going to potentially keep me from being at Shea every night in October. I had my freedom, and the Mets had the division title.

KEEPING SCORE: The Mets were in first place for all but one day of the 2006 season. After losing their second game of the season on April 5, they fell into second place but moved back into first place the next day and remained there the rest of the season.... Valentín, signed as a free agent in the off-season, batted .271 in 137 games in 2006 with 18 home runs.... The division clincher was Trachsel's 15th victory of 2006 and his last in a Mets uniform. He signed with the Baltimore Orioles as a free agent after the season.

ELIMINATION DAY

METS 9 DODGERS 5
GAME 3, NATIONAL LEAGUE DIVISION SERIES
OCTOBER 7, 2006, at DODGER STADIUM, LOS ANGELES

WHILE I'M NOT this person anymore, there was a time where I was a true Yankees hater. When Chris "Mad Dog" Russo led the crack committee of Yankees haters back in the day on WFAN, as a listener I felt like one of them, and who could blame me? I grew up in the midst of the Yankees dynasty and felt the indignity of losing to them in a World Series in which their fans partied in my house. I also went to high school on Long Island, which is supposed to Mets country, surrounded by arrogant Yankees fans. You cannot blame me for being a full-blown hater of the pinstripes and everything they stood for. There is no doubt that the 2004 collapse against the Red Sox was the beginning of my softening stance against the Yankees, but over the next few years the hatred still ran deep in my soul.

The 2006 season was like no other in modern New York baseball history...not since 1956 had New York teams lead their respective

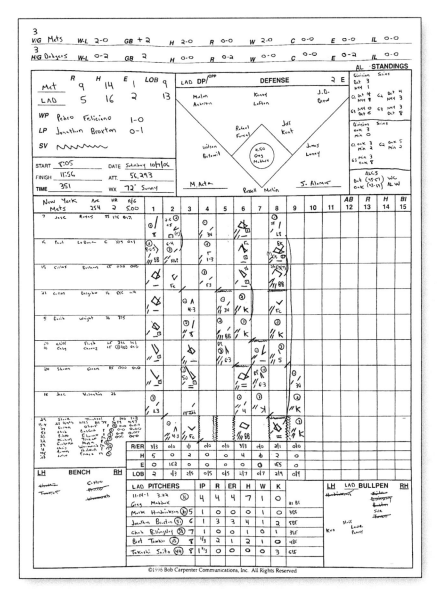

leagues in wins. Those fans in the 1950s were obviously spoiled by the outrageous success of the Yankees, Giants, and Dodgers, where there were five Subway Series over the course of six seasons. Well in 2006 the Mets and Yankees had rekindled the '50s magic as they both finished with a league-leading 97 wins. It was certainly different than 2000, but the Mets-Yankees rivalry was back! On the radio,

	1	2	3	4	5	6	7	8	9	R	H	E	LOB
Mets	3	0	1	0	0	3	0	2	0	9	14	1	9
Dodgers	0	0	0	2	3	0	0	0	0	5	16	2	13

STADIUM/CAP. Dodger Stadium

UMPS: Hirschbeck, Winters, Barrett, 2B, O'Nora 3B, 1B Kulpa, HP, Cooper

DEFENSE

Mets DP / OPP

Cliff Floyd — Carlos Beltran — Shawn Green

Jose Reyes — Jose Valentin

David Wright — 3.00 Steve Trachsel — Carlos Delgado

R. Donnelly

Paul Lo Duca

M. Duncan

NL STANDINGS

Division Series
LAD 0
Met 2

G1 LAD 5 Met 6 — G2 LAD 1 Met 4

Division Series
SH 2
SD 0

G1 SH 5 SD 0 — G2 SH 2 SD 0

G3 SD 3 SH 1

Division Series
2-0 Met

Game 3

★ Mets sweep Series ★
Advance to 1st NLCS since 2000

| | | | 3 of 5 | |
| Shawn Green | steals 6th inn Rally | 228 | 118 | |

Los Angeles Dodgers	Ave 235	HR 1	R/G 3.00	1	2	3	4	5	6	7	8	9	10	11	AB 12	R 13	H 14	BI 15
15 Rafael Furcal																		
7 Kenny Lofton																		
21 Marlon Anderson																		
12 Jeff Kent																		
7 J.D. Drew																		
55 Russell Martin																		
10 Wilson Betemit																		
24 James Loney																		

				1	2	3	4	5	6	7	8	9	10	11	12	13	14	15
R/ER				olo	olo	olo	2|2	3|3	olo	olo	olo	olo						
H				1	1	0	4	4	2	1	2	1						
E				1|1	0	0	0	0	0	0	0	0						
LOB				2	0|2	1|3	1|4	3|7	2|5	1|10	2|12	1|13						

LH BENCH RH

Repko, Hall, Martinez

Met PITCHERS		IP	R	ER	H	W	K	
Steve Trachsel	(37)	3 1/3	2	2	6	1	2	178 BF
Darren Oliver	(21)	4 1/3	3	3	3	0	0	56 BF 18R
Chad Bradford	(53)	5	0	0	0	1	1	2 BF
Pedro Feliciano	(25)	1/3	0	0	0	0	1	2 BF
Guillermo Mota	(93)	6	2	0	0	3	0	1	9 BF
Aaron Heilman	(43)	8	1	0	0	2	0	0	5 BF
Billy Wagner	(13)	9	1	0	0	1	0	2	4 BF

LH Met BULLPEN RH

©1996 Bob Carpenter Communications, Inc. All Rights Reserved

doing overnights at the FAN, there was a constant Mets vs. Yankee fans battle among the callers and a natural debate over which team was better. Every show I did turned into callers going at it with each other about the two teams. Eddie from Staten Island would be pissed about what Short Al from Brooklyn had to say about his team and vice versa. I forget the name of the caller, but one dude called me up in late September with a very funny line. "Hey, Evan," the caller said, "I want you to go to the store and buy two bottles of champagne and a box of tissues. One bottle for when you win the division series, one bottle for when you win the pennant, and then use the box of tissues for when the Yankees beat your team again in the World Series."

The back and forth all summer long was priceless. Then when the playoffs finally started, it was a battle for attention, which was tough to ignore. Getting to be on New York radio during those times was pretty special as both teams were legit World Series contenders. When the playoffs finally began, the Mets were matched up with the 88-win Los Angeles Dodgers, who settled for the wild-card spot. The Yankees were facing a Detroit Tigers team that had choked away the AL Central by losing their last five games before they too settled for the wild-card. The Mets had jumped out to a 2–0 series lead against the Dodgers, while shockingly the Yankees had just lost back-to-back games against the Tigers and were now one loss away from an elimination nobody saw coming. The day before, while the Mets enjoyed an off day, the former Yankee (and Met) Kenny Rogers dominated his way to a win, putting the Yankees on the brink. On Saturday October 7, 2006, the stage was set for an epic day...the Yankees had a chance to be eliminated and the Mets were a win away from closing out the division series.

I'll never forget sitting in my Long Island City apartment watching Jeremy Bonderman absolutely mow down the Yankees lineup that was nicknamed before the series by Tigers manager Jimmy Leyland as "Murderers' Row and Cano." This was the famous day where Joe Torre desperately dropped Alex Rodriguez to eighth in the batting order and it provided no spark. I had a few friends over that night, and as we celebrated the Yankees elimination, it was on to the main event of the evening. Could the Mets sweep the Dodgers and move on to the NLCS? An old rival in Greg Maddux made the start, and the Mets jumped all over him, giving Steve Trachsel an early lead that he would very quickly flush down the toilet. Up 4–0, Trachsel gave up two in the fourth and three in the fifth as he was chased from the game. Jeff Kent was supplying all of the offensive damage for the Dodgers in this series as he tormented his former team. His two-run home run off Darren Oliver tied it before Pedro Feliciano came in and walked future Met James Loney with the bases loaded. But right after giving up the lead, the feisty 2006 Mets responded. The top of the order of José Reyes, Paul Lo Duca, and Carlos Beltrán supplied RBI singles that gave the Mets a three-run lead they would never relinquish. The final four innings of this game was a countdown to party. When Billy Wagner finally got pinch-hitter Ramon Martinez to hit a little foul pop up to right field, the sweep was complete and the Mets were going to the NLCS for the first time since 2000. It also capped off a day that saw the Yankees eliminated and the Mets moving on—an image one could only try to picture in our deep imagination. The great Bob Huessler, who was a big part of that old crack committee, greeted me the next night when I came in to do the overnight show with, "How did you enjoy your elimination day?" Saturday, October 7, 2006, will always be a special holiday for us Met fans and Yankees haters, an event we don't get very often, but aptly named Elimination Day.

KEEPING SCORE: Kent went 8-for-13 in the series (.615).... For the Mets, Carlos Delgado had six hits in the three games, including a home run in Game 1.... Ramon Martinez played 19 games for the Mets in 2008–09.

METS LOSE GAME 7 AT HOME

CARDINALS 3 METS 1
GAME 7, NATIONAL LEAGUE CHAMPIONSHIP SERIES
OCTOBER 19, 2006, at SHEA STADIUM

GAME 7... GAME 7... I've heard many people say that those two little words are two of the most magical words in the English language when they are connected to each other. There is magic and mystique to the idea of a winner-take-all game—the heroes that are created, the memorable moments that occur in those games. But to me, *Game 7* is a phrase that haunts my dreams. To that point in my sports fan life, I had only experienced one Game 7. That occurred a few years earlier when my beloved New Jersey Nets got blown out in a Game 7 in Detroit against the Pistons. The game was over before it started, and all hope of a third straight NBA Finals appearance was eviscerated rather quickly. But for the New York Mets, the only Game 7 I could remember is the one that never happened but should have. In 1999 the Mets blew multiple leads after staging an incredible comeback against the Braves in Game 6 but came up short (*see* "It Can't End Like This," p. 95). Game 7 in that series is the coulda/shoulda game that never occurred. But in 2006 the stage was set for the most dramatic introduction to a Game 7 one could fathom. Unfortunately, it would also feature the worst and most nightmarish ending my brain could conjure.

Here is what kills me the most about this game: there were signs throughout that this was *our* game, this was *our* year. Take everything from the first inning as an example. Go down and look at what Albert Pujols did in the top of the first inning. Before you look, I guarantee as a Mets fan you won't even remember this until I bring it up. Albert Pujols reached second base on a two-base error. It was a high, easy popup to Carlos Delgado at first base, and he simply dropped it. So think about it...we were in a rocking Shea Stadium and Albert Pujols popped up to secure what should have been an

A hand-kept baseball scorecard for a St. Louis Cardinals vs. New York Mets game.

	R	H	E	LOB
StL	3	6	1	6
Met	1	4	1	11

WP Randy Flores 1-0
LP Aaron Heilman 0-1
SV Adam Wainwright 4

START 8:20 DATE Thursday 10/19/06
FINISH 11:43 ATT. 56,357
TIME 3:23 WX 67° Overcast

©1996 Bob Carpenter Communications, Inc. All Rights Reserved

easy 1-2-3 inning for the 25-year-old Oliver Perez. Oliver was making this start on only three days' rest and had completed a regular season in which he was 3–13 for the Pirates and Mets with a 6.55 ERA. His Game 4 start was a rocky one in which he gave up three home runs and five runs over 5⅓ innings. A dropped popup seems like something that could have destroyed the young lefty, and I was

	1	2	3	4	5	6	7	8	9	R	H	E	LoB
Cardinals	0	1	0	0	0	0	0	0	2	3	6	1	6
Mets	1	0	0	0	0	0	0	0	0	1	4	1	11

STADIUM/CAP. Shea Stadium

NL STANDINGS

©1996 Bob Carpenter Communications, Inc. All Rights Reserved

convinced it would. But Perez calmly got Juan Encarnación to fly out to right field to end the inning. Then in the bottom of the first inning, David Wright, the face of the franchise, came through with a clutch RBI single to drive in Carlos Beltrán, who had started a two-out rally with a double, with the first run of the game. *Boom.* We are gonna win this fuckin' game.

But there was a slight problem, and his name was Jeff Suppan. Suppan was a 31-year-old journeyman right-hander who had the Mets' number. He had our number in Game 3 when he hurled eight brilliant innings, allowing only three hits, en route to an easy 5–0 Cardinals win, and he had our number again after that first inning. Jeff Suppan was an *average* pitcher and was an *average* postseason pitcher until this point. The crowd was chanting loudly at him and it never bothered him. In fact, maybe this dude from Oklahoma thrived on it. But more than anything else in this game, the Mets' inability to hit Suppan helped to write our obituary. Now let's just get to the elephant in the room: Endy Chavez. Before we get to the catch, here was my first guess from that night and I stand by it to this day. Oliver Perez should never have faced Scott Rolen in the sixth inning to begin with. The Mets bullpen had become one of the strengths of this team, especially with their questionable rotation. Chad Bradford needed to be in this game. I thought Willie Randolph had mostly done a really good job managing his deep pen, but he made a big mistake not pulling the hook on Perez right there and going to his sidearming righty. But Perez stayed in, and we all know what happened. Scott Rolen hit the shit out of a ball and Endy Chavez made a miraculous leaping catch, robbing Rolen of a two-run home run. Not only that, he promptly threw the ball in to help turn an inning-ending double play punctuated by a Carlos Delgado fist pump. We all thought the same thing, and I was dumb enough to say it out loud—"We are going to the fuckin' World Series."

But let's not forget, the Mets still couldn't hit Suppan since that first inning RBI single by Wright and needed to take advantage of the momentum of Endy's catch in the bottom of the sixth inning. I mean, it's still a 1–1 game. This half-inning may haunt me even as much as the game's conclusion. With a runner on first and one out, David Wright hit a ground ball to the best defensive third baseman of my generation, Scott Rolen, who proceeded to do the unimaginable and throw the ball away. The modern-day Brooks Robinson had committed a *huge* error to put runners on second and third in a tie game. After the Cardinals intentionally walked Shawn Green,

José Valentín came up with a chance to give us the lead. He struck out on a pitch in the dirt and the top of the inning's hero, Endy Chavez, swung at the first pitch and hit a lazy fly ball to center field. My stomach dropped...are we going to the World Series? My confidence had just taken a major hit.

The last few innings of this game I can replay in my head anytime I want to depress myself. Willie Randolph having no confidence in Billy Wagner to pitch the ninth and sticking with Aaron Heilman, who then gave up the game-winning home run to Yadier Molina... going for it all with Cliff Floyd as a pinch-hitter instead of using Tom Glavine to lay down a bunt in the ninth...and as bad as the Beltrán K was, the José Reyes lineout to center actually haunts me more. Off the bat, I thought for a split-second that Reyes' line drive was going to go up the alley...it did not. It nestled into the glove of Jim Edmonds, and it felt like I just got kicked in the stomach. The Beltrán at-bat was quick and painful. Strike one looking...foul ball on pitch two and the infamous breaking ball from Adam Wainwright to freeze him for strike three. Leaving the building that night you could eavesdrop on the Cardinals celebrating and hear a pin drop. I depressingly went to Wendy's after the game to get a No. 6 (a spicy chicken sandwich), and for some reason they were out of it. This normally wouldn't bother me, but on the night my sports fandom got kicked in the balls? I then went to the old Kaufman Astoria Studios to host the overnight show. There would be no more painful night than that evening, where I had to spend four hours going over one of the worst sports nights of my fandom.

KEEPING SCORE: Suppan held the Mets to just one run in 15 innings (0.60 ERA) in his two starts and was named the Most Valuable Player of the NLCS.... Beltrán had gone 3-for-9 with the bases loaded in 2006, with all three hits being home runs.... The Cardinals, who had won only 83 games during the regular season, went on to beat the Detroit Tigers in the World Series, four games to one.

ARE THE METS COLLAPSING?

PHILLIES 11 METS 10

AUGUST 30, 2007, at CITIZENS BANK PARK, PHILADELPHIA

IN MY FIRST year of doing middays at WFAN with Joe Benigno, we were quickly forming a very cool relationship. We were both diehard Mets fans and were open to traveling to see our favorite teams play. In late August the Mets and Phillies were playing a four-game series at Citizens Bank Park in Philadelphia that included a Thursday afternoon finale. Joe and I thought it would be awesome if after our show Wednesday we headed down to Philly and went to Wednesday night's game. Then after sleeping over, we could do our Thursday show from the ballpark, leading up to the *Mets Extra* pregame show, which would allow us to see the Thursday afternoon game in person too. Joe and I would make many a road trip over the years to see the Mets, NBA Finals games, and the Jets in the postseason, but this was our maiden voyage in taking a midday show road trip.

The Mets were following up their 2006 season with a solid but sort of disappointing season thus far. Yes, the Mets were in first place all year long to this point, but there felt like something was missing about this team. The Mets entered this four-game series with a 73–56 record and led the Phillies by six games in the NL East. Before our trip, we watched the Mets lose the first two games, including a heartbreaking second game in which they blew a 2–0 lead in the eighth inning before losing on a two-run home run by Ryan Howard off Guillermo Mota in the 10th. Our first night there we saw the Met bats remain cold as they got stymied by the ageless Jamie Moyer and lost 3–2. The pressure was now on going into the finale of this series...would the Mets really get swept? Going into this game we talked on the air about how winning today would save what could be a disastrous week in Philadelphia. This felt like a huge swing game in terms of how close this pennant race would actually get.

I felt good going into the game based on who was starting for the Mets. Orlando "El Duque" Hernandez was having a very solid season in his second year with the Mets. A year earlier, he got hurt right before the postseason was set to begin, and so the Mets went into battle without a man who had proven to be a very reliable

STADIUM/CAP. Citizens Bank Park

	1	2	3	4	5	6	7	8	9
Mets	0	0	0	3	0	0	5	0	
Phillies	2	0	3	0	3	0	0	1	2

NL STANDINGS

U M P S

2B
3B 1B
HP

4 of 4
Season Series
9-6 Phi (15 of 18)

Met DP/OPP   DEFENSE   E

Endy Chavez   Carlos Beltran   Shawn Green

Jose Reyes   Ruben Gotay

David Wright   Nos Orlando Hernandez   Carlos Delgado

Mike Difelice

Philadelphia Phillies	Avg. 277	HR 168	R/G 5.42	1	2	3	4	5	6	7	8	9	10	11	AB 12	R 13	H 14	BI 15
11 Jimmy Rollins ss																		
26 Chase Utley 2b																		
5 Pat Burrell lf																		
6 Ryan Howard 1b																		
33 Aaron Rowand cf																		
Greg Dobbs 3b																		
28 Jayson Werth rf																		
51 Carlos Ruiz c																		

	R/ER	2/2	0/0	3/3	0/0	3/3	0/0	0/0	1/1	2/2					
	H	2	1	3	1	4	1	1	1	3					
	E	0	0	0	0	0	0	0	0	0					
	LOB	0/0	1	1/2	2/4	2/6	1/7	1/8	1/9	2/11					

LH   BENCH   RH

Iguchi
Helms
Coste
Sti
Nunez
Victorino

Met PITCHERS		IP	R	ER	H	W	K
Orlando Hernandez	(36)	3	5	5	6	1	2
Aaron Sele	(40)	4	1⅓	3	3	5	2	1
Scott Schoeneweis	(60)	5	⅓	0	0	0	0	1
Pedro Feliciano	(25)	6	2	0	0	2	0	1
Billy Wagner	(13)	8	1⅓	2	3	4	2	2

LH   Met BULLPEN   RH

postseason arm. This afternoon in late August felt like the biggest start El Duque had made as a Met—since the Mets had easily won the division in 2006, there had been no pennant race. When I think of Orlando Hernandez's Mets tenure my thoughts will always go right to him injuring himself before the 2006 Division Series before anything else, but I should think of the way he crapped the bed on this important afternoon. He allowed three home runs in the first three innings to Ryan Howard, Mets killer Pat Burrell, and Aaron Rowand. The Mets looked destined to be swept as they trailed 5–0. But this painful afternoon was going to provide us with many twists and turns before we would finally get kicked in the balls.

The Mets railed to tie the game 5–5 in the fifth inning, and then Aaron Sele proceeded to immediately give three runs right back. Trailing 8–5 in the eighth inning, the Mets put together what could have been a season-changing rally. They scored five times in the inning, aided by big hits from Marlon Anderson and Endy Chavez. The Mets still left guys on base, so despite the five-run rally and taking the 10–8 lead, they should have been up by more, and deep down I knew this would kill us at some point. Realizing the importance of this game, Willie Randolph did something he never did, he handed the baseball to Billy Wagner looking for a six-out save. Look, I have respect for everything that Billy Wagner accomplished in his career. He was no doubt an elite regular season closer, and the numbers back it up. But he sucked in a big spot. He sucked in the playoffs throughout his career, and on his Thursday afternoon with the Mets desperate for a win, guess what he did? Up 10–8 he allowed a solo home run in the eighth inning to Pat Burrell (what else is new), his second of the game, which cut the lead to a run. Then in the ninth inning, with the Mets only two outs away from victory, Wagner gave up the tying hit to Tadahito Iguchi and the winner to good buddy Chase Utley. The Phillies walked off the Mets to sweep the series, cutting their deficit to only two games. Walking out of that building was torture...it was a very hot day and the game lasted four hours, plus the Phillies fans could be relentless in their taunts.

The following day on WFAN, Joe and I engaged in a heated Mets debate that aged very poorly for me. He was convinced the Mets were choking, and I wasn't quite sure of it yet, despite how brutal the sweep was. Joe reasoned that Mets history told him the collapse was inevitable...I did not understand that point at all! Yes, the Mets had disappointed us many times over the years, but they had never actually collapsed. Later in the day, even Chris Russo came to my defense, saying I had clearly defeated Joe in our debate. I appreciate Mad Dog standing up for me as a rookie full-time host, but he was as wrong as I was. "I can feel it, bro. We are going to blow this freakin' division," Joe said loudly. This may have been the most prophetic thing Joe B ever told me on air.

KEEPING SCORE: This was the fourth of five straight appearances, including two blown saves, in which Wagner gave up a run.... The Phillies won the season series from the Mets 12–6 and the NL East by one game.

A TRIP TO D.C. TO SAVE THE METS

METS 8 NATIONALS 4

SEPTEMBER 19, 2007, at RFK STADIUM, WASHINGTON

WE ALL KNOW the numbers...it will now live in Mets history as well as MLB history for the rest of time. In 2007 the Mets had a seven-game lead with 17 games to go and somehow managed to blow the NL East. On September 12, the Mets had just defeated the Atlanta Braves while the Philadelphia Phillies were shut out 12–0 by the Colorado Rockies, giving the Mets the now famous seven-game lead. From there the Mets would get swept (again) by the Phillies and lose the first two games to the lousy Washington Nationals. The Mets' lead in the NL East was now down to just 1½ games. I went to work that day with a plan. Something needed to spark the Mets, and I was desperate enough to think that my getting in a car and driving to Washington, D.C., would be the spark they needed. Of course, this wasn't going to matter to Mets catcher Paul Lo Duca, who probably started hating me and Joe from his weekly spots with us or get Carlos Delgado going, but as a desperate fan who was on his way to going to 62 of 81 Mets home games that year, in my delusional mind being there in person might help change things. I remember Mike and the Mad Dog so getting a kick out of this 24-year-old rookie full-time host taking his fan desperation to these levels, that they called me up during my trip down to sorta interview me and also mock me a bit. Nine months into my midday show tenure with Joe Benigno, this was my first appearance with Mike and Chris.

As I pulled into RFK Stadium, I made first pitch with some time to spare. Our show ended at 1:00 PM, and I immediately got into my car and headed down I-95 to my former stomping grounds. The other thing I felt good about was the fact I had a good record in D.C. when seeing the Mets play. It was a small sample size, but to this point the Mets were 4–0 when I saw them play at RFK Stadium.

I bought tickets from the ticket window before the game started and got an awesome seat. The Nationals were a bad baseball team playing in a dilapidated ballpark, plus I was looking for only a single ticket. When you combine those factors, it was going to be quite easy to find an affordable ticket with an incredible view. I sat behind the Mets dugout about 10 rows off the field as the Mets got set to try and end their five-game losing streak.

Mike Pelfrey took the mound for the Mets that night, and at this point in Big Mike's career he was an unproven rookie struggling in his first full year in the majors. The Mets took the early lead on a sacrifice fly by Lo Duca. I really liked Paul, but I'm not sure he felt the same way about me. He was a weekly guest with me and Joe throughout the season, and as things turned bleak, our questions became more pointed and tougher. He had been ejected from a game back in June, and I remember we were pushing him hard on what happened. Our interview style was that of fans, which could get ugly when things weren't going well. Lo Duca had a very strong 2006 season, but he wasn't quite the same player the following year and was open about some issues facing the locker room that year that probably led to his departure after this season ended. Pelfrey promptly blew the early lead when he allowed two runs in the bottom of the second, including a two-out single to the opposing pitcher, Matt Chico, which put the Nats up 2–1. Luckily the bats showed up on this night, as they put up eight runs on 12 hits and gave the Mets what turned out to be a comfortable win by the score of 8–4. The bleeding had stopped for the night as they snapped their five-game losing streak.

Making a day trip to Washington, D.C., is always much easier in theory than the practicality of it. When I leave the WFAN offices at 1:00 PM to make a 7:00 PM game, it's nice and easy. But the issue is what happens when the game is over? The three-plus-hour game ended at 10:19, and by the time I got to my car that night it was about 10:45, and then there was the four-and-a-half-hour trek back to Queens. I always say this when making long sports trips: it's a fine trip after a win. I'll never forget when I drove back from

Toronto after the Nets beat the Raptors in Game 7 of the 2014 play-offs, it was so damn sweet that I didn't mind the nine-hour drive. On this Wednesday night in September as I drove back up I-95, I was relieved. The Mets were back up by 2½ games, and it felt as if the crisis had been averted. Little did I know, my traveling was only beginning.

KEEPING SCORE: This would be the very last game that the Mets played at RFK Stadium before Washington moved into Nationals Stadium the following season.... The Nationals, who finished in fourth place in the NL East with a 71–91 record, were a deciding factor in the division race due to the fact that they beat the Mets in five of their seven meetings in September, while losing five of their six games against the Phillies down the stretch.

THE 2007 COLLAPSE U.S. TOUR

MARLINS 8 METS 7 (10 INNINGS)

SEPTEMBER 20, 2007, at DOLPHIN STADIUM, MIAMI

AFTER BEING IN Washington, D.C., the night before in a desperate attempt to save the Mets from collapse, I walked into Kaufman Astoria Studios for my WFAN show the following morning bleary eyed from my late-night excursion. The Mets had temporarily stopped the bleeding and were now heading to Florida to take on the Marlins. That morning I sat in the office of my two bosses, Mark Chernoff and Eric Spitz, as they asked me about how my adventure went. As I was talking about all the boring intricacies of my trip, I could see an idea pop into Mark's head. "Hey, how about you follow the Mets to Florida now?"

I wasn't sure if he was kidding or not, but as a single 24-year-old in my first year working full-time at WFAN, who the hell was I to say

Baseball scorecard (Bob Carpenter Communications, Inc.) — New York Mets at Florida Marlins, September 20, 2007. Mets 7, Fla 8 (10 innings). WP: Taylor Tankersley (6-1). LP: Jorge Sosa. Start 7:05, Finish 10:57, Time 3:52, Att. 15,132, WX 87° Clear.

©1996 Bob Carpenter Communications, Inc. All Rights Reserved

no to this idea? "Sure, let me check what flight I could make." Bingo! I found one...a flight that could get me out of LaGuardia Airport at 2:30 PM and land me in Fort Lauderdale at about 5:30, which would give me plenty of time to get to the ballpark. All I needed was clothes! Luckily, a friend of mine was able to do me a solid and go over to my apartment and pack me some clothes for the trip down to sunny Florida. The radio station paid for my flight down, but I needed a place to stay, and my sister living down there made that part easy. What a whirlwind 24 hours I was now staring at—a Wednesday midday show, drive to D.C. for a game that night, drive back to Queens, do another midday show, fly to Florida for Mets-Marlins, and then do the midday show on Friday from studios down in Florida. Nine months into my first full year on middays with Joe Benigno, I was slowly going from Joe's annoying new, young partner, to the psycho who was traveling with the Mets.

I arrived in South Florida with no hitch in my flight plans and quickly jumped into a cab as I headed to what was then known as Dolphin Stadium to see the Mets battle the Marlins. After the win against Washington the night before, the Mets were now back to being 2½ games up on Philadelphia as they began a four-game series against the Marlins. The pitching matchup for this game would be the same as the one that would define the season a few weeks later—Tom Glavine vs. Dontrelle Willis. I found a single ticket in the seats I adore, about 20 rows up and directly behind home plate. I worked feverishly to get my scorebook ready for first pitch as I sipped a nice cold beer. It appeared early on that my magic was working! Moises Alou hit a two-run double in the first inning, and the Mets had grabbed an early 2–0 lead. Holding a 3–0 lead in the fifth inning, the overrated Tom Glavine would do something he had also done in Game 5 of the NLCS in the prior season...blow a lead. This time it was Miguel Cabrera who got the big hit, a three-run home run, as the Marlins went up 4–3 and knocked Glavine out of the game.

As I sat in my seat behind home plate on this warm night in Florida, an uneasiness came over me. I was now officially tired from all the travel and frustrated as the Mets continued to trail by one run as the innings went by. Finally down to their final two outs they rallied dramatically in the ninth inning against Marlins closer Kevin Gregg as Marlon Anderson cleared the bases with a three-run triple! The Mets tacked on one more run to take a seemingly commanding 7–4 lead into the bottom of the ninth. There was one major problem I noticed: Billy Wagner was not coming into this game to nail down the save. Just a few years before Twitter became a bastion of sports information, I furiously texted my Mets text chat back at home to find out what the hell was going on. I would later find out after the game that Wagner was dealing with back spasms and was unavailable. Pedro Feliciano and Jorge Sosa then proceeded to blow the three-run lead and force extra innings. The 10th inning would be a quick death as two batters into the frame the Marlins walked it off on a Dan Uggla RBI double. The Mets had managed to blow multiple three-run leads in collapsing against the Marlins. I walked out of the stadium in a comatose state, now fearing the collapse was indeed back on. As I entered my sister's apartment, her boyfriend (and now my brother-in-law) said something to me that was very innocent, but in the moment rubbed salt in the wounds. "Don't worry, Evan, I won't bring up the game. Your sister warned me how seriously you take these games, so don't worry, I won't say anything about the game."

By saying you aren't going to bring up the game, guess what you are doing? You are bringing up the freakin' game! I was a hell of a lot more upset at the crappy Mets than I was at him, but still it only added more pain. I was now emotionally spent as I lay my head down on the couch in my sister's living room. I was pissed, I was exhausted, and I was damn worried. Even my magic mystery tour didn't appear to be saving the choking New York Mets.

KEEPING SCORE: Losing pitcher Jorge Sosa, who had gone 13–3 for the Braves two years earlier, was in the Mets rotation earlier in the season and had gotten off to a 6–1 start but faded after that. This loss brought his final record to 9–8. He did not make a start after July.

THE JOHN MAINE ONE-HITTER

METS 13 MARLINS 0
SEPTEMBER 29, 2007, at SHEA STADIUM

IT WILL GO down in history as one of the most dominant, clutch, and yet depressing pitching performances in Mets history. At the time, we didn't know the depressing part, but while it was happening John Maine was potentially making himself a Mets legend. The Mets' collapse had finally hit its crescendo the night before as they lost their fifth straight game and dropped out of first place for the

V/G M.rlins	W-L 70-90	GB		H		R		E 31-39	C 18-20	W 12-22	IL 9-9
H/G Mets	W-L 87-73	GB	1	H 40-39		R 47-34		E 34-36	C 28-12	W 17-18	IL 8-7

STANDINGS

	R	H	E	LOB
Fla.	0	1	3	2
Met	13	19	0	12

WP John Maine 15-10
LP Chris Seddon 0-2
SV ~~~~~~~

START 1:10 DATE Sept. 29, 2007 Saturday
FINISH 4:13 ATT. 54,675
TIME 303 WX 73° Sunny

Met DP/OPP DEFENSE

PITCHERS

Met PITCHERS	IP	R	ER	H	W	K
John Maine 22-19 4.27	7⅔	0	0	1	2	14
Willie Collazo	⅓	0	0	0	0	0
Carlos Muniz	1	1	0	0	0	1

©1996 Bob Carpenter Communications, Inc. All Rights Reserved

first time since May 15. With only two games left to go in the season, the Mets had lost control of their own destiny. With only two games to go in the season, the Mets were now trailing the Phillies by one game in the NL East. Not only did they need to find a way to win the last two games, but they needed some help. This day, the second-to-last day of the regular season, would give us hope and provide one of the great teases in Mets history.

Scorecard — Mets vs Marlins at Shea Stadium. Handwritten notations include:

STADIUM/CAP. Shea Stadium

	1	2	3	4	5	6	7	8	9
Marlins	0	0	0	0	0	0	0	0	0
Mets	2	3	3	0	2	1	1	1	X

UMPS: Rapuano, Hickox, West, Buckner

2 of 3 Season Series 10-6 Met (17 of 18)

Castillo thrown out in 5th brackets empty. Moments later during pitching change Bonds. C Miguel Olivo chases Reyes at 3rd. Maine retires 17 in a row. Maine pitches 7⅔ no hit innings

©1996 Bob Carpenter Communications, Inc. All Rights Reserved

I walked into Shea Stadium on this gorgeous Saturday afternoon expecting doom—and who the hell could blame me? After winning three of four from the Marlins to increase their NL East lead to 2½ games, the Mets returned home to close the season with a seven-game homestand against some bad baseball teams. The Nationals, Cardinals, and Marlins were all on their way to sub-.500 seasons, so the Mets were set up to close this race out. But a funny thing happened on the way to inevitability: the Mets resumed their month-long choke. They got swept by Washington, giving up an ungodly 32 runs in three games, then lost a makeup game against the Cardinals, before losing the opener against Florida. We were now desperate for something positive. In Game 161, the Mets offense supplied it by jumping all over Marlins pitching and putting the game out of reach early with eight runs in the first three innings. Then the focus turned to John Maine. Maine was in the midst of his finest major league season and was putting together the most dominant pitching performance of his career. He struck out seven straight guys at one point (he would finish with 14), and it became noticeable early that Maine had yet to allow a hit. Through the years of no Mets pitcher throwing a no-hitter I started to rationalize that the longer the drought went on, the more I figured that when it did happen, it would occur in an epic moment. Would Game 161 in the midst of a collapse count as an epic no-hitter?! Damn right it would!

In the fifth inning, with the Mets expanding their lead even more on Lastings Milledge's second home run of the game, Luis Castillo appeared to be thrown at a couple times. After the second pitch went behind him, Luis started gesturing to the mound and all the benches emptied. Even though the game was out of reach, it was nice to see the Mets show some damn fight for a change. And fight they did, because after Castillo walked, the pitcher who caused the anger, Harvey Garcia, was being pulled from the game. During the meeting at the mound, Marlins catcher Miguel Olivo charged at José Reyes, the runner at third base, and the brawl was on. The crowd loved it, and in the moment I loved it...but in the back of my mind, there was one small fear. The Marlins should have nothing to play for in Game 162; don't give them any motivation to actually care. Either way, the brawl ended, and now all of the attention was on the John Maine no-hit bid. With two outs in the eighth inning and a 1–2 count on backup catcher Paul Hoover, who had replaced the ejected Olivo, Shea Stadium was shaking it was so loud. In all my years of watching Mets baseball and praying for a no-hitter to break the curse, I had never seen one taken into the ninth inning, and here was Maine one pitch away from doing just that. Hoover then unleashed a swinging bunt that, off the bat, I knew it would end up in no man's land. The Marlins had their first hit in the cheapest of fashions. Maine was promptly pulled from the game to a standing ovation. I wish Hoover had drilled a ball in the gap or something, because having the no-hit bid end on a hit like that really stinks. What didn't stink was that the Mets finally won a damn game and they did it very easily, but now they needed help.

Right after the game, I drove a few miles to the WFAN studios where Joe and I hosted a special late Saturday afternoon show to recap the huge Mets win and look ahead to Sunday. This was freakin' perfect, what better way to let out the emotion of the day and nervousness of the night then by having an on-air therapy session. As we did our show, we watched the Phillies battle the Nationals with huge implications. If the Phillies lost, the Mets would regain control of their playoff destiny. We lived and died on every pitch as we also did a Mets pep rally. When the final out was recorded and the Nationals upset the Phillies, we were both euphoric. The Mets had pulled even in first place again and would have everything in their hands as they played Game 162 at Shea Stadium. From baseball depression in the early afternoon to a new sense of hope by early evening, the 2007 Mets weren't dead yet. Key word being *yet*.

KEEPING SCORE: Maine's victory was his 15th of the season, a career high.... Hoover had only eight at-bats (with three hits) in three games after joining the Marlins as a September call-up. He then appeared in 13 games for Florida the following year before playing a total of 12 games for the Philadelphia Phillies in 2009 and 2010.

COLLAPSE COMPLETE

MARLINS 8 METS 1

SEPTEMBER 30, 2007, at SHEA STADIUM

I WAS CONFIDENT. What a schmuck I was back in 2007—but I'm being honest here, I truly was confident. The Mets had stopped the bleeding 24 hours earlier when John Maine threw the game of his life and the Mets went into Game 162 tied for first place in the NL East. The playoff scenario going into the final game of the season had some similarities to 1999. Winning the game didn't guarantee the Mets a playoff spot, but it did lock in playing another game. It could mean a one-game playoff for the NL East, and even the possibility of losing that game and going into a one-game playoff for the NL wild-card spot. But everything was predicated on the Mets taking care of business. Tom Glavine was on the mound, and if there was a guy who would not be intimidated by huge spot like this, logic would tell you Glavine would be up for the challenge. Tom Glavine would make 164 starts as a Met over five full seasons, but his final start of his Mets career would be the game that would define him.

Shea had a buzz on this gorgeous Sunday afternoon. The sun was shining and the ballpark was 100 percent packed, which was always a sight to behold. There was certainly tension in the air, but considering what had happened just one day earlier, I don't think I was the only one who had confidence going into this affair. Despite the Mets' September swoon, the day before was magical. John Maine tossed a one-hitter, and the Phillies miraculously lost! When Miguel Cabrera singled in the first Marlins run, I was annoyed but not quite panicking. When Cody Ross lined a ball down the right-field line, my stomach dropped. Two runs scored, and then in a sign of things to come, Ross scored when the Mets threw the ball all over the place, and he had himself a "Little League" three-run home run that was officially scored a double. The Mets were now down four runs before you could blink, and boos were raining down loudly on Shea

V/G Marlins W-L 70-91 GB 18 H 36-45 R 34-46 E 31-40 C 18-20 W 12-22 IL 9-9

H/G Mets W-L 88-73 GB Tw/ Phi H 41-39 R 47-34 E 35-36 C 28-12 W 17-18 IL 8-7

AL STANDINGS

	R	H	E	LOB
Fla	8	11	0	8
Met	1	5	1	10

WP Logan Kensing 3-0
LP Tom Glavine 13-8
SV ~~~~~~

START 1:11 DATE Sept. 30, 2007 Sunday
FINISH _____ ATT. 54,453
TIME _____ WX Sunny

Mt DP/OPP   DEFENSE   E

Moises / Alou — C-115 / B.Horn — Loshings / Miller jr

Jose Reyes — Luis Castillo

David Wright — 4.23 Tom Glavine — Carlos Delgado

Bo Porter   Ramon Castro   Andy Fox

©1996 Bob Carpenter Communications, Inc. All Rights Reserved

Florida Marlins	Avg	HR	RBI	1	2	3	4	5	6	7	8	9	10	11	AB 12	R 13	H 14	BI 15
3 Hanley Ramirez ss	267	201	25051														

M't PITCHERS | IP | R | ER | H | W | K |
Tom Glavine 302-198 3.49 | 1/3 | 7 | 7 | 5 | 2 | 0 |
Jorge Sosa | 1 1/3 | 0 | 0 | 1 | 0 | 4 |
Orlando Hernandez | 3 | 1 | 0 | 0 | 1 | 0 |
Scott Schoeneweis | 4 1/3 | 1 | 1 | 2 | 1 | 2 |
Guillermo Mota | 7 | 2 | 0 | 0 | 1 | 0 |
Aaron Heilman | 9 | 1 | 0 | 0 | 0 | 1 |

LH BENCH RH

LH Mt BULLPEN RH

Stadium. Okay...deep breath. It's 4–0 and it looks bad, but it ain't over. Just get the final two outs of the first inning, and let's regroup. Glavine then gave up a single, walked a guy, and then another single to load the bases with one out. The opposing pitcher, but decent hitter Dontrelle Willis then came up. I couldn't believe what I was watching—the dude with loads of playoff experience was shitting the bed right before our eyes in a must-win game. Yet I was still

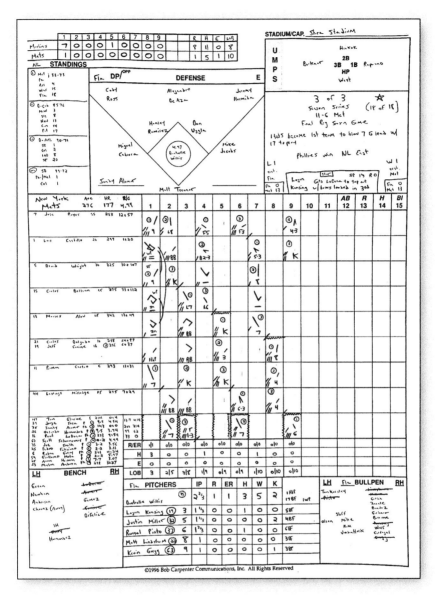

holding out hope that Glavine could escape this and keep it 4–0. Ahead of Willis 1–2, Glavine proceeded to plunk him to force in a run. Are you freakin' kidding me? At this point, the boos were deafening as Willie Randolph had to mercifully take the baseball from Tommy and get his old washed-up ass out of the game. As I've said, I don't boo, but I never had such a strong urge to let out the loudest boo of my life for Glavine as he walked off the mound with his don't-give-a-crap look on his face.

Now we needed Jorge Sosa to somehow escape this mess Glavine created. When he struck out the dangerous Hanley Ramirez, there was hope he could keep this 5–0. But then Dan Uggla and his fat face smoked a two-run double to make it 7–0. When the inning mercifully ended, I looked at my dad in disbelief. Did that first inning really happen? Did the Mets just allow a baseball team playing for nothing to score seven runs in the first inning against our supposed most reliable starter?

Ever the optimist I once was, I told my dad this bottom of the first inning was essential. Respond with three runs and you're back in this game. So this is the underrated part of this baseball game that truly kills me to this day. In the bottom of the first inning, down 7–0, the Mets mounted a rally. They scored a run on a wild pitch and had the bases loaded with two outs for Ramon Castro. The Mets were legit a base hit away from making this a game again. On 2–0, Castro *just* missed it. He hit a ball that I thought for a split second off the bat had a chance to get out for a grand slam. Instead it died in left field and was caught by Cody Ross to end the inning. It's true, we talk about the Mets losing Game 162 in 2007 in the first inning, but it wasn't only lost in the top of the first, but the failed opportunities in the bottom of the inning as well. The funeral of the 2007 season didn't come without other teases. As the Mets kept the Marlins run total at 7, they blew more chances to score. With two on and two out in the second inning, David Wright struck out. In the third, with the bases loaded and two out after Willis walked his fifth batter of the game, he was replaced by Logan Kensing, who retired pinch-hitter Paul Lo Duca on a ground ball. Think about it—despite the awfulness of Tom Glavine, the Mets left eight guys on base in the first three innings of this game. We all blame Tom, but the offense choked away numerous big opportunities early in that game too.

The final six innings were a death march. Shea Stadium had turned into a morgue as we were all left to ponder how this once-promising season turned so bad so quickly. Only one year earlier, this team was a hit away from the World Series, and now we would be at home fuming in October. When Luis Castillo struck out in the ninth, the Marlins had secured an 8–1 win to end the game and season. We walked out of Shea somberly, and this was as disgusted as I'd ever been to end a season in my Mets life. We have had some bad losses, some devastating losses to end seasons, but not like this. Not an all-time choke followed by a lifeless Game 162. The season was over, and so was Tom Glavine's Mets career now defined by this horrific performance. When you try and go back to define Glavine's time with the Mets with a level head, it's almost impossible to look past how it started and how it ended. A boo-filled Mets debut on Opening Day in 2003, and an embarrassing, season-ending, can't-get-through-the-first-inning disaster in 2007. Horrible! To this day Game 162 in 2007 still ranks among the worst efforts in Mets history.

KEEPING SCORE: Glavine finished his Mets career with a 61–56 record and an ERA of 3.97 and rejoined the Braves for his final season in 2008.... The game also marked Willis's last with the Marlins, as he was traded with Cabrera to the Detroit Tigers after the season. Although he didn't get the win in Game 162, Willis went 11–3 against the Mets during his career with the Marlins.

WITH A TORN MENISCUS

METS 2 MARLINS 0

SEPTEMBER 27, 2008, at SHEA STADIUM

DURING THE LONG winter of 2007 into 2008 I hardly realized the practical joke Major League Baseball decided to play on us Mets fans. The 2008 regular season would finish up against the same team in the same location that spoiled the conclusion of the 2007 season. The Mets were scheduled to play the Florida Marlins in a cruel antic

V/G Marlins	W-L 83-76	GB 6½	H 45-36	R 39-40	E 39-30	C 19-20	W 20-16	IL 5-10

H/G Mets	W-L 88-72	GB 2	H 47-32	R 41-40	E 39-31	C 20-20	W 20-15	IL 9-6

AL STANDINGS

	R	H	E	LOB
Fla	0	3	0	5
Met	2	6	0	6

WP John Jintana 16-7
LP Ricky Nolasco 15-8
SV ~~~~~

START 1:45 DATE September 27, 2008 Saturday
FINISH 4:02 ATT. 54,920
TIME 2:17 WX 67° Rain

Met DP/OPP — DEFENSE

Daniel Murphy · C. Ross Beltran · Ryan Church · Jose Reyes · Ramon Martinez · David Wright · 4.09 John Santana · Carlos Delgado · Bo Porter · Andy Fox · Ramon Castro

Florida Marlins	AVG 255	HR 206	R/G 4.82	1	2	3	4	5	6	7	8	9	10	11	AB 12	R 13	H 14	BI 15
2 Hanley Ramirez SS																		
31 John Baker C																		
3 Jorge Cantu 1B																		
14 Josh Willingham LF																		
6 Dan Uggla 2B																		
12 Cody Ross CF																		
15 Wes Helms 3B																		
27 Jeremy Hermida RF																		

	R/ER	0|0	0|0	0|0	0|0	0|0	0|0	0|0	0|0	0|0					
	H	1	0	0	0	1	0	0	0	1					
	E	0	0	0	0	0	0	0	0	0					
	LOB	0	0	0	1	3|4	0|4	0|4	0|4	1|5					

LH BENCH RH
Gonzalez · Andino
McPherson · Amezaga

Met PITCHERS	IP	R	ER	H	W	K
John Santana	108-51-1 3.13	9	0	0	3	3	9

LH Met BULLPEN RH

©1996 Bob Carpenter Communications, Inc. All Rights Reserved

that (little did I know) would haunt my dreams in ways that were worse than the previous season.

The 2008 season was a weird one...as they struggled through the first few months, clearly having some kind of choke job hangover, the Mets decided in a controversial way to fire manager Willie Randolph in the middle of the night. Coincidentally, my former radio partner Joe Benigno and I had picked that June interleague series in Anaheim to follow the Mets out West. I'll never forget Joe B in a ripped T-shirt with his boxers on loudly proclaiming to me and our producer at the time, Gregg Giannotti, that "Willie is gone, bro." Though the Mets were bumbling their way to a 34–35 start, the fact they had won the night earlier calmed our "fire

226 | MY METS BIBLE

Willie" beliefs for the evening, so waking up to his ouster came as a surprise. I like Willie and definitely thought, and still think, he deserved another shot to manage. But I also believed that the Mets needed to try something to spark the team, and that included a change in the manager's office. It clearly worked, because the Mets shortly thereafter took off and eventually climbed back into first place in the NL East.

When September began, the Mets were up by two games in the division on the same rival from a year earlier, the Philadelphia Phillies. Unfortunately, the Mets started feeling the injury bug in a big way, led by the loss of Billy Wagner. That led Aaron Heilman to being the closer most of August, before waiver-trade pickup Luis Ayala took over through most of September. The Mets were clearly a flawed team as they battled in a second straight tooth-and-nail pennant race, but unlike a year earlier, this Mets team wasn't collapsing. Were they playing great baseball in the heart of the pennant race through September? Absolutely not. But this by no means was the same free-fall that we had witnessed a year earlier. They were playing .500 baseball throughout the homestretch and went into the final weekend of the season in a very good spot to make the playoffs. The Mets were playing a huge four-game series against the best team in the National League that year, the Chicago Cubs, prior to the weekend. They finished the series and split by walking off the Cubs when Carlos Beltrán came through with a monstrous hit in the ninth. The Mets went into the final weekend one game behind the Phillies for the division, but in a deadlock with the Milwaukee Brewers for the wild-card spot. The Brewers were playing three games at home against the Cubs, who had everything wrapped up in the NL Central, while the Phillies were at home against the very bad Washington Nationals. The division felt like a long shot, but the wild-card was right in front of the Mets to win. Just win games against the Florida Marlins as you are closing down Shea Stadium. Yes, the Marlins were drastically better than they were a year earlier, but you are still at home with your playoff destiny in your hands...no excuses!

I had been in Arizona for the Giants-Patriots Super Bowl in February 2008 when the news broke that the Mets had acquired soon-to-be 29-year-old, two-time Cy Young Award winner Johan Santana. Like most Mets fans, I was ecstatic at acquiring an elite starting pitcher in the midst of his prime to bolster a team that came off a colossal division collapse a year earlier. I figured the year before couldn't happen again when you had a monster like Johan taking the baseball every five days.

When the Mets opened up the weekend series against the Marlins that would not only end the season but close down Shea Stadium, everything felt eerily similar to 2007. The Mets lost Game 1 to the Marlins and were essentially non-competitive. Mike Pelfrey gave up two runs in the first inning, and the offense was completely limp. Simultaneously, the Milwaukee Brewers took care of business, and destiny was out of the Mets' hands right off the bat. So far the Friday nights in 2008 had mirrored exactly what had happened in 2007.

As I entered Shea Stadium for the Saturday afternoon game against the Marlins, not only did the Mets need to pick their asses up off the ground, they needed help. As Johan was warming up in right field, I repeated to my dad what I had said throughout the week about Johan Santana: "This is why he's here." He's not here just to compete for Cy Youngs, he's here to put the team on his back and carry us home. On this rainy, disgusting September afternoon, unbeknownst to us, with a torn meniscus in his knee, Johan Alexander Santana Araque told us desperate Mets fans to jump aboard his back. Johan made a nifty play in the first inning, fielding a comebacker to work around a two-out single, then pitched a 1-2-3 second and a 1-2-3 third. Over next few innings his defense backed him up—first it was David Wright, and then Carlos Beltrán made an awesome clutch catch that could have set up a big inning. Johan was fired up every time he struck someone out, and barked off the mound when he escaped a bases-loaded, two-out jam in the fifth. It was clear that Johan wasn't going to let Jerry Manuel take the baseball from him.

He was nursing a 2–0 lead late into the game. When Santana struck out Dan Uggla with a runner on second and one out in the ninth, Shea Stadium was rocking. I joined the crowd in chanting "Jo-Han," *clap-clap*, "Jo-Han," *clap-clap*, as he was now one out away from pitching a shutout. All the while, when we looked up at the right-center field scoreboard, we saw something beautiful and hopeful: CUBS 5 MLW 1. The Mets, much like a year earlier, were about to grab back destiny on a magical Saturday. The Santana masterpiece was not without drama—the final batter, Cody Ross, drove a ball to deep left that chased Endy Chavez to the halfway point of the warning track. But on this rainy afternoon in Queens, the ball died and landed safely into the glove of Endy to secure the win. Johan Santana on three days' rest, with a torn meniscus in his knee had just delivered one of the more gutty and clutch performances you'll ever see. I walked out of Shea Stadium with hope and optimism, but what I didn't realize or even think about at the time was that it was possible I was leaving the old Shea Stadium after a win for the final time. Truth be told, chanting the name of Johan while walking down the long corridors of Shea Stadium would indeed be the last time I walked out of that old ballpark happy.

KEEPING SCORE: The two Mets runs came on Carlos Delgado's first-inning sacrifice fly and Ramon Martinez' RBI double in the fifth off Ricky Nolasco.... Santana finished his first season as a Met with a 16–7 record and a 2.53 ERA, best in the majors. He finished third in Cy Young Award voting behind Tim Lincecum of the San Francisco Giants and Brandon Webb of the Arizona Diamondbacks.

CLOSING SHEA STADIUM

MARLINS 4 METS 2

SEPTEMBER 28, 2008, at SHEA STADIUM

IF AN INCREDIBLE pennant race wasn't enough, closing a venue that I grew up in was going to put me over the edge emotionally. I was 11 months old on June 21, 1984, when my parents took me to Shea Stadium for the first time. I obviously can't remember a thing about that afternoon, but I do know that the Mets defeated the Philadelphia Phillies that day by a score of 10–7. Apparently I was a terror at this game and it kept my parents from taking me to another game for just about two years. But on April 20, 1986, at the age of two years and 10 months, I returned to Shea to see the Mets beat the Phillies again, 8–0. I went to five more games in 1986, six more in 1987, and another six in 1988. While I have zero recollection of any of this, my dad did an incredible job of keeping careful records on games attended, so I know that I grew up at Shea before I knew what an actual baseball was.

I then spent my formative years going day in and day out with my dad to just about every Mets home game. Other than my actual home in Woodmere, New York, I spent more time at Shea Stadium than any other place on earth. Now, at the age of 25 and 859 games later, I was staring into the abyss of never walking into this old building again. Unfortunately, there would be no clean farewell, where you knew this was the final game at Shea, because the Mets had major playoff uncertainty on this Sunday afternoon. If the Mets defeated the Marlins, there would 100 percent be another game at Shea—combined with a Brewers loss, the Mets would advance to the NLDS; a Brewers win, on the other hand, would mean a one-game playoff at Shea the next day. But if the Mets lost, they needed the Brewers to also lose to stay alive. How can you possibly celebrate the closing of a building when you don't actually know if the building is closing!?

©1996 Bob Carpenter Communications, Inc. All Rights Reserved

On this potentially historic day, my sister, Stacy, who now lived in Florida, few black to New York to join us. In our blue seats on the loge level, her name was etched everywhere, because as a kid she loved to carve it into our four season seats. My dad would tell me that Stacy was an angel as a kid going to games and would enjoy them; but as she grew older, she was no longer a baseball fan. We had an extra ticket, and my mom had zero interest in going to such a high emotion kind of game. So we decided to invite someone we had deep respect for and someone who I know could call a co-worker. The legendary Steve Somers joined the Roberts group at Shea for Game 162. Steve was freakin' Elvis walking around Shea that day, as people would constantly yell, "Hey, Shmooze, we love you!" While my sister was all about the emotions of saying goodbye to Shea, my father, Steve, and I were mostly in pennant race mode.

Here we were back at Shea, one year later in virtually the same position as 2007, facing a win-and-you're-in situation. Oliver Perez was getting the baseball this year as compared to Tom Glavine, and the opponent was another Marlins lefty, this time Scott Olsen. For the first five innings, Oliver delivered in a big way, as he had in Game 7 in 2006. He held the Marlins to only one base hit and kept them off the scoreboard. The problem was that the Mets again couldn't hit the freakin' ball and weren't even threatening against Olsen. Finally, the Marlins broke through in the sixth inning, knocking Perez out of the game and scoring two runs. The following sequence I can see over and over in my head. Carlos Beltrán stepped to the plate in the bottom of the sixth inning with the Mets down 2–0 and hit a 1–0 pitch to deep left-center field; Shea Stadium collectively stood up as the ball kept going and going, finally landing in the bleachers in left-center for a shocking, game-tying, two-run home run. Only two years removed from taking a third strike that seemingly was going to define his Mets tenure, I thought in that moment Beltrán was erasing it. "If we win this game," I said in a hoarse voice to my dad and Steve sitting behind me in our season ticket seats in loge box 325, "we are going to end up building a fuckin' statue for this man." I shouldn't have said it. I should have known better. When Endy Chavez made a sparkling catch to keep the game tied to end the seventh inning, it was impossible to not immediately think about his catch in 2006. Finally, in the top of the eighth inning our collective hearts would be shattered when Scott Schoeneweis allowed a pinch-hit home run to Wes Helms. If that wasn't bad enough, Luis Ayala then promptly entered the game and allowed the second half of the back-to-back home runs when he gave up a bomb to Dan Uggla. In this moment, I knew our fate. We all knew our fate.

The bottom of the eighth inning saw a two-out rally that died when Carlos Delgado lined out to left field with two on against the ageless Arthur Rhodes. We were now three outs from defeat, and it was the former Mets farmhand Matt Lindstrom trying to stick the sword straight through our hearts. Down to our final out and representing the tying run at the plate, Ryan Church would become the answer to the trivia question I hope to never receive. Ryan hit a fly ball to center field that for a split second I thought might get out, but I soon realized that the baseball had as good a chance of leaving the park as Piazza's fly ball did to end the 2000 World Series. When the ball was squeezed by Cameron Maybin, our season was officially over (the Brewers had finished beating the Cubs a half hour earlier). I buried my head in my hands. We were promptly reminded that a ceremony would soon follow where we would now officially say goodbye to Shea. The Mets brought almost every single available former player back in this tear-jerking ceremony as they walked onto the field and touched home plate. Doc Gooden, Darryl Strawberry, Willie Mays, and of course, such standard-bearers as Tom Seaver and Mike Piazza were all in attendance. I had a tear in my eye watching the whole thing, but it was also very, very painful. You couldn't ignore the fact we'd just witnessed the Mets lose a pennant race in some kind of funky clown mirror type shit from a year earlier. That ceremony, while incredibly well done, was extremely painful to watch. There has been much controversy about having it done after the game when the Mets were eliminated, and while it sucked no doubt, that ceremony wouldn't have been as touching if it had been done prior to the final game. So, while I acknowledge how difficult it was to sit through, I also didn't necessarily think the alternative was much better. Piazza and Seaver walking through the center-field door to depart was incredibly well done. As much as we all love to kill the Wilpons and say "LOL Mets," we have to admit the ceremony, while suffering from awful timing, was a masterpiece.

I walked as slowly as humanly possible departing Shea that day. There were two major sets of emotions running through my body—the disappointment of the season and the sadness of saying goodbye to my old home. An era of my life and Mets baseball was officially ending.

KEEPING SCORE: The Brewers defeated the Cubs 3–1 as Ryan Braun hit a tiebreaking two-run home run in the bottom of the eighth and CC Sabathia pitched a complete game. With the Mets loss, the Brewers officially clinched the wild-card.... The Mets finished with a record of 1,859–1,713 (.520) in their 45 seasons at Shea.

OPENING CITI FIELD

METS 4 RED SOX 3, RED SOX 9 METS 3 (EXHIBITIONS), PADRES 6 METS 5

APRIL 3, 4, 13, 2009, at CITI FIELD

FOR TWO YEARS while sitting at Shea Stadium, we could look straight ahead into center field and see our future. Citi Field was being built brick by brick right before our eyes. I was in the minority, but I was not looking forward to this monumental change for a few reasons. First was sentimentality. I grew up at Shea, and while it was a dump, it was *our* dump. I saw the Mets fill the building for the last few years and didn't see the need for a new stadium. Nicer bathrooms would be cool and all, but did we really need a new stadium to supply that? I also had the selfish fear concerning where my season ticket would be. Growing up at Shea, we sat in loge box 325, which was such a unique level. For those who sat there, you know what I mean. You would sit insanely close to the field with a bit of height that very few other stadiums could offer. As I looked at replicas of the new Citi, I didn't see that exact same seat anywhere. The transition to Citi also meant a transition of me taking over the season tickets from my father. At 24 years of age, it was time! The free ride was over! Our seats at Shea were behind home plate but slightly to the left so we could actually see inside the visitors dugout. My father had mentioned that the only minor thing he would tweak about our seats would be to move slightly to our right so the dugout we could peek into would be the Mets dugout. I wanted to come through for my dad!

On April 3, 2009, I was finally going to see our new home. The Mets were opening up Citi Field with two exhibition games against the Boston Red Sox. A few times before this, the Mets would play exhibition games at Shea right before Opening Day, with the last time being six years earlier against the Orioles. I regretted going to that game and grew to strongly dislike the stadium games before Opening Day. Part of the appeal of the opener is walking into your building for the first time in months, smelling the hot dogs and seeing that beautiful green grass, and I thought doing that a few days early for a dress rehearsal took part of the mystique away from Opening Day. This situation was very different, though, as we were opening up a brand-new stadium. Walking in our new home for the first time brought some very mixed emotions. I loved the Jackie Robinson Rotunda and thought it was very cool that we honored not only a baseball and New York legend but an American icon. But outside of that beautiful area of the ballpark, the rest of the stadium simply ignored that a baseball team played there. I couldn't find a Mets logo anywhere—no pictures of Mets legends, no clubs named after Mets icons, no orange, no blue, *nada*. The Mets would later go on and eventually fix this miscarriage of justice, but first impressions matter, and a first glance at Citi Field would not tell you that the New York Mets resided there.

As we sat down in section 323 at the new Citi Field, I knew immediately that I let my dad down. While we could now see into the Mets dugout, we were further to the left of home plate than I planned. I spent the first few innings of the first game and then the next few weeks trying to convince myself that the new seats were awesome, but deep down I knew they were not. Two months later I was able to successfully move our season tickets to my permanent home ever since in section 318, but the first few months was me playing mental gymnastics with our new view. The only thing I vividly remember about those first two games against the Red Sox was the fact that Oliver Perez was booed off the mound in Game 2. This

V/G	P.dres	W-L 5-2	GB +1 LAD	H 5-2	R 0-0	E 0-0	C 0-0	W 5-2	IL 0-0
H/G	Mets	W-L 3-3	GB 2	H 0-0	R 3-3	E 1-2	C 2-1	W 0-0	IL 0-0

AL STANDINGS

	R	H	E	LOB
50	6	9	0	9
Met	5	7	1	5

WP Edward Mujica 1-1 *1st NL Win
LP Brian Stokes 0-1
SV Heath Bell 4

START 7:11 DATE April 13, 2009 Monday
FINISH 10:22 ATT. 41,007
TIME 311 WX Clear 54°

Met DP/OPP 0   DEFENSE   E9 1 E

Daniel Murphy — Carlos Beltran — Ryan Church

Jose Reyes — Luis Castillo

David Wright — 4.01 Mike Pelfrey — Carlos Delgado

Glen Hitrin

Brian Schneider

San Diego Padres	Avc 237	HR 6	RBI 4.29	1	2	3	4	5	6	7	8	9	10	11	AB 12	R 13	H 14	BI 15
33 Jody Gerut cf															4	2	2	1
2 David Eckstein 2b															4	1	3	2
24 Brian Giles rf															5	0	1	1
23 Adrian Gonzalez 1b															5	1	1	1
7 Chase Headley lf															3	0	0	0
5 Kevin Kouzmanoff 3b															5	0	1	0
4 Nick Hundley c															4	0	0	0
15 Luis Rodriguez ss															3	1	0	0
27 Walter Silva P															2	1	1	0
45 Edward Mujica P															1	0	0	0
46 Cla Meredith P															1	0	0	0
50 Duaner Sanchez P																		
21 Heath Bell P															37	6	9	5

R/ER		3/3	o/o	o/o	1/1	1/o	e/o	o/o	o/o			
H	2	4	1	0	1	1	0	0	0			
E	0	0	0	0	0	0	0	0	0			
LOB	2	1/3	1/4	1/5	o/5	1/6	1/7	2/1	o/1			

LH	BENCH	RH
	Hairston	
	Blanco	

Met PITCHERS	IP	H	R	ER	W	K	
19-20 4.35 Mike Pelfrey	5	8	5	5	2	3	
Brian Stokes	6 1/3	0	1	0	0	0	
Pedro Feliciano	6 2/3	1	0	0	0	0	
Sean Green	7	1	0	0	0	1	
J.J. Putz	8	1	0	0	2	0	
Francisco Rodriguez	9	1	0	0	0	1	

LH	Met BULLPEN	RH
	Feliciano	

©1996 Bob Carpenter Communications, Inc. All Rights Reserved

was still considered a spring training game, but Perez was fresh off signing a new contract to remain with the Mets, which was met with mixed opinions, so the pressure was on. Perez walked four batters in the first inning and then got chased when he allowed the first home run in Citi Field history. The grand slam made it 6–0 Red Sox and led to Oliver Perez being taken out of the game and being greeted with the most vitriolic boos one could garner. The guy who hit the grand slam, which will go down in the record books as the first home run at Citi Field, would actually later play for the Mets. Despite signing a two-year, $20 million contract with the Mets in 2019, this man would not only never hit a home run for the Mets, he would never record even a single base hit...you may remember Jed Lowrie.

Nine days later, we would return to Citi Field for the home opener, and all the juice was completely gone. When you combine the fact that I was in the building already for multiple games, the season was already a week old, and the game was played at night instead of its customary 1:10 PM start, this didn't feel like Opening Day. While the place was packed and people were cheering on the home team, you could tell immediately that it didn't have the same sound as the old Shea Stadium. It also didn't help that, in the first regular season at-bat at Citi Field, the visiting team's leadoff hitter smacked a home run to right. Jody Gerut went yard off Mike Pelfrey, and then the Padres would go and tack on three more runs in the second inning. The highlight of the game was the dramatic game-tying three-run home run by David Wright in the fifth inning. While the place didn't have the energy of Shea, that swing and the reaction by the Mets faithful did come close to recreating the magic and loudness of Shea. It was fitting that David would hit the first long ball by a Met in the new digs, but it was also a sign of the year to come that the Mets would promptly give the lead right back in the top of the sixth when Pedro Feliciano balked in the go-ahead run after Ryan Church couldn't catch a fly ball in right field. Yes, a two-base error and a balk led to the winning run scoring and the Mets losing the inaugural game at Citi Field. It took a while, and I now love Citi Field, but when it first opened in 2009, love would certainly not be the word to describe my feelings toward the new place.

KEEPING SCORE: Georgetown and St. John's had played the first game at Citi Field a week before the Mets faced the Red Sox. Future Mets second baseman Joe Panik played for the Johnnies in that contest.... The Mets went 41–40 at Citi Field in 2009 and finished fourth in the NL East with an overall 70–92 record.

LIVE IN L.A. FOR
THE RYAN CHURCH GAME

DODGERS 3 METS 2 (11 INNINGS)
MAY 18, 2009, at DODGER STADIUM

MY LONGTIME midday partner Joe Benigno and I loved to travel! In 2008, we went to Los Angeles to see an NBA Finals game and the Mets play a series in Anaheim against the Angels. We were treated to a Mets win and the firing of Willie Randolph in the middle of the night, but we had so much fun we decided to do it again one year later. Our producer at the time was Gregg Giannotti, who has blossomed into a star at our radio station, now hosting the morning show with Boomer Esiason. He joined us as we went back to the West Coast for a second straight year. This time it would be another Lakers postseason game, and we'd see the Mets at Dodger Stadium. Gio and I went to Lakers-Rockets on the Sunday night before the Mets would open a series against the Dodgers. We also decided to live it up by getting a room at the Beverly Hills Hilton and renting a convertible so we could really live that L.A. lifestyle while on the road. Our trip got off to a wild start when we met a nice woman poolside at the hotel named Tatiana who wasted no time showing us a picture of a famous NFL player's genitalia that she had on her phone. The trip was off to a rollicking start!

While I had been to many a stadium at this point in my life, this was my first-ever trip to the famous Dodger Stadium. It is such a unique ballpark. You walk in and you're immediately in the upper deck and instantly see that gorgeous view of the mountains in the distance. Even though it's an older ballpark, it just doesn't feel very old and weathered like other aged stadiums appear. Before the opener of the series, we did a special show live from the press box at Dodger Stadium leading into the Mets pregame show. After the show, I promptly went to get a bite to eat and missed out on a life-changing event that Gio and Joe B got to experience. They both ran into the legendary Vin Scully, and before they could even introduce themselves, Vin went into a remarkable soliloquy. "You know, guys," Vin said in his recognizable tone, "your baseball team has a catcher named Omir Santos. Well, I had never heard that name before, so I while I was eating dinner tonight, I needed to learn more. A few of the workers are of Latino descent, so I asked them

©1996 Bob Carpenter Communications, Inc. All Rights Reserved

what *omir* means. They then began to chuckle and informed me that *omir* means 'penis.' So, fellas, you guys have a catcher named Penis." Joe and Gio were laughing hysterically as they repeated the story to me a few minutes later. The most iconic voice in baseball history wanted to explain that our baseball team had a catcher named Penis. (After further review, *omir* does not mean what Vin thought it meant in Spanish.) You couldn't make it up if you tried.

Forgettable Met Tim Redding recovered from allowing two runs in the first inning and pitched a very solid game as he kept the game close into the later innings. With two outs in the eighth, Gary Sheffield dramatically tied the game up for the Mets with a two-run single. I've always said that, when you are in a visiting ballpark, you need to not act like a jackass because you invite trouble if you do. With this being my first game at Dodger Stadium, I didn't know what to expect from Dodgers fans, but I promptly learned that they are a rough fan base with plenty of shit-starters. I saw a few Mets fans sitting in front of me have Dodger Dogs thrown at their head when they celebrated the Sheffield hit. You need to know the art of celebrating quietly, which I had perfected over the years, so I quickly realized that I needed to use that skill tonight at Dodger Stadium.

Despite the Mets' dramatic comeback, this game felt destined for the Mets to lose in walk-off fashion. In the top of the 11th inning at about 10:20 local time, so about 1:20 AM back in New York, an infamous Metsian moment was about to occur right before my eyes. Angel Pagan hit a majestic fly ball to deep right-center field. As soon as the ball left the bat, I couldn't control myself as I quickly jumped into the air to watch that beautiful tiny white pearl float deep into the California night. It bounced up against the wall, and Ryan Church easily scored to give the Mets an extra-inning lead. As I wrote down the Pagan triple in my scorebook, I shockingly heard the roar of the crowd. *What the hell is going on?* I thought. When I glanced up, I saw the Dodgers walking off the field and Dodgers fans high-fiving all over the place. I was forced to ask one of those douchey Dodgers fans what the hell happened. Church had missed third base and was called out. Things became even more brutal in the bottom of the 11th when Carlos Beltrán couldn't catch a ball in center, and just when I thought the Mets were going to escape a bases-loaded, no-out jam, Jeremy Reed, who had essentially never played first base in his life, threw a ball away to end the game. This was freakin' painful, only made worse by having to now walk out of Dodger Stadium.

While I am still bothered by losses, I can't explain why this one affected me in a way that was uncommon for a regular season game.

When Gio, Joe B, and I got in the car to drive back to the hotel, I was completely inconsolable. At the end of the day, this was a only a regular season game in May, but for reasons I can't fully explain I was devastated as if this game were in the midst of October. I legit wouldn't even communicate with G or Joe for over an hour as I stewed in anger over the horrific loss I had just witnessed. Finally, my mood began to change courtesy of the guy who now has great success in New York morning radio. Gio started doing his Mike Francesa imitation, which I always found funny, but on this night he needed to bring it up a few notches. So this time it was Mike Francesa saying some of the most vile things as he described the scene of a porn movie. Between how spot-on Gio's Francesa imitation was, and the hilarious material coming out of his mouth, I not only began laughing, but it was a belly laugh. I had totally forgotten why I was so angry. Who cares that Ryan Church had the ultimate brain fart? I was listening to fake Mike Francesa say the most grotesque but hilarious things. While I won't give details, you can use your imagination.

KEEPING SCORE: Sheffield had joined the Mets for his final major league season, and his first home run for the team was the 500th of his career.... Church, who had battled two concussions a year earlier, was traded to the Atlanta Braves two months later for Jeff Francouer, another right fielder. The Braves let Church go at the end of the year, and he spent his last big league season with the Pittsburgh Pirates and Arizona Diamondbacks in 2010.

THE OMIR SANTOS GAME

METS 3 RED SOX 2

MAY 23, 2009, at FENWAY PARK

WHEN THE METS' 2009 schedule came out, I was pretty excited to see that there was not only a trip to Boston on the docket but a weekend series to boot. That meant the timing would be right for me and the old man to make a return trip to Beantown. We had gone for the interleague series of 1998 and 2000, back when it seemed like the NL East took on the AL East every single season. Fenway Park is always cool to visit, especially when you walk around what used to be known as Yawkey Way (now Jersey Street) and just enjoy the sights and sounds of the old-time ballpark. The only issue with Fenway is that it feels almost impossible to find a really good seat. Because it's an old-time park, you still have poles set up that can lead to a restricted view and the seats are very small and uncomfortable. But hey, I only go there rarely, so who the hell am I to complain?

I have been to thousands of games in my lifetime, but these had to have been the worst seats imaginable. We were tucked away in the right-field corner, with a pole blocking part of our view a few rows ahead of us. It was my first game at Fenway since 2000, so despite the awful view, I was still pumped to just be in the building. The Mets were in the midst of a long road trip that kicked off out West, which included us seeing them firsthand in Los Angeles, and now they were wrapping things up in Boston. The Mets struck first with an RBI single by Gary Sheffield, but the Red Sox instantly responded with a two-run single off the bat of Kevin Youkilis. After that, both starting pitchers, Mike Pelfrey and Josh Beckett, settled in for a good old-fashioned pitchers' duel. Finally, in the ninth inning the game would write a drama that would be memorable to a lot of Mets fans more than a decade later. Down to our final out and trailing 2–1 with Gary Sheffield on first base and facing Red Sox closer Jonathan Papelbon, who had converted his first 11 save opportunities of the

V/G Mets W-L 22-17 GB 1½ H 12-8 R 10-11 E 10-8 C 7-5 W 4-6 IL 1-0

H/G Red Sox W-L 25-17 GB ½ H 16-5 R 9-12 E 16-6 C 5-2 W 4-8 IL 0-1

NL STANDINGS

Bos DP/OPP 0 DEFENSE EI I E

	R	H	E		LOB
Met	3	6	0		5
Bos	2	6	1		5

WP Pedro Feliciano 1-1
LP Jonathan Papelbon 0-1
SV J.J. Putz 2

START 7:10 DATE May 23, 2009 Saturday
FINISH 9:59 ATT. 37,871
TIME 2:49 WX clear 55°

Jason Bay — Jacoby Ellsbury — J.O. Drew

Nick Green — Dustin Pedroia

Mike Lowell — 7.56 Josh Beckett — Kevin Youkilis

Rocco Shinos — Luis Alicea

Jason Varitek

New York Mets	Avc	HR	RIG	1	2	3	4	5	6	7	8	9	10	11	AB 12	R 13	H 14	BI 15
28 Daniel Murphy 1b 256 3012															4	0	0	0
16 Angel Pagan RF 400 061															4	0	0	0
15 Carlos Beltran DH 347 6429															4	1	1	0
10 Gary Sheffield LF 257 311															3	1	1	1
5 David Wright 3b 353 3129															4	0	0	0
1r Jeremy Reed CF 324 002															4	0	1	0
4 Omir Santos c 254 1413															4	1	2	2
6 Ramon Martinez ss 063 002															4	0	1	0
1 Luis Castillo 2b 0811															2	0	0	0

Mike Pelfrey 4-1 4.61 7 0 / 41 46 11 17

R/ER	H	E	LOB

		1	2	3	4	5	6	7	8	9			
R/ER	1/0	0/0	0/0	0/0	0/0	0/0	0/0	0/0	2/2		33	3	6	3
H	2	0	0	0	1	0	2	0	1				
E	1E1	0	0	0	0	0	0	0	0				
LOB	1	0/1	0/1	0/1	2/3	0/3	2/5	0/5	0/5				

LH BENCH RH
Church — Tatis Castro
JH Reyes
DL Schneider 15 — Corn — Delgado 15

Bos PITCHERS	IP	H	R	ER	W	K	117
93-64 3.86 Josh Beckett	8	8	5	1	0	1	5
Jonathan Papelbon 59 9 0-11 0.95	1	1	1	2	2	1	2

LH Bos BULLPEN RH
Okajima — Delcarmen — Saito — Ramirez — Masterson
Lester — Penny — Mastabara — Wakefield

©1996 Bob Carpenter Communications, Inc. All Rights Reserved

year, the little-known catcher Omir Santos drove a ball to deep left field. From my vantage point buried in the right-field corner, it was tough to see, but I was able to catch the ball fly deep into the air as it approached the Green Monster, and it was obvious to me that it was not going to be caught. Then mass confusion hit as the ball appeared to bounce off the top of the wall. Sheffield could not score from first base, and while the Santos blast was shocking, it didn't tie the game

	1	2	3	4	5	6	7	8	9			R	H	E	LB
Mets	1	0	0	0	0	0	0	0	2			3	4	0	5
Red Sox	2	0	0	0	0	0	0	0	0			2	6	1	5

STADIUM/CAP. Fenway Park 1912

Interleague Play — 2 of 3 — Susun Series — 1-0 Met — RF (2 of 3)

Replay: Santos 2B in 9th ruled HR

©1996 Bob Carpenter Communications, Inc. All Rights Reserved

because it was a double. Jerry Manuel quickly came out to claim he thought it was actually a home run, and Fenway Park had an audible buzz as the building essentially was arguing with itself over whether this was a home run or a double off the top of the Monster. Because our seats were so awful, one positive was that there was a small TV screen hanging under the overhang right above us. It was still tough to see if the ball had cleared the fence, but what we did know is that the umpires were discussing it. After a lengthy meeting, they decided to go to replay and the wait continued. Though there was no action on the field and we were simply waiting for a few old guys to end their meeting, the ballpark had an electricity as we awaited the verdict. After what felt like the longest replay delay in MLB history, umpire Joe West's finger flew through the air to signal that indeed it was a two-run home run by Omir Santos.

With Francisco Rodriguez not available, J.J. Putz, Omar Minaya's other big off-season acquisition to fix the Mets' bullpen issues, was asked to come on and save the game. He walked the leadoff hitter, Youkilis, and then the Mets defense saved his ass. First David Wright made a great play on a smash by Jason Bay and was helped out by Luis Castillo holding second on his off-kilter throw. After J.D. Drew lined out to right, the game ended when little-remembered Ramon Martinez made a sparkling play at shortstop on a ball hit by Mike Lowell. The Mets had won a classic in Boston that for the time being made me move on peacefully from how brutal the loss in L.A. had been the night Ryan Church missed third base. Sometimes you try to draw conclusions early on in a season based on how brutal or amazing some wins and losses have been, and 2009 was a weird one. The Mets were sitting a little bit over .500 and already had some brutal and great wins, so I wasn't sure where this year was going to take us. A few short weeks later, they would endure a loss that would make the Ryan Church game feel like Mickey Mouse stuff, and would be a clear indication that 2009 would not be a year I would tell my kids about glowingly.

KEEPING SCORE: Santos's 91 games caught (74 starts) were the most among the four catchers the Mets used in 2009, his only season with the team.... Papelbon only blew two more saves the rest of the season and finished with 38.... Putz's save was his second and last one for the Mets. He was placed on the injured list in early June and never pitched for them again.

THE LUIS CASTILLO GAME

YANKEES 9 METS 8

JUNE 12, 2009, at YANKEE STADIUM

THE ONLY THING remembered about this game was the disgusting conclusion, and trust me we will get to my emotions on that in detail, but first let's not forget how ridiculous this baseball game was. This was the first Subway Series game played at the new Yankee Stadium, which had opened a few months earlier. It wasn't the sexiest pitching matchup ever, as Livan Hernandez started for the Mets and Joba Chamberlain for the Yankees. Joba was still the center of a huge debate on our radio station concerning his role. Should he be a reliever so he could recreate his dominance from 2007, or should the Yankees see what he could be as a starting pitcher? Joba threw a million (okay, a hundred) pitches in four innings and couldn't throw strikes. The Mets trailed 1–0, then took a 2–1 lead, then trailed 3–2, then retook the lead at 6–3, and then promptly gave up the lead when Hideki Matsui, the first batter Jon Switzer faced after relieving Hernandez, hit a three-run home run to put the Yankees up 7–6. The Mets tied it in the seventh and took the lead in the eighth on a two-out double by David Wright off Mariano Rivera. So it was a classic back-and-forth affair, a real entertaining baseball game. Then Francisco Rodriguez took the mound trying to protect a one-run lead in the ninth. To this point the man known was K-Rod had been perfect as the Mets closer. He was 16-for-16 on saves and had a microscopic 0.61 ERA. But this was his moment of truth...protect a one-run lead against the hated New York Yankees. Mets closers are defined by what they do in the big moment, and even though this was mid-June, when you're facing the Yankees it's a big moment. Are you Armando Benitez? Or are you gonna be the guy we can trust to the hand the ball to in the biggest of spots?

So here we were...bottom of the ninth, up by one, facing the vaunted Yankees offense. First up was Brett Gardner, and Frankie calmly got him to pop up. One out. Then came the old nemesis,

V/G Mets W-L 31-27 GB 4 H 18-11 R 13-16 E 18-12 C 7-8 W 4-6 IL 2-1

H/G Yankees W-L 34-26 GB 2 H 18-11 R 16-15 E 12-16 C 13-5 W 8-3 IL 1-2

NL STANDINGS

	R	H	E	LOB
Met	8	7	1	9
NYY	9	9	1	5

WP Mariano Rivera 1-2
LP Francisco Rodriguez 1-1
SV ~~~~~

START 7:09 DATE June 12, 2009 Friday
FINISH 10:55 ATT. 47,967
TIME 346 WX Clear 77°

©1996 Bob Carpenter Communications, Inc. All Rights Reserved

Derek Jeter, to the plate. He swung at a 2–2 pitch and ripped a single back up the box. Jeter then stole second base, setting up the tying run in scoring position with one out for the pinch-hitter Johnny Damon. Frankie struck out Johnny to the pleasure of about 25 percent of the building, who were rooting for the Mets. I was sitting along the third-base line in the upper level and pumped my fist as

Damon went down on strikes. But, oh shit, look who's coming up. Mark Teixeira had gotten really hot after a slow start in his first season as a New York Yankee. Mark had also hit a bomb back in the third inning, so I could envision him parking one right here, but I also had another wild thought. Maybe you walk Mark to face Alex Rodriguez? I wasn't aware of the specific numbers, but I knew through the playoff battle of 2005 that Alex had terrible numbers against Francisco. So why not put Mark on base and go after the slumping A-Rod. It goes against normal thought to put the winning run on base, but I was more scared of Teixeira parking one into the upper deck than Alex lacing a double up the alley. When Frankie fell behind Tex 3–0, the decision was easy. Just put him on base. So here we were—first and second, two out, one-run lead. K-Rod vs. A-Rod. What a freakin' game.

There are few regular season games in the middle of June that can stick with someone as much as this freakin' game. The 20 or so seconds that occurred around this moment are etched in my brain forever. Again, Francisco Rodriguez, who had not blown a game yet as Mets closer, was staring down Alex Rodriguez with the tying run in scoring position and the winning run on first base. When Frankie got Alex to pop the ball in the air to short right field, my friend Chad sitting next to me put his arm on my shoulder and said, "Congratulations." I responded with a gasp of, "Holy shit, bro, he's in trouble." That trouble manifested into a full-fledged nightmare scenario. Luis Castillo dropped the ball, and Mark Teixiera raced around the bases to win the game. I sat in my seat at Yankee Stadium in shock and awe. I uttered, "Not again," referring to the loss in L.A. when Ryan Church infamously missed third base. I was in a trance as I attempted to leave a rocking Yankees Stadium, and I proceeded to do something I do sorta regret to this day. I told Chad to find his own ride home, because I could not sit in a car next to him after suffering a loss like this. That game, that moment, that feeling fully defines the era of the early Citi Field years.

KEEPING SCORE: The Mets rebounded the next afternoon, beating Andy Pettitte 6–2, but dropped the rubber game Sunday 15–0 as Johan Santana was knocked out during a nine-run fifth inning.... The downward spiral continued, and the Mets dropped under .500 by the end of June, finishing the season 70–92, their first losing season in five years.... Castillo would be released two springs later with a year remaining on his four-year contract and the Mets eating the remaining $6 million he was owed.

The

2010s

THE LONGEST GAME

METS 2 CARDINALS 1 (20 INNINGS)

APRIL 17, 2010, at NEW BUSCH STADIUM, ST. LOUIS

IT WAS A late Saturday afternoon in April, and I made a simple request of my girlfriend at the time and to my family who were going to take us out to dinner. "Hey, guys," I said, "the Mets play at 4:00 PM, it should be over by 7:00–7:30, so let's go out after." No issue...an 8:00 PM dinner on a Saturday night in New York City was perfect. We plan, and the baseball gods laugh. This game not only is the single longest baseball game I've ever scored, but it taught me a very important life lesson that would benefit me down the road— DVR is a thing and it should be used!

When I sat down for this game, it was still early, but the Mets were off to a very bad start. After a disappointing 2009, the Mets had followed it up with a 3–7 start to the season as they played the middle game of a three-game weekend series against the St. Louis Cardinals. A night earlier they had nursed a 1–0 lead into the seventh inning before giving up a grand slam to journeyman Felipe Lopez, would then blow multiple chances to score, and lost a frustrating 4–3 game. Nothing seemed too unusual about this game in the early going—the Mets couldn't hit, and Johan Santana was brilliant. Jaime Garcia started the game for the Cardinals and actually kept the Mets hitless until the top of the sixth when Angel Pagan

Cont.

V/G Mets	W-L 3-7	GB 5	H 2-4	R 1-3	E 2-4	C 0-1	W 1-2	IL 0-0
H/G Cardinals	W-L 7-3	GB +2 P:1 Cards	H 3-1	R 4-2	E 1-0	C 6-3	W 0-0	IL 0-0

STANDINGS

20 inn	R	H	E	LOB
Met	2	9	2	13
Stl	1	15	0	22

Stl DP/OPP

DEFENSE

WP Francisco Rodriguez 1-0
LP Joe Mather 0-1 ★ 1st MLb SS
SV Mike Pelfrey 1 ★ 1st ML Save

START 4:14 DATE April 17, 2010 (Saturday)
FINISH 11:07 ATT. 43,709
TIME 653 WX Clear 63°

DEFENSE positions: Adam Craig / Joe Mather / Ryan Ludwick / Brenden Ryan / Skip Schumaker / Felipe Lopez / Blake Hawksworth / Albert Pujols / Yadier Molina

New York Mets	H/AB 4/47	HR 0	R 0	16	17	18	19	20	6	7	8	9	10	11	AB 12	R 13	H 14	BI 15
7 Jose Reyes	53	0/6	0ro															
1 Luis Castillo	2b	2/5	0ro															
5 David Wright	3b	0/4	0ro															
44 Jason Bay	LF	0/6	0ro															
12 Jeff Francoeur	RF	0/6	0ro															
4 Henry Blanco	C	0/2	0ro															
32 Jenrry Mejia P / 22 Raul Valdez P / 75 Francisco Rodriguez P / 34 Mike Pelfrey P																		
16 Angel Pagan	cf	1/4	0ro															
35 Mike Jacobs	1b	0/1	0ro															

	R/ER	0/0	0/0	0/0	1/1	1/1							
	H	1	1	1	0	2							
	E	0	0	0	0	0							
LOB		1/8	0/8	1/9	3/12	4/13							

LH BENCH RH
NO
ONE

DL
Murphy 15
Beltran 15

Stl PITCHERS	IP	H	R	ER	W	K	
Blake Hawksworth ⑭ ㉗	2⅓	2	0	0	1	3	108f
Ryan Franklin ㉛	17	1	1	0	0	0	38f
Felipe Lopez ③	18	1	1	0	1	0	40f
Joe Mather ㉓	19	2	2	2	3	0	128f 116P

LH Stl BULLPEN RH
Franklin
Staff
Penny
Lohse
Wainwright
Cupalate

singled leading off the inning. The game remained scoreless as both starting pitchers left after seven brilliant frames, Santana striking out nine, and Garcia allowing just that one hit. The game trudged into extra innings and it was still 0-0. At this point, I started to panic. What the heck was I supposed to do? My girlfriend and I had been together for about a year, so she knew I was a little insane, but still, was I really going to push back dinner plans? I pulled the "don't

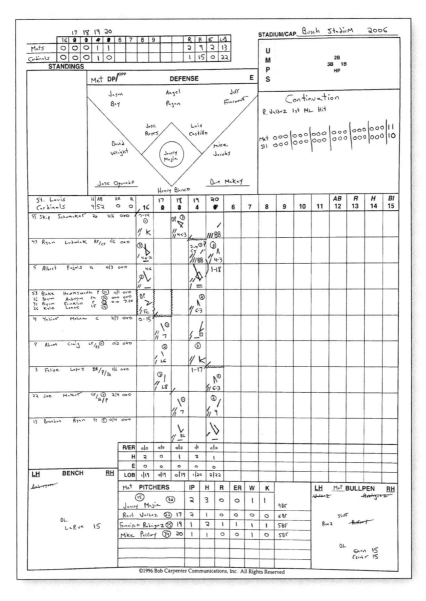

worry, guys, the game will end soon" line for multiple innings, and before I knew it the clock had struck 9:00. Our plans to go out for dinner now started to evolve into ordering in food. I didn't come up with the idea, but with the Mets locked into a thrilling 0–0 game deep into extra innings, I really liked the sound of having the food brought to us and the game remaining on.

I'm not sure what inning it was, but at some point the food came, we ate, and my parents disappeared. I was on the couch scoring this insane game, and I'm not even sure what my girlfriend at the time was doing, probably reading a book. The game was so long and crazy that Tony La Russa had double-switched cleanup hitter Matt Holliday out of the game in the 11th and so the slot in the batting order protecting the great Albert Pujols was now being held down by the pitcher's spot. This led to Pujols not being pitched to at all in the 12th and 14th innings when he came up with men on base and a chance to walk it off. After the Mets finally took the lead in the 19th inning on Jeff Francoeur's sac fly, Albert came up with one out and nobody on base. They decided to finally pitch to him, and he rocked a double off Francisco Rodriguez and eventually scored on a two-out hit by Yadier Molina to tie the game back up. This game was certifiably drunk! My girlfriend was now passed out on the couch next to me as the game moved into the 20th inning. Pagan led off with his third hit of the game and scored when José Reyes delivered a sacrifice fly that gave the Mets a 2–1 lead. And since the Mets were left without any relievers, they summoned Mike Pelfrey to come out of the pen and try to record his first career save. With two men on and two outs, the drama hit a fever pitch as Ryan Ludwick came up with Albert Pujols looming on deck. Pelfrey made the big pitch he needed to and got Ludwick to ground out to second and end the damn game.

I was relieved and also in awe of the beautiful artwork I had made with my scorecard. Since my Carpenter book only goes to 16 innings, I need to flip the page, which I had done numerous times, but never had it gone that long into page two. As I breathed a sigh of relief from nearly seven hours of baseball, I started to realize that this was my lowest moment. While I wasn't a dick about it, I had basically watched my parents and girlfriend at the time cancel our Saturday night in order to watch an April baseball game. I felt disgusted with myself as I sat on the couch recalling the evening I'd just had. At 26 years old, a life epiphany was coming over me: I love the Mets, baseball, and scoring games, but from this day forward I wouldn't let something like this ever happen again. By the time I met the love of my life, I had gotten these pathetic moments out of my system. Never would I make her sit around and watch seven hours of baseball instead of going out to dinner. So I remember this 20-inning classic for two important reasons—the length of game and that I got most of the bad Evan out of my system before meeting the woman of my dreams.

KEEPING SCORE: The Mets have played five games of 20 innings or more in their history, and this game was the only one they've managed to win.... Pelfrey's save was the only one of his major league career.... The Cardinals used 10 pitchers and the Mets nine (Santana, Ryota Igarashi, Pedro Feliciano, Fernando Nieve, Hisanori Takahashi, Jenrry Mejia, Raul Valdes, Rodriguez, and Pelfrey).

NETS AND METS PAIN CONVERGE

BRAVES 3 METS 2

MAY 18, 2010, at TURNER FIELD, ATLANTA

BASEBALL IS MY first love, and the Mets are the team that got me into sports as a young kid. Then I learned about the Jets and Nets, and they soon became an obsession of mine as well. While I watch every game and every second of each of my three big teams, whenever I'm posed the question of which team I love the most, I can give a straight answer. If on the die-hard fan meter I'm a 9.8 with the Nets and Jets, I ring at a 9.9 with the Mets. So, while the Mets will always be my first and true love, the passion runs incredibly deep for both the New York Jets and the now Brooklyn Nets. Sometimes the multiple passions will converge for all the right or, in this case, all the wrong reasons.

```
40
V/G Mets   W-L 19-20   GB 6      H 14-8   R 5-12   E 8-12   C 5-5   W 6-3   IL 0-0
39
H/G Braves W-L 18-20   GB 6½     H 10-6   R 8-14   E 3-10   C 8-5   W 7-5   IL 0-0
```

AL STANDINGS

	R	H	E	LOB
Met	2	5	1	3
Atl	3	7	0	7

WP Billy Wagner   3-0
LP Pedro Feliciano 1-2
SV

START 7:10   DATE Tuesday May 18, 2010
FINISH 9:56   ATT. 27,119
TIME 246   WX Clear 79°

ATL DP / OPP   DEFENSE

Melky Cabrera   Nate McLouth   Jason Heyward

Yunel Escobar   Martin Prado

Chipper Jones   4.04 Kris Medlen   Troy Glaus

Brian McCann

Chip Hale   Reggie Shines

AL STANDINGS
TB 28-11 ✓
NYY 22
Tor 5 ✓
Bos 7
Bal 16

Mn 24-15 ✓
Det 2 ✓
CWS 7½ ✓
Cle 8
KC 9

Tex 21-18
Oak 2
LAA 3½
Sea 6½

New York Mets	Avg 245	HR 30	R/G 4.36	1	2	3	4	5	6	7	8	9	10	11	AB 12	R 13	H 14	BI 15
7 Jose Reyes SS 221 0•11																	
1 Luis Castillo 2b 257 0•11																	
23 Chris Carter LF 400 0•3 / 19 Gary Matthews Jr. PH/LF 173 0•1																	
5 David Wright 3b 270 8•26																	
29 Ike Davis 1b 271 3•10																	
21 Rod Barajas c SCRATCHED / 16 Angel Pagan cf 271 2•17																	
16 Angel Pagan CF Moved / 12 Jeff Francoeur RF																	
12 Jeff Francoeur RF / 4 Henry Blanco c																	
57 Johan Santana p 143 0•0 / 44 Jason Bay rm / 25 Pedro Feliciano p / 32 Jenrry Mejia p																	

	R/ER	0|0	0|0	0|0	0|0	2|2	0|0	0|0	0|0	0|0							
	H	0	0	0	1	2	0	1	0	1							
	E	0	0	0	0	0	0	0	0								
	LOB	0	0	1	0|1	0|1	0|1	1|2	0|2	1|3							

LH BENCH RH
Corr
Tatis
Barajas
SH
Matthews Jr.
OL
Murphy 15
Bottom 15

ATL PITCHERS	IP	H	R	ER	W	K	90 P
4-6 3.77 Kris Medlen (58)	6⅓	4	2	2	2	6	248F 2HR
Peter Moylan (58)	⅔	0	0	0	0	0	10F
T.Kashi Saito (40)	8	1	0	0	0	0	3BF
Billy Wagner (13)	9	1	1	0	0	2	4BF 1wP

LH ATL BULLPEN RH
O'Flaherty   Chavez
Venters   Moylan
Wagner   Saito
             Kimbrel
SP.15
Hanson
Lowe
Kawakami
Hudson

©1996 Bob Carpenter Communications, Inc. All Rights Reserved

In 2010, the New Jersey Nets were a godawful basketball team. On opening night that season the Nets blew a 16-point fourth-quarter lead against the T-Wolves and lost at the buzzer on a Damien Wilkins put-back. From there the Nets would lose 17 more in a row and start the season an ungodly 0–18. They fired their coach (Lawrence Frank) and used an interim for a few games (Tom Barrise)

	1	2	3	4	5	6	7	8	9		R	H	E	LOB
Mets	0	0	0	0	2	0	0	0	0		2	5	1	3
Braves	0	0	2	0	0	0	0	0	1		3	7	0	7

STADIUM/CAP. Turner Field   1997

2 of 2
Season Series   (5 of 18)
4-0 Met
Nets get screwed in lottery
Wright K's in his
15th consec. game

©1996 Bob Carpenter Communications, Inc. All Rights Reserved

before finally settling on GM Kiki Vandeweghe. I watched every painful second of a season that seemed to hit a new bottom each week. When it was all said and done, the Nets finished 12–70, putting up the worst record in the league. While this was happening, I spent the season daydreaming about Kentucky point guard John Wall, who was clearly going to be the consensus No. 1 overall pick in the upcoming draft. Despite that, I never once rooted against the Nets in order to secure the worst record and the most Ping-Pong balls in the NBA lottery. The system had shown me time and time again that finishing with the worst record really didn't guarantee you anything. So rooting against my team and hoping for more losses was not something that appealed to me. But let's not kid ourselves, as I watched every second of Yi Jianlian, Courtney Lee, Terrence Williams, Rafer Alston, and the rest of my horrific team, I feared May 18. May 18 would be the day where I would learn my destiny. Was this season of pain and embarrassment going to at least conclude with John Wall as my gift?

I was so damn stressed out on this random Tuesday in May that I did something I very rarely do when watching a big sporting event. I got my favorite alcoholic beverage, Maker's Mark, and started going to town. This was the night that was going to dictate the future of my basketball team for the next decade, and I needed to calm my nerves. The other thing I did was get my scorebook out to score the Mets vs. Braves! The Mets were sitting at 19–20 and had a chance to take a brief two-game series from the Atlanta Braves after winning the night before behind Mike Pelfrey's seven strong innings. Johan Santana took the mound for the Mets against Kris Medlen. By the time we got to about 8:00 PM, I was now very buzzed, but I'm very proud of the stellar penmanship I maintained on my book. As Troy Glaus took Santana deep in the third inning to give the Braves a 2–0 lead, it was go time. I kneeled down in front of my TV as we had reached the top three picks that were about to be revealed. The next logo that would come up would be the team that finished third. Besides my New Jersey Nets, the Washington Wizards and Philadelphia 76ers were the remaining teams with a chance to win the lottery. Both teams finished with far superior records than the Nets and had much lower odds of winning this thing. As the old Nets logo appeared on the screen, my stomach dropped. I began verbalizing my pain and frustration with four letter words. After watching the team brutalize its fans with 70 losses, they had missed out on the hypothetical generational player in John Wall and would be picking third. All that suffering was for naught and even the strong buzz from Maker's Mark couldn't help contain my emotions. I sat back down on my couch and quickly tried to emotionally move on back to the Mets. I thought marking this occasion in my book by writing, "Nets get screwed in lottery," would be therapeutic and a reminder of this dark night. Over a decade later, I need no reminder.

Even though one thing has zero to do with the other, I was 1,000 percent certain the Mets were now going to lose this game to the hated Atlanta Braves. Even when they tied the game in the fifth courtesy of solo homers by Ike Davis and Angel Pagan, I still knew that eventually the cherry on top would come. After blowing scoring chances in the seventh and ninth innings, that final nail in the coffin to the evening came in a typically painful way. The Braves had first and second with nobody out in the ninth inning when Jenrry Mejia got Melky Cabrera to hit a chopper to third base. David Wright would make this play nine out of 10 times, but this time unleashed a wild throw into the runner that got past Davis at first base and went into the right-field corner. The winning run scored and the Braves had won the game 3–2. That John Wall wouldn't be a Net and the face of the Mets made a game-losing error all on the same night didn't seem fair. For most Mets fans you probably don't remember this game. The 2010 season was a forgettable one, and this game, while painful in the moment, was also something you would move on from within 48 hours. But for me this game stuck with me because of what that night entailed. It was a night where the pain of the Nets and Mets converged over a few drinks of Maker's Mark.

KEEPING SCORE: For the record, the Wizards won the first pick and drafted Wall, who became a perennial All-Star.... The Nets' consolation prize with the third pick was Georgia Tech guard Derrick Favors, who would be traded during his rookie season to the Utah Jazz in a blockbuster deal for All-Star guard Deron Williams.... To top things off, the winning pitcher for the Braves was ex-Met Billy Wagner, who struck out Wright and Davis with the go-ahead run on third base in the top of the ninth.

JOHAN SANTANA'S NO-HITTER

METS 8 CARDINALS 0
JUNE 1, 2012, at CITI FIELD

MY BIGGEST FEAR for most of my life was NONO FOMO—the fear of missing out on seeing the Mets' first no-hitter in the history of the franchise. Any home Mets game I'd happen to miss going to, there would be a secret I would hold with me—rooting for the opponent to get a base hit so I don't have to worry about missing history. June 1, 2012, was a Friday night, and I asked my friend Nick to join me at Citi Field to watch the Mets take on the Cardinals. Little did I know we'd be witnessing something I could never picture actually happening.

Usually, I would think about a no-hitter right from the get go—a Mets starting pitcher gets through one clean inning, and my mind would begin to wander. For some bizarre, unexplainable reason on this night, even with Johan Santana on the mound, my mind didn't go there. It took until the top of the fifth before my eyes darted down to my scorebook to notice the zero next to hits. It was easy for this to sneak up on you because Johan wasn't particularly dominant and had issued a few BBs. As Johan continued to twirl hitless innings, I was faced with a huge dilemma. What to do I do with my father, who is sitting at his house in upstate New York, probably waiting to start the Mets game late so he could skip through commercials? Could I allow him to be delayed? He has been to thousands and thousands of Mets games and has been waiting for the impossible too. Before the top of the seventh inning, I picked up my cell phone and called him. "Hey, Dad, I don't want to get into details, but start the Mets game and move quickly." I could tell, based on his response, that he knew exactly what was going on. When Mike Baxter put his career on the line to make a stupendous catch on Yadier Molina's drive to left field in the seventh, I started to think, *Holy shit, this is gonna happen.* I called my dad again— "*Quicker*...move it, move it."

Scorecard — Cardinals vs. Mets, June 1, 2012

WP Johan Santana 3-2
LP Adam Wainwright 4-6

R H E LOB
StL 0 0 0 5
Met 8 8 0 5

START 7:13 FINISH 9:48 TIME 2:35 ATT. 27,069 WX Cloudy 66°

Met PITCHERS: Johan Santana — IP 9, H 0, R 0, ER 0, W 5, K 8

"Okay, okay, I get it," he responded.

As the ninth inning began, I turned to my friend Nick and told him, "Here is my phone, God forbid this happens, please record it." He nodded in agreement. Nick had moved from New Orleans to New York City in 2004 and quickly adopted the Mets as his baseball team because he couldn't stand the Yankees and he knew his pal Evan would take him to games frequently! But he got it—he knew

STADIUM/CAP. Citi Field   2009

	1	2	3	4	5	6	7	8	9		R	H	E	LB	
Cardinals	0	0	0	0	0	0	0	0	0		0	0	0	5	0-2
Mets	0	0	2	0	3	3	0	X			8	8	0	5	3-7

NL STANDINGS

All-Time   1 of 4
368-330 11 Season Series (1 of 7)
StL   3-3
1st No hitter in Met History !!

Johan NO Hitter
Santana

New York Mets	AVG 260	HR 36	R/C 4.31	1	2	3	4	5	6	7	8	9	10	11	AB 12	R 13	H 14	BI 15

StL PITCHERS

		IP	H	R	ER	W	K	
Adam Wainwright	70-40-3 3.07	6 1/3	6	7	7	3	6	95 P
Jim Freeman	7	2/3	1	1	1	2	1	58
Michael Cleto	8	1	1	0	0	0	2	48

©1996 Bob Carpenter Communications, Inc. All Rights Reserved

what this meant. I will remember the final moments of this night like it was yesterday. When Johan fell behind David Freese 3–0, I screamed, "Walk him and get me that piece of shit, Yadier Molina!" Nothing could make up for 2006, but, sure, why not let him make Mets history by being the final out. Strike one, Strike two...one strike away from a freakin' no-hitter. In this moment, I knew it was happening, there was no hesitation. Strike three...I jumped in the air with my scorebook in my arm and began to tear up. If you aren't a Mets fan, you don't get it. If you are a Mets fan, no explanation is necessary on why this was so emotional. That night I didn't want to leave Citi Field. That night Citi Field became our home. To that point, what emotional moment happened in that ballpark? Don't tell me Gary Sheffield's 500th home run! There was nothing. But on this random June night in 2012, Citi Field got its soul. The controversial hit by the Cardinals' Carlos Beltrán that was ruled foul in the sixth inning wasn't a thought in my mind that night. Being at the game I didn't fully realize the call was missed as blatantly as it was by the third-base umpire. I have now spent pointless hours debating with smartasses the merits of Johan's no-hitter. But to me it's an open-and-shut case—we finally witnessed a Mets no-hitter! And from that day forward, I never had to secretly root for that first opponent hit ever again.

Now let's address the elephant in the room, the thing my former radio partner, Craig Carton, would bring up to me every single time we talked about this magical night. Is it really a no-hitter? Isn't this really a one-hitter because Carlos Beltrán had a clear base hit down the left-field line ruled a foul ball? A couple of things—as I said, on that night this thought never went through my mind. A part of that is, when you are sitting at a game you aren't privy to replays, so most of the time you aren't aware of a bad call unless it's painfully obvious. While sitting with my season ticket in the Excelsior level that night at Citi Field, while it did look like it could have been called fair, our naked eyes didn't make it as obvious as the replay would show. So the entire night wasn't clouded in controversy; we were rocking Citi Field rooting on the first no-hitter in Mets history. Did I see the replay when I got home? Absolutely. Did I think it was a bad call? Of course! I'm not blind. But I'm also not one to recreate baseball history because there was an obvious missed call. The Kansas City Royals won the 1985 World Series despite a missed call; the New York Yankees won Game 1 of the 1996 ALCS and went on to win the series despite an obvious missed call. Bad calls are not new, but what was new was to somehow discredit this moment and achievement because of a bad call. Let me make this perfectly clear...there is *zero* cloud over this no-hitter. It was a no-hitter! Period. Stop. The debate over Johan throwing 134 pitches in that game affecting the rest of his career is absolutely fair, but anyone suggesting this isn't a "real" no-hitter is a hater trying to mock us. Why I took time to address this right now is actually sad on my part. I guess it shows the haters have won. Okay, fine, you got me...but nobody can take away our first no-hitter in franchise history.

KEEPING SCORE: The Mets had gone 8,019 games without a no-hitter since coming into the league 60 years earlier.... The losing pitcher was 2006 nemesis Adam Wainwright, who gave up seven runs, including a three-run home run to Lucas Duda.... Santana had missed the 2011 season after undergoing shoulder surgery, dealt with an ankle injury and back inflammation later in 2012, and was shut down for the season in August. He suffered another shoulder injury the following spring and never pitched again.

HARVEY'S BETTER

METS 7 NATIONALS 1
APRIL 19, 2013, at CITI FIELD

THE METS FRANCHISE has gone through periods of darkness in their history and certainly during my time as a fan. One of the tougher periods was the post-Madoff, early Citi Field years. The Wilpons never treated the Mets like a small market team, so usually the criticisms of spending were merely about not being as aggressive as the Yankees, more than not being an upper- echelon spending team as a whole. In 2009, the Mets had the second highest payroll in baseball; in 2010, it dropped to fifth; in 2011, it went down to seventh; then to 14th in 2012; and when we got to 2013, it had collapsed to 23rd in baseball. In just a four-year period, the Mets went from a legit big-market team to a franchise that was being outspent by more than half the league.

There is one tiny positive to sucking, which the Mets had been doing now for going on five seasons, and that was getting high draft picks. As Paul Wilson proved to us two decades earlier, you can pick as high as you want, but you still have to select the right guy! Well, after having a very disappointing 2009, the Mets selected seventh in the 2010 amateur draft and picked a kid named Matt Harvey, a right-handed pitcher from the University of North Carolina. As with all bad teams, you start to look toward the future with hope while watching the terrible baseball. Certain prospects come with hype and attention, while others may come out of nowhere upon making their debut, but Matt was certainly the former. I even remember traveling to Binghamton one weekend just to see the kid pitch a Double A game. When Matt was called up in 2012, he pitched very well, with a 2.73 ERA in 10 starts and certainly gave us the hope we were looking for.

Matt's 2013 season got off to an incredible start, as he won his first three starts, allowing only two runs, so when he walked onto the mound at Citi Field for only his second Citi start of the year, we were certainly excited to see him pitch before us. His opponent on this evening was a man whose hype upon being called up three years earlier made Matt Harvey look like a no-name prospect. Stephen Strasburg had one of the more talked about prospect debuts I recall in my lifetime! And to Strasburg's credit, his debut was electric, and you could certainly see what the hype was all about. After missing time early in his career, he broke through with a monster 2012, but the Nationals made a controversial decision to hold him out of the 2012 postseason in the name of protecting his arm. So Strasburg, fair or not, was now known as an electric arm who didn't pitch when the games actually mattered. Either way, Harvey going up against Strasburg was a very cool early season duel on paper, featuring the next generation of arms. Helped out by some bad Nats defense, the Mets took an early 2–0 lead, and Matt Harvey continued his dominance.

He allowed only one hit through five innings (a double by Strasburg, of all people) and completed seven outstanding innings of one-run ball that actually raised his ERA through four starts to 0.93. But what made this game truly memorable is what we as fans did in the bottom of the sixth inning. After Ike Davis and Lucas Duda hit home runs against Strasburg to give the Mets a 4–0 lead, a loud sound

STADIUM/CAP. Citi Field 2009

	1	2	3	4	5	6	7	8	9	R	H	E	LOB	
Cardinals	0	0	0	0	0	0	0	0	0	0	0	0	5	0-2
Mets	0	0	0	2	0	3	3	0	X	8	8	0	5	3-7

UMPS: Culbreth 2B, Johnson 3B, 1B Barksdale, HP Cederstrom

All-Time 1 of 4
368-330 11 Season Series (1 of 7)
STL 3-3

1st No hitter in Met History!!

Johan NO Hitter
Santana

Ist No Hitter in Met History!!

started to ring down from the seats at Citi. "Har-vey's better!" *clap-clap-clap-clap*, "Har-vey's better!" I certainly didn't start the chant, but you can bet your ass I very quickly joined in! It was such a unique thing to say, but what made it awesome is that it felt like for the first time in Citi Field's history we were actually happy. Since 2009, things had been so bleak, and here we were singing at the top of our lungs, showing pride in a homegrown Met's performance. Davis and Duda homered again in the eighth inning against Drew Storen, and the Mets completed the 7–1 win when Bobby Parnell got the final three outs. A sound permeated Citi Field as we walked out that was truly awesome. Leaving Shea, the place would be loud after wins as we walked out of the building, but this was a maiden voyage for Citi. The "Let's Go, Mets!" chants were joined in by louder and drunker "Har-vey's better!" chants. There were only about 27,000 people at Citi that night, but I swear to this day walking out was as loud as I'd ever heard it. In its fifth year of existence, Citi Field was starting to develop its soul, it was starting to feel like Shea. It just needed a reason to, and finally we were starting to see small signs of life in this franchise. We as a fan base were desperate for hope. Matt Harvey was providing it, and we were eating it up. "Harvey's Better" Night at Citi Field may not seem like much. The Mets were 8–7, and 2013 would be another under-.500, non-playoff season, but we were starting to see what was growing and began realizing that our days of darkness might soon be ending. April 19, 2013, was the day you could feel the tide slowly starting to turn.

KEEPING SCORE: Harvey would soon be joined by another highly touted pitching prospect, Zach Wheeler, who pitched well after being called up in June.... Unfortunately, a month after starting the All-Star Game (see following chapter), Harvey's 2013 season would be cut short when he suffered a partially torn ligament in his elbow, and he would miss the entire 2014 campaign.

ALL-STAR GAME COMES TO CITI

AMERICAN LEAGUE 3 NATIONAL LEAGUE 0

JULY 16, 2013, at CITI FIELD

LIKE MOST KIDS who love baseball, I thought the All-Star Game every summer was awesome. What was not to love? It was chance to see the stars of baseball all together on one field, and an opportunity to show great pride in the one or two players who are representing your favorite team on this national stage. In the days before the MLB app and our ability to see all the great players of the game whenever we wanted to, the All-Star Game was a unique experience. But for most of us, there comes a day when the All-Star Game loses its luster and becomes a boring exhibition game that you may not even watch anymore. While I still find myself watching the game every year, the end of my innocence occurred in 2002, when commissioner Bud Selig shrugged his shoulders and allowed a tie to take place when managers Joe Torre and Bob Brenly both misused their bullpens and had no arms left. While the gimmick of making the game "count" for home-field advantage in the World Series certainly worked on me and kept my interest, the game was never the same to me after that one ended in a tie.

One of the perks of being a season ticket holder is not only having your exact same seat for 81 games, but guaranteeing those same seats for the playoffs. Obviously, the Mets wouldn't comply with that whole playoff thing in most seasons, but upon opening a brand new ballpark in 2009, the rumors were rampant that the Mets would at least get something they had not had in more than 40 years, and that's to host an All-Star Game. My dad took me to Philly in 1996 for the All-Star Game, and it was very cool. We sat in the outfield at the old Veterans Stadium, and I remember Mike Piazza (in his days before becoming a Met) hitting a home run. But getting to host an All-Star Game would be so much cooler, espe-cially knowing we would be sitting in our very own seats for the midsummer classic. Plus, remember where we were in the course of Mets history—the team had finished under .500 every single season since Citi Field opened in 2009. So, as we entered year five of Citi Field, the team was perennially bad and honestly hadn't played a big game yet in the new park. Santana's no-hitter was far and away the most magical moment, but who could see that coming? So at least

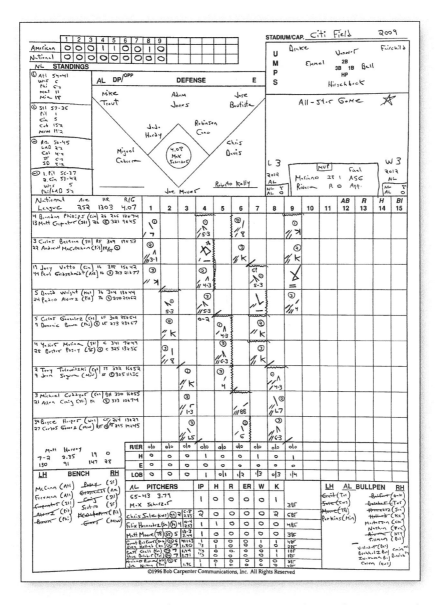

the All-Star Game would bring some hype to the stadium, even if it was unrelated to the Mets. Little did we know that, going into the 2013 season, we would actually have something to go nuts about besides the All-Star Game—Matt Harvey was becoming a cult hero right before our eyes. Soon after that "Harvey's Better" game, Matt would continue his magical year and give some fans memories of

Doc Gooden in 1985 with his pure dominance. He was not only going to clearly be an All-Star, but he was making a very compelling case that he should start the game itself. NL manager Bruce Bochy made the decision and played to the hometown crowd by giving us exactly what he wanted. He announced that Matt Harvey and not Clayton Kershaw would start the game. He even said that the location of the game didn't even factor into the call and that Harvey deserved the nod over Kershaw, even if the game weren't going to be in New York. We can parse the numbers all we want, but clearly the right call was going with the hometown guy. Clayton Kershaw, who to his credit is one of the most dominant pitchers of this era, got a little sensitive about it and said that Bochy's comments were hurtful. Hurtful, my ass...you're a future Hall of Famer who'll win numerous Cy Young Awards and you're getting teary about not starting the All-Star Game? Bottom line is this: for Mets fans who have had very little to cheer about over the years, this was something unique for us, so let us be happy. There is no doubt that Matt starting this game added hype to it and pumped us up a bit.

We gave Harvey a standing ovation as he took the mound, but it took about 30 seconds for the inning to go haywire. He allowed a first-pitch double to Mike Trout, and then on his second pitch to crosstown rival Robinson Cano, drilled him in the knee. Yankees fans on Twitter were pissed and thought Harvey had hit Cano on purpose. Meanwhile my immediate concern was that Harvey had put himself in a tough first-and-second, no-out jam right off the bat. I know it shouldn't matter, but there was pride on the line here. The last thing I wanted to see was Matt not get through the first inning and embarrass himself on a national stage. Cano left the game, and the arguments on Twitter become fierce, debating the intent of Harvey. Luckily, Matt calmly got the next three hitters out, stranding the two runners, and topped it off with a 1-2-3 second inning. Harvey had a very successful All-Star debut in front of his home crowd, the first of many All-Star appearances...right?

The story of the night, though, was another New York baseball player. Mariano Rivera was going through his retirement tour and was pitching in his final All-Star Game. With the American League leading 3–0 in the eighth inning, AL manager Jim Leyland decided to go to Mo for the eighth and not the ninth. Rivera received a standing ovation as he walked in, and I was honestly conflicted on what to do. Of course, I have great respect for Mo, but he's the freakin' enemy. He's the one who was on the mound for one of my worst moments when he got Mike Piazza to fly out to end the 2000 World Series, as well as countless other times he closed the Mets out to win a Subway Series game. As he jogged in, I ended up giving him a polite golf clap. This game didn't matter all that much to me in terms of winning and losing, so why not respect this legend as he jogged in? What I didn't fully understand was why Leyland didn't let him pitch the ninth, as opposed to Joe Nathan, who ended up getting the final three outs. Either way, Mo had his moment and the AL secured the 3–0 win on a hot steamy night at Citi Field. The whole evening was a success—and now I went back to hoping we could see a crowd like that again for a playoff game. I'd have to wait a couple more years for that.

KEEPING SCORE: Harvey was joined in the starting lineup by Mets third baseman David Wright, who went 1-for-3.... Kershaw would finally start an All-Star Game in 2022—in his home park, Dodger Stadium.... As part of the All-Star Game festivities, Citi Field hosted the Futures Game two days earlier with Mets prospects Noah Syndergaard and Rafael Montero as the starting pitchers.

DEGROM'S DEBUT

YANKEES 1 METS 0

MAY 15, 2014, at CITI FIELD

THERE IS SOMETHING so exciting and hopeful about a prospect being called up and making his major league debut. In the old days, we would never see highlights of the kids being called up, just the black-and-white stats in *USA Today Baseball Weekly*. Now we get daily updates and can even watch the kids play before they make their Queens debut. During the early Citi Field era, as I like to call it, that was the only hope we had—young players saving us. Matt Harvey and Zack Wheeler were the first of the bunch, but in May 2014 we were treated to a doubleheader of young hype. The Mets were calling up young pitchers to make their debuts in back-to-back games.

From day one it was all the same for Jacob deGrom. Let's go back to that week in 2014 and remember how it all began for Jake, and you'll know exactly what I'm talking about. The Mets were in the midst of a four-game home-and-home series with the Yankees and called up a couple of young arms. The ballyhooed prospect with all the hype was Rafael Montero, who replaced Jenrry Mejia in the rotation and pitched decently in his first start (three runs in six innings) but came up short to the Yankees. The next night was the turn for the guy who would probably go right back down to the minors because he wasn't as highly regarded as Montero and had originally been called up to work out of the bullpen. Jacob deGrom would make that idea impossible as he went out and pitched seven brilliant innings against the Yankees as a replacement for starter Dillon Gee, who was placed on the disabled list a day earlier. There was only one slight problem for Jake; he made the mistake of allowing one run, and that was enough for the Yankees to claim a 1–0 win. You see what I mean? Disrespected from day one and given zero run support from the beginning. Who knew those two things would continue for the next nine seasons as a Met?

40
V/G Yankees W-L 20-19 GB ½ H 9-10 R 11-9 E 11-9 C 0-0 W 5-6 IL 4-4
40
H/G Mets W-L 19-20 GB 3 H 9-11 R 10-9 E 7-12 C 5-7 W 4-3 IL 3-3

AL STANDINGS

	R	H	E		LOB
NYY	1	6	0		6
Met	0	3	0		6

WP Dellin Betances 2-0
LP Jacob deGrom 0-1
SV David Robertson 7

START 7:12   DATE Thursday May 15, 2014
FINISH 10:16   ATT. 40,133
TIME 304   WX Overcast 68°

Met DP/OPP   DEFENSE

Eric Young Jr. — Chris Young — Curtis Granderson
Ruben Tejada — Daniel Murphy
David Wright — 3.77 Jacob deGrom — Lucas Duda
Juan Centeno

E

① Bal 20-18
Bos] ½
NYY
Tor 1½
TB 3½

② Oct 24-12
KC
CWS
Cle] 7
Min

③ o-K 25-16
LAA 3
Sea 4½
Tex 5
Hou 11

New York Yankees Avg .266 HR 38 R/G 4.44

Met PITCHERS:
Jacob deGrom 0-0 --- IP 7 H 4 R 1 ER 1 W 2 K 6 91 P 25 BF
Scott Rice (56) IP ⅓ H 0 R 0 ER 0 W 2 K 1 3 BF
Jeurys Familia (27) IP ⅓ H 0 R 0 ER 0 W 0 K 0 1 BF
Josh Edgin (66) IP ⅓ H 0 R 0 ER 0 W 0 K 0 1 BF
Jenrry Mejia (58) IP 1 H 1 R 2 ER 0 W 0 K 1 4 BF

BENCH LH / RH
Johnson / Ryan
Suzuki / Murphy
JH
Place Beltran on DL
DL Beltran 15

©1996 Bob Carpenter Communications, Inc. All Rights Reserved

I'm a Jacob deGrom fanboy, that I admit, and it still burns my soul that he wasn't made a career Met, but on this day in May I had no idea about what was about to be born. I do remember the excitement of seeing the Mets call up young arms and throw them right in the mix of the Subway Series. Unfortunately, Matt Harvey had had Tommy John surgery and was lost for the entire 2014 season, but there were still young pitchers to be excited about. Zack Wheeler was already here, Noah Syndergaard was a hot prospect, and now two more arms were being called up. What made deGrom's start also unique is that he was facing a Yankee who joined him in making his major league debut. Chase Whitley got the ball for the Yankees, and so under the microscope of the playoff-like atmosphere of the Subway Series, we were getting dual major league debuts. Jake did not dominate this start by any stretch but gave us a preview of the moxie he would provide in tough spots. He also showed us early on he could handle the bat, when he picked up a hit in his first major league at-bat and then laid down a perfect sacrifice bunt in his second. What was so damn frustrating was not just that our offense did nothing but that it went from red hot to ice cold. In the first two games of the series at Yankee Stadium, the Mets had won 9–7 and 12–7. They then game back to Citi and got shut out by Masahiro Tanaka and couldn't scratch out a damn run against Chase Whitely and company, who held the Mets to only three singles. What's funny to look back on is that the Mets' best rally came courtesy of deGrom himself. In the third inning, Jake singled in his first major league at-bat, which chased Ruben Tejada to third base. So the Mets were set up with first and third with only one out and the top of the order coming up. Unfortunately, Eric Young Jr. popped up and Daniel Murphy would strike out looking to strand the runners. On the other hand, deGrom would make one fatal mistake, though that didn't come until the seventh inning when he allowed the eventual game-winning hit to Alfonso Soriano, a two-out double that scored Brian McCann. The Mets did put runners at the corners with two outs in the eighth, but David Robertson came in and got David Wright to ground out. It was an incredibly frustrating game, but also a very hopeful game. We saw a glimpse of the future with Jake. But little did I know we'd also witness the first night of many nights when the Mets would give deGrom no support.

KEEPING SCORE: deGrom's first Mets catcher was Juan Centeno, who would appear in 14 games for the Mets in 2013 and '14.... deGrom finished his Mets career in 2022 with the lowest ERA in Mets history (2.52), ranks fourth in strikeouts (1,607), is tied for fifth in wins (82), seventh in starts (209), and eighth in innings pitched (1,326). He also won four of his five postseason starts.... Whitley went 4⅔ innings, one out short of qualifying for the win, which went to Dellin Betances. Whitley made 24 appearances for the Yankees (12 starts) in 2014 and bounced between the majors and minors until 2018, also spending time with the Tampa Bay Rays and Atlanta Braves.

CHRIS HESTON NO-HITS THE METS

GIANTS 5 METS 0

JUNE 9, 2015, at CITI FIELD

IT'S AN OLD cliché about baseball, but it's so true. When you walk into a ballpark on any given night there's a chance you are going to see something you've never seen before. On a Tuesday night in June as the Mets returned home from a West Coast trip, my 64-year-old father was about to witness something he had never seen in the thousands of games he had attended. The Mets were sitting four games above .500 and playing mediocre baseball after they got off to a great start to the 2015 season, winning 11 straight games in mid-April. The constant issue the Mets were facing was coming from the limp bats that couldn't score runs consistently. All you had to do was look at the lineup Terry Collins was putting out every night and you could see the issues. Ruben Tejada batting second!? Michael Cuddyer, who was fast becoming a free-agent bust, was batting cleanup? It wasn't a stretch to say that one of the better Mets hitters in this lineup was the pitcher, Noah Syndergaard. The Mets went into games at this point in the season needing dominant pitching performances to win games consistently. And that's what they were getting! Jacob deGrom was quickly proving his rookie season was no fluke, Matt Harvey looked great coming off Tommy John surgery, and the rookie Syndergaard was showing early promise. But the offense was the problem, and they had a habit of making mediocre pitchers look dominant, and on this night, they most certainly did that.

Who the hell is Chris Heston? It's a fair question to have been asked going into this game. He was a 27-year-old rookie right-hander who had won five career games. I pride myself on knowing about 95 percent of the players on MLB rosters, but Heston was not someone I was overly familiar with. The only reason I even knew he had five career wins wss because I put the career stats in the pitcher box of my scorecard. I was excited to be at this game because the Mets had

59
V/G Giants W-L 32-26 GB 1 H 16-14 R 16-12 E 6-5 C 6-4 W 16-16 IL 4-1
59
H/G Mets W-L 31-27 GB+½ W-S H 21-8 R 10-19 E 21-11 C 4-10 W 3-4 IL 3-2

AL STANDINGS

	R	H	E	LOB
SF	5	13	0	8
Met	0	0	0	2

WP Chris Heston 6-4
LP Noah Syndergaard 2-4
SV ~~~~~

Met DP/OPP — DEFENSE — E

START 7:12 DATE June 9, 2015
FINISH 9:44 ATT. 23,155
TIME 232 WX clear 81°

just spent the last week and a half on the road, and my dad was in town and able to go to the game. By this point, my parents had moved to upstate New York, so my dad's Mets attendance was nowhere near what it had been in the late '90s when we would push toward 70-plus games per season. Now he was hovering around 15–20 games a year, still a healthy number, but enough games missed to potentially miss out on big moments. In 2012, when Johan Santana did the impossible in pitching the Mets' first no-hitter, he was back home in Copake Falls, New York, while I feverishly called and texted him about the craziness going on before my eyes. As a Mets season-ticket holder since the mid-1970s, he had probably been to more than 2,000 games and still had yet to witness a no-hitter in person.

Without breaking a sweat, Chris Heston breezed through the Mets lineup, retiring the first 10 batters he faced. At this point in the fourth inning, with the Mets trailing 3–0 and Heston helping his cause with a bases-loaded single, he hit Tejada and Lucas Duda back-to-back, and the Mets were set up with runners at first and second. We were thinking rally, but there was one big problem, and that was the human rally killer, Michael Cuddyer, was the next batter. When Cuddyer promptly bounced into a double play, I glanced over at my dad and made a comment that was sarcastic but turned out to be prophetic: "This nobody is gonna no-hit us, isn't he?" As the Giants slowly expanded the lead with solo home runs by Matt Duffy and Joe Panik, the Mets we're doing the cha-cha—1-2-3, 1-2-3, 1-2-3. Was this really going to happen? Were the Mets actually going to get no-hit?

Heston wasn't walking anybody, he wasn't mucking it up to the point where it would be easy to forget the Mets hadn't yet recorded a base hit. Going into the final frame, he had pitched seven 1-2-3 innings, and the only two base runners had come from those hit batsmen back in the fourth. As we entered the ninth inning, the Mets were trailing 5–0, and the question I had for my dad was a simple but complicated one: "Do you want to see a no-hitter?" This game was clearly over, and after spending more than 2,000 games at Shea Stadium and now Citi Field, I could understand if he wanted to witness history. "No way," he said. "Not this way." I was lucky enough to see Johan Santana break the Mets' no-hitter curse a few years earlier, which will always be special in my heart. But Chris Heston doing it to the Mets was certainly going to go down differently. After he hit Anthony Recker, the leadoff hitter in the ninth inning, to break his steak of retiring 13 in a row, he struck out Danny Muno and then Curtis Granderson. It was all up to the light-hitting Ruben Tejada as an audible buzz filled the half-empty stadium. The stadium was now cheering every strike call, and groaning after every ball call. It was tough to tell if that was coming from the Giants fans who had overtaken the stadium or Mets fans rooting on history. Heston threw a fastball right down the middle that was called strike three, and history was made. The Mets had been no-hit, and my father had broken his streak. It wasn't Seaver, and it wasn't Gooden...it was Chris Freakin' Heston.

KEEPING SCORE: Heston's gem was the first no-hitter against the Mets since Darryl Kile of the Houston Astros threw one at the Astrodome in September 1993 and the seventh overall at their expense.... Washington's Max Scherzer threw the eighth on the next-to-last day of the 2015 season (*see* "The Missing Scorecards," p. 377).... Heston went 12–11 as a rookie, won just one more game after that, and was out of the majors two years later after moving on to the Seattle Mariners and Minnesota Twins.

SWEEPING THE NATIONALS OUT OF FIRST PLACE

METS 5 NATIONALS 2

AUGUST 2, 2015, at CITI FIELD

THERE HASN'T BEEN a five-day period with more emotion, ups, downs, and everything in between than the days surrounding the trade deadline of 2015. When the Mets were losing a lifeless game to the Padres on Wednesday, the story became the rumored trade with the Milwaukee Brewers for Carlos Gomez and Wilmer Flores crying on the field because he thought he was being dealt there. Soon after the game the big deal (reportedly also involving Zach Wheeler) for Gomez fell through, and even though history has told us it was a major blessing in disguise, I was pissed at the time. I blamed Mets ownership for making an excuse about Gomez's health as a way to kibosh the deal. On Thursday afternoon with Joe and I on the air filling in for Mike Francesa, the Mets managed to blow a 7–1 lead that was capped off when Justin Upton smoked a ball through the

Scorecard: Washington Nationals vs. New York Mets, August 2, 2015

103 V/G Nationals W-L 54-48 GB +1 Met H 28-19 R 26-29 E 27-19 C 10-16 W 9-4 IL 8-9
105 H/G Mets W-L 54-50 GB 1 H 37-18 R 17-32 E 26-17 C 9-17 W 14-12 IL 5-4

	R	H	E	LOB
Was	2	8	0	5
Met	5	8	0	5

WP Noah Syndergaard 6-5
LP Jordan Zimmermann 8-7
SV Tyler Clippard 18

START 8:11 DATE August 2, 2015
FINISH 10:53 ATT. 35,374
TIME: 242 WX Clear 81°

raindrops for a two-out, three-run home run off Jeurys Familia that put the Padres up 8–7. When filling in for Mike, we would have to navigate a Mets game going on while also hosting a five-hour talk show—no easy task for two die-hard fans. After a long rain delay, Craig Kimbrel recorded the last three outs, and the Mets had lost a brutal game.

The next day Joe Benigno and I hosted the afternoon show from New York Giants camp as we refreshed Twitter every few seconds because the MLB trade deadline was that day at 4:00 PM. Right at the buzzer we celebrated the acquisition of Yoenis Cespedes from the Detroit Tigers. That night I was so emotionally drained from the previous 72 hours, I did something so rare I can count it on one hand—I chose to not score the Friday night game against the Nationals. As I walked into our old Long Island City apartment that night with the Mets game on DVR, I bawled out crying. I wasn't crying over anything specific, I legit just needed to let out some big-time tears. I swear to you, I wasn't crying over the Cespedes trade, or the loss to the Padres, or being stuck at Giants camp during the MLB trade deadline, I just needed to let out emotions from everything combined. That led me to just calmly starting the Mets game with no scorebook in my lap. We all know how that turned out. Late in the evening Wilmer Flores had his defining Mets moment when he walked off the Nationals with an extra-inning home run. I still remember vividly trying as hard as I could to not wake my sleeping wife next to me as Wilmer rounded the bases. That game is probably the most significant game during my Mets fandom that I do not have a scorecard of.

The next two nights at Citi Field were magical. On Saturday, the Mets pulled to within a game of the first-place Nationals, and on Sunday night a third straight victory and series sweep would put them in a tie atop the NL East. I walked into Citi Field that evening with my wife brimming with confidence. After bawling my eyes out a few days earlier from the roller coaster of the previous few days, now all of a sudden there was a different feel. Noah Syndergaard put the Mets in an early hole by allowing a solo home run to the second batter of the game, Anthony Rendon, but I remained steadfast in my confidence as they now faced a deficit against Jordan Zimmermann. Boy, was my faith rewarded, because in the third inning the Mets unleashed a blitzkrieg, all coming with two outs. Curtis Granderson, Daniel Murphy, and Lucas Duda all hit bombs, giving the Mets a commanding 5–1 lead. Syndergaard cruised through the Nationals lineup and pitched a stellar eight innings before handing the ball over to Tyler Clippard. As former National Clippard recorded the final out to secure the sweep, Citi Field was rocking. In year seven of this building, we were experiencing our first true contender, and the sounds bouncing off that stadium reflected that excitement. Raucous "Let's go, Mets!" chants filled the corridor as we departed Citi

Field with a confidence we had not had in years. The Mets were now in a first-place tie in the NL East, but after what had just happened it felt like a hell of a lot more. There was still nearly two months left in this season, but that weekend at Citi, which had followed the craziness of the trade deadline, was going to define the 2015 Mets.

KEEPING SCORE: The Mets took over sole possession of first place the next night with a 12–1 win over the Marlins in Miami and never looked back. They steadily built their lead to 6½ games by the end of August, but the Nationals cut the lead to four games heading into another three-game series, this one in Washington beginning on Labor Day. The Mets came from behind to win all three games. They rallied for three runs in the seventh to win the opener 8–5. They fell behind 7–1 the next night, then rallied for six runs in the seventh inning to tie it before Kirk Nieuwenhuis smashed a pinch-hit homer the following inning to win it. In the third game, they overcame a great pitching performance by Stephen Strasburg thanks to a game-tying pinch homer by Kelly Johnson in the eighth inning and a two-run homer by Cespedes off Drew Storen for a 4–2 victory and a three-game sweep that stretched their division lead to seven games.

THE METS WIN THE DIVISION

METS 10 REDS 2

SEPTEMBER 26, 2015, at GREAT AMERICAN BALL PARK, CINCINNATI

JUST BECAUSE something is inevitable doesn't mean it's not exciting. Yes, the Mets made it clear for a few weeks that they were going to win the 2015 National League East, but with the magic number at one and the champagne on ice, the excitement level was still through the roof for the inevitable party. There are a few things that made clinching the NL East in 2015 so freakin' special. The obvious

Baseball scorecard (Bob Carpenter Communications, Inc. scorebook):

Standings (top):
- I/SS V/G Mets — W-L 97-67 GB +8½ W+S H 48-30 R 37-37 E 46-24 C 11-20 W 21-12 IL 9-11
- I/S4 H/G Reds — W-L 63-90 GB 33½ H 34-42 R 29-48 E 16-14 C 32-38 W 8-25 IL 7-13

AL STANDINGS

Line score:
	R	H	E	LOB
Met	10	10	1	6
Cin	2	13	1	11

WP Matt Harvey 13-7
LP John Lamb 1-4
SV

START 4:11 DATE Saturday September 26, 2015
FINISH 7:08 ATT. 32,293
TIME 2:57 WX overcast 58°

DEFENSE (Cin): Adam Duvall, Jason Bourgeois, Jay Bruce, Ivan DeJesus, Brandon Phillips, Todd Frazier, Joey Votto, John Lamb (4.78), Tucker Barnhart

New York Mets AVE 247 HR 167 R/G 4.25

Batting lineup:
- 3 Curtis Granderson RF .259 24+68
- 5 David Wright 3b .307 44-14
- 52 Yoenis Cespedes CF/LF .294 35+105
- 28 Daniel Murphy 2b .294 17+70
- 7 Travis d'Arnaud C .271 12+41
- 21 Lucas Duda 1b .245 24+66
- 23 Michael Cuddyer LF .267 10+39
- 4 Wilmer Flores SS .264 16+59
- 33 Matt Harvey P .115 12-7 2-7 2.71
- 43 Addison Reed P
- 46 Tyler Clippard P
- 55 Kelly Johnson PH
- 27 Jeurys Familia P

R/ER, H, E, LOB totals rows.

LH BENCH RH:
- Johnson (LH) / Lagares, Campbell, Herrera, Uribe, Tejada, Plawecki, Recker (RH)
- Monnell, Conforto, Nieuwenhuis

Cin PITCHERS:
Cin PITCHERS	IP	H	R	ER	W	K	
1-3 4.60 John Lamb (47)	2	3	5	5	2	4	11BF 2HR
Carlos Contreras (55)	3	2	2	2	3	2	10BF
Colin Balester (51)	5	3	0	0	2	2	11BF
Ryan Matthews (71)	1	0	0	0	0	0	3BF
Burke Badenhop (33)	1	5	3	3	0	0	7BF 1HR

LH Cin BULLPEN RH: Parra, Chapman, Cingrani, Finnegan, Simpson, Iglesias / Villarreal, Hoover, LeCure, Diaz, (struck-through names)

©1996 Bob Carpenter Communications, Inc. All Rights Reserved

---

was the drought this team had had. After running away with the division in 2006, the Mets collapsed in 2007, lost a brutal race in 2008, and had been nowhere close to contention for the following six seasons. On top of that, if you are my age, 2006 was the only division championship you've seen! In 1988, when the Mets won 100 games en route to the East title, I was five years old and can't remember a

STADIUM/CAP. Great American Ball Park

	1	2	3	4	5	6	7	8	9						
Mets	4	1	2	0	0	0	0	0	3						
Reds	0	2	0	0	0	0	0	0	0						

NL STANDINGS

Ⓐ Met 87-67 #1
WAS 8½s
Mia 20
Atl 25
Phi 29

Ⓑ P-StL 77-57 #6
P-Pit 3 w7
P-Cub 7½
Miw 32
Cin 33½ L6

Ⓒ LAD 87-CC · #2
SF ½
Arz 13½
SD 15½
Col 23½

Ⓓ 1.Pit 94-60
2.Cub 81-64

3 of 4
Season Series (6 of 7)
5-0 Met

☆ Mets clinch NL East ☆
Cin division title
8th playoff appearance

Mets clinch NL East

| Cincinnati Reds | Ave | HR | RIG | 1 | 2 | 3 | 4 | 5 | 6 | 7 | 8 | 9 | 10 | 11 | 12 | AB 13 | R 14 | H 15 | BI |

PITCHERS

Met PITCHERS	IP	H	R	ER	W	K	
Matt Harvey 24-17 2.56	㉝	6⅔	9	2	2	0	6
Addison Reed ㊼	7⅓	1	0	0	0	0	
Tyler Clippard ㊺	8	1	1	0	0	1	1
Jeurys Familia ㉗	9	1	2	0	0	0	1

thing. So if you were born after 1980, there is a real good chance that your memories of division titles only included the 2006 season. This team was also unique in that a division title certainly didn't look or feel likely as the their limp offense held the team back. After starting the season 15–5, the Mets played mediocre baseball, including a seven-game losing streak in late June that dropped them below .500

at 36–37. Even at the trade deadline, they sat at a very average 52–50, and the only reason they were still in a race is because the rest of the division was struggling too. So even as late as August 1, this felt like an average baseball team. The other issue that popped up was the Matt Harvey conundrum. Out of the clear blue sky in early September, Harvey's agent, Scott Boras, had declared that Matt had a strict innings limit and there was a chance he would not pitch in the playoffs. "Are you fucking kidding me?!" I and every other Met fan screamed. The Dark Knight, who was having a tremendous season coming off Tommy John surgery, wasn't going to pitch in the playoffs? This has to be some sick joke. Luckily, a few days later, Harvey wrote an article in the *Players' Tribune* that clarified his status for October. While the Mets would lighten his workload in September with the division seemingly in hand, he would indeed be unrestricted for the postseason run.

After all that drama, here we were on a Saturday afternoon with the Mets one win away from winning the NL East. It was a late afternoon start in Cincinnati, 4:00 PM, and my wife and I had plans to go to a friend's party later that evening. Harvey was on the mound making just his third start since Scott Boras opened up that can of worms three weeks earlier. The Mets had started to restrict his pitch count a bit, so the idea that Harvey could be on the mound as the Mets clinched the division was very, very unlikely. The potential drama from this game was taken out very early when Lucas Duda crushed a first-inning grand slam off a rookie named John Lamb to set the tone for what kind of day this would be. Even after Harvey gave two runs back in the second, Michael Cuddyer of all people cracked a two-run double the following inning that put the Mets up 7–2. The exclamation point on this three-hour party was David Wright hitting a ninth-inning home run. David was still the face of this team and had missed a huge chunk of time, but was back and playing every day at the perfect time of the season. He had only played a handful of games in April before going on the shelf. When he returned in late August, he supplied a baseball and life moment I will never forget. In his first at-bat after missing 115 games, he dramatically hit a home run against the Phillies at Philadelphia. This was also five days before my wedding, and during the at-bat my soon-to-be wife was not so pleased with my lack of help in planning the wedding. She was giving me an earful as I tried to watch David's at-bat. When he crushed it to left, I jumped off the couch in excitement. She was even less pleased than before, to put it mildly. But David's dramatic return will forever be connected to one of the first fights my wife and I ever had. Thank you, David, for making that brutal fight a little more bearable. Jeurys Familia came on to make the party official, and in a sense of irony I wouldn't pick up until the following year, he struck out Jay Bruce to make winning the NL East official. I hugged my wife in celebration, and we had a celebrity toast of some nice wine we had bought. I teared up a bit thinking about the season and how special it was to watch my team win the NL East. There were obviously bigger fish to fry now, but the 162-game accomplishment of winning the division was worth enjoying. That night we went out partying, and I don't remember much...but I do remember the feeling of embracing my wife with a tear in my eye. The Mets were the 2015 NL East champions!

KEEPING SCORE: Harvey struck out six batters in six innings to win his fifth straight decision.... The Mets traded for Bruce in 2016, traded him to the Cleveland Indians in 2017, brought him back as a free agent in 2018, then traded him after that season to the Seattle Mariners in the Edwin Diaz trade. He then moved on to the Philadelphia Phillies before finishing his career with the Yankees in 2021.

THE RETURN OF OCTOBER BASEBALL

METS 3 DODGERS 1
GAME 1, NATIONAL LEAGUE DIVISION SERIES
OCTOBER 9, 2015, at DODGER STADIUM, LOS ANGELES

NINE YEARS is a long freakin' time. Do the math, and that's more than 3,000 days and a lot of meaningless baseball games. But the drought was about to end. After getting red hot in August and September, the Mets turned the 2015 NL East into a rout as they secured the franchise's first division championship and postseason appearance since 2006. When the Mets' season ended in heartbreak fashion on that October night in 2006 at Shea Stadium, the expectation was that we would be back very shortly with a chance to redeem ourselves for how things ended. That day never came, and it served as a sports life lesson that you should never take success for granted because it's fleeting and may elude you for a long time. Well, this had been a long-ass time, but the drought was over. The Mets were in Los Angeles to face a Dodgers team that only won two more games than the Mets in winning the NL West. The great Clayton Kershaw would not only be facing the Mets but his postseason demons as he took on the second-year right-hander Jacob deGrom.

While I loved that the often-disrespected Jacob deGrom was getting the Game 1 nod, it came with a little bit of an asterisk. Matt Harvey was still viewed by most Mets fans as the ace of the team but was not getting the ball for the playoff opener for reasons that didn't have to do with his regular season performance. A month earlier, a major controversy erupted when his agent, Scott Boras, talked about Matt protecting his arm and not pitching the postseason because of an innings limit. While avoiding the postseason would have been a Strasburg-like disaster, it seemed like the compromise was that while he would pitch in October, the Mets would be strategic about how often he threw. So deGrom would pitch Game 1 and Noah Syndergaard would pitch in Game 2, with both being legit possibilities to throw multiple times in the best-of-five series. Harvey would then start only one time in the series by pitching Game 3. Even though

A hand-filled baseball scorecard (©1996 Bob Carpenter Communications, Inc. All Rights Reserved). Mets vs. Dodgers at Dodger Stadium, NLDS Game 1. Mets 3, Dodgers 1 (visible inning line scores). Defense positions include Michael Cuddyer, Yoenis Cespedes, Curtis Granderson, Ruben Tejada, Daniel Murphy, David Wright, Jacob deGrom (3.43), Lucas Duda, Travis d'Arnaud. Dodgers lineup: Carl Crawford, Howie Kendrick, Corey Seager, Adrian Gonzalez, Justin Turner, Andre Ethier, A.J. Ellis / Jimmy Rollins, Joc Pederson. Pitchers: Clayton Kershaw, Pedro Baez, Chris Hatcher, Joel Peralta, Chris Hatcher. Mets pitchers: Jacob deGrom, Tyler Clippard, Jeurys Familia.

Jake had statistically been the best pitcher of the staff, the perception had not changed that Matt was *the* guy. But in order to protect his workload, he was getting Game 3.

I went into this game and series having zero idea what to expect. This was still a young Mets team that had put it all together over the last few months, and there wasn't an October track record to look back on. Despite Kershaw's postseason bumps, I still could only think back to how Kershaw dominated the Mets a few months earlier, flirting with a perfect game at Citi Field. The Mets couldn't hit Clayton early, but it didn't matter as deGrom was matching him with zeroes of his own. The Dodgers were putting base runners on against deGrom, but Jake would just pile up strikeouts to work his way out of trouble. Before I knew it, I looked down at my score-card and noticed that the deGrom K total was getting obscene very early. When he struck out Corey Seager to end the fifth inning, his total had already reached 10. Meanwhile, Daniel Murphy was about to write an October script none of us saw coming, and he started it with a shocking long ball against Kershaw to break the tie in the fourth inning.

Jake was making the 1–0 lead hold up as he somehow managed to work through any trouble he had in front of him, which usually involved a hit by Justin Turner. Finally, the top of the seventh inning would be a Monday morning quarterback's dream. Up 1–0 with runners on first and second with one out, Terry Collins had a huge decision to make—should he keep deGrom in to lay down a bunt, or should he go for the jugular and use a pinch-hitter? I pleaded at the TV to allow Jake to remain in the game, and somehow my prayers from thousands of miles away worked! Jake stayed in and laid down a bunt to advance the runners, and when Curtis Granderson drew a walk (the third of the inning allowed by Kershaw), Dodgers manager Don Mattingly did something I also hoped would happen. With Kershaw laboring, Mattingly pulled him in favor of right-hander Pedro Baez to take on David Wright with the bases loaded. While there is no doubt Kershaw was on his last legs, I still would rather see Wright against a reliever than Wright against an all-time great arm. I vividly remember David working the count full and telling my wife sitting next to me, "This feels like the game." Could the Mets really just win a game 1–0? I felt like they needed the cushion, and they needed it right now. On 3–2, David hit a line drive right back up the box that fell onto the beautiful Dodger Stadium green grass and into center field. Lucas Duda and Ruben Tejada scored, and the Mets would get the insurance I was begging for to make it a 3–0 game. Jake would reward the decision to let him hit by pitching a 1-2-3 seventh inning, which put an exclamation point on a brilliant postseason debut—7 IP, 0 runs, 13 Ks...damn! The game would not end without drama when closer Jeurys Familia was needed to record a four-out save. He came in, up 3–1, with Justin Turner at the plate as the tying run. Familia calmly got Turner out and then made things stress-free in the ninth with a 1-2-3 inning, retiring Andre Ethier, Jimmy Rollins, and Joc Pederson on ground balls. The Mets had taken Game 1 in Los Angeles, and as I closed my scorebook well after 1:00 AM, I took a deep breath. That old October playoff rush was back, and it felt so damn good after a win.

KEEPING SCORE: It was the Mets' first postseason victory since defeating the Cardinals 4–2 in Game 6 of the 2006 NLCS behind John Maine.... The Mets had advanced to the championship series that year by defeating the Dodgers in a three-game sweep.... Wright was the only Met to appear in both the 2006 and 2015 postseasons.

THE CHASE UTLEY GAME

DODGERS 5 METS 2

GAME 2, NATIONAL LEAGUE CHAMPIONSHIP SERIES

OCTOBER 10, 2015, at DODGER STADIUM, LOS ANGELES

I TOOK A major risk before Game 2 of the 2015 NLDS. After watching Jacob deGrom dominate and the Mets take a 1–0 lead in the best-of-five series, I decided to change locale for my viewing experience of the second game. My wife and I were visiting my folks upstate, so while it was cool I was going to watch this pivotal playoff game with my dad, I knew that I was risking screwing up the juju of the victory from my Long Island City apartment. It was another late-night start, but honestly they could have started this game at 2:00 AM and it wouldn't have mattered to me. Let's freakin' go! The Mets were up 1–0 in the series, and with rookie Noah Syndergaard on the mound they had a chance to take a stranglehold. I'm not a believer in the theory of "house money" games. Granted, even if the Mets lost Game 2, they would have done their job by getting a split in Los Angeles. But that's not how I view things, especially in the midst of a series. While a split is nice, you know what's even nicer? Taking the Dodgers' spirit and putting them one loss away from extinction. Losing this game risked giving the Dodgers new life and new hope.

I felt very, very good when Yoenis Cespedes and Michael Conforto hit solo home runs off Zach Greinke in the second inning, giving the Mets a quick 2–0 lead. But besides the early offense against a pitcher who somehow sported a ridiculous 1.66 ERA during the regular season, I was very encouraged by what Syndergaard was doing early on. Noah was still a very young, inexperienced rookie and escaped some damage in the second and third innings that kept the lead at two runs. Noah was showing great poise in his first career postseason start. Even in the fourth inning, when he gave up back-to-back doubles to Justin Turner and Andre Ethier, he still managed to limit the damage by only giving up one run to maintain the lead. Noah held on to that 2–1 lead all the way into the seventh inning... the inning that would change everything. The inning that would live in Mets history, that would take a nondescript Met to new heights, and would take a Mets heel and make him arguably the biggest villain in Mets history.

With runners on first and third with one out and the Mets nursing a one-run lead, Bartolo Colon relieved Syndergaard and got Howie Kendrick to hit a humpback line drive to second baseman Daniel Murphy, who fielded it off one hop and flipped to shortstop Ruben Tejada, who was making a 360-degree turn as he caught the ball and touched second base (or so we thought). Chase Utley barreled into him, allowing the tying run to score, breaking up the double play, and subsequently breaking Ruben Tejada in the process. I jumped up to scream, "Illegal slide!" hoping the umpires would

Scorecard (Bob Carpenter Communications scorebook):

V/G Mets — W-L 1-0 — GB +1 — H 0-0 — R 1-0 — E 0-0 — C 0-0 — W 1-0 — IL 0-0
H/G Dodgers — W-L 0-1 — GB 1 — H 0-1 — R 0-0 — E 0-1 — C 0-0 — W 0-0 — IL 0-0

AL STANDINGS

	R	H	E	LOB
Met	2	5	0	1
LAD	5	7	0	6

WP Zack Greinke 1-0
LP Noah Syndergaard 0-1
SV Kenley Jansen 1

START 9:07 DATE October 10, 2015 (Saturday)
FINISH 12:31 ATT. 54,445
TIME 324 WX Clear 90°

LAD DP/OPP DEFENSE

Carl Crawford — Enrique Hernandez — Andre Ethier
Corey Seager — Howie Kendrick
Justin Turner — (3.00 / 2.... Greinke) — Adrian Gonzalez
Yasmani Grandal

New York Mets — Avg 161 — HR 1 — R/G 3.00

New York Mets	AB	R	H	BI
3 Curtis Granderson RF	12	13	14	15
5 David Wright 3b				
28 Daniel Murphy 2b				
52 Yoenis Cespedes CF				
21 Lucas Duda 1b				
7 Travis d'Arnaud C				
30 Michael Conforto LF				
11 Ruben Tejada SS / 4 Wilmer Flores SS				

34 Noah Syndergaard P
40 Bartolo Colon P
43 Addison Reed P
44 Jon Niese P
47 Hansel Robles P
55 Kenley Jansen P

	1	2	3	4	5	6	7	8	9
R/ER	0/0	2/2	0/0	0/0	0/0	0/0	0/0	0/0	0/0
H	1	2	0	1	0	1	0	0	0
E	0	0	0	0	0	0	0	0	0
LOB	0	0	0	0	0	0	0	0	1

LH BENCH RH
Nieuwenhuis — Plawecki
Johnson — Legares
Cuddyer
Flores

LAD PITCHERS	IP	H	R	ER	W	K		
Zack Greinke	7	5	2	2	0	8	238F 2HR	110 P
Chris Hatcher	1	0	0	0	0	2	3BF	
Kenley Jansen	1	1	0	0	0	1	4BF	

LH LAD BULLPEN RH
Avilan — Baez — Peralta — Garcia
Wood — Hatcher
Howell

Starters:
Anderson
Kershaw

rule a DP and end the inning. We could see immediately that Tejada was in major pain as he lay on the ground. Utley promptly got up and jogged to the Dodgers dugout, proud of what he had accomplished. As Tejada lay in pain, the umpires decided to review the play to see if Tejada had come off the bag a millisecond too early. "Are you freaking kidding me!" I screamed to my dad. "There is no way they can

STADIUM/CAP. Dodger Stadium

	1	2	3	4	5	6	7	8	9
Mets	0	2	0	0	0	0	0	0	
Dodgers	0	0	0	1	0	0	4	0	x

NL STANDINGS

DEFENSE

NLDS Game 2
1-0 Met

Tejada rolled off field after Utley took out Slide in 7th.

LAD CH
Utley out at 2nd in 7th is overturned even though he never touched 2nd.

	Los Angeles Dodgers												AB	R	H	BI

©1996 Bob Carpenter Communications, Inc. All Rights Reserved

Met PITCHERS		IP	H	R	ER	W	K
Noah Syndergaard		6⅓	5	3	3	4	9
Bartolo Colon		7	0	0	1	1	0
Addison Reed		7⅓	2	1	1	0	0
Jon Niese		7⅓	0	0	0	0	1
Hansel Robles		8	1	0	0	0	2

overturn this!" So my focus was not on Utley being dirty or even the pain Tejada was in. I was consumed with the idea that the umpires were going to rule Utley safe at second and in a tie game give the Dodgers runners at first and second with only one out, as opposed to just a runner on first with two outs. As Tejada was carted off the field, the umpires inexplicably ruled that Utley was safe. So the guy who committed the play that fractured Tejada's right leg and *never* touched second base was going to be awarded the bag? This moment felt like a series-turning point, and I was fuming. Adrián González and Justin Turner would make us pay with back-to-back doubles off Addison Reed. The Dodgers took a lead they would never relinquish and go on to win the game, changing the trajectory of the series.

Now let's get to Utley. I don't like Chase, never liked Chase, and he will always go down as a Mets killer, but my anger on this night was directed at the umpires more than him. Utley did (while dirty) what we want all our players to do, play the game hard and try to win at all costs. The fact is, the umpires flat out missed *two* calls on this play. First, it should have been ruled an illegal slide since he didn't even begin his slide until he was essentially at second base. But if you're going to miss that, you certainly can't overrule the call on the field and have him called safe. Both decisions completely changed the trajectory of Game 2. I don't believe Utley intended to hurt Tejada on the play, but he was playing the game the way he had for his entire career—he was focused on blowing up the double play opportunity. If no one gets hurt on this play, I don't think he gets suspended, nor does he get the backlash from Mets fans that he's gotten. Chase Utley is now more known for this play than the destruction he caused the Mets as a killer in Philadelphia. In the process, Ruben Tejada sort of became a cult hero! He received a rousing standing ovation at Citi Field when he returned sporting a Mets cane.

This loss felt worse in the moment than it would turn out to be, because the Mets would win the series, but on this Saturday night I was pissed and worried. Pissed at the umpiring crew, pissed at Addison Reed, and pissed at myself. Because, after all, maybe Utley doesn't destroy Tejada's leg if I'm watching this game at home in LIC!

KEEPING SCORE: Utley appealed his two-game suspension and remained active for the rest of the series. MLB then dropped the suspension the following spring. During his 16-year career with the Phillies and Dodgers, Utley had more runs scored (116), hits (197), and home runs (39) against the Mets than he did against any opponent.... The Mets released Tejada during spring training in 2016, and he went on to play for the St. Louis Cardinals and Baltimore Orioles before returning to play six games for the Mets in 2019.

METS IN FIVE

METS 3 DODGERS 2
GAME 5, NATIONAL LEAGUE DIVISION SERIES
OCTOBER 15, 2015, at DODGER STADIUM, LOS ANGELES

I HAD NO idea what to expect—no gut feeling, no premonition, simply no clue—going into the winner-take-all Game 5 of the National League Divisional Series. I had nothing. The Mets were two and a half months removed from being a struggling .500 team, and now they were looking to close out the NL West champions at Dodger Stadium. The Mets had won Game 1 when deGrom out-dueled Kershaw, lost Game 2 hampered by a brutal umpiring call, blew the Dodgers out in Game 3 by scoring 13 runs, and squandered a chance to close out the series at Citi by losing Game 4 to Clayton Kershaw. So now it was set up to be a win-or-go-home game with Jacob deGrom taking on Zack Greinke. I'm not a spiritual person, yet that didn't stop me from desperately asking the baseball gods for a favor. "Dear Babe Ruth, Ty Cobb, and Satchel Paige: Just give me Game 5.... If you give me Game 5, I won't ask for anything else from this season, but please deliver me this win tonight." Of course, I was lying! Sure, I wanted to win Game 5, but as soon as that concluded, I would be begging for the NLCS, then I'd beg even more for a world championship, but in the moment all I needed was a tiny victory in a winner-take-all game. Because I was too young for 1986 and 1988, this was only my second winner-take-all game in my postseason history as a Mets fan, and the other time, 2006, didn't exactly go well.

5
V/G Mets W-L 2-2 GB even H 1-1 R 1-1 E 0-0 C 0-0 W 2-2 IL 0-0
5
H/G Dodgers W-L 2-2 GB even H 1-1 R 1-1 E 2-2 C 0-0 W 0-0 IL 0-0

AL STANDINGS

	R	H	E	LOB
Met	3	7	1	6
LAD	2	6	0	8

WP Jacob deGrom 2-0
LP Zack Greinke 1-1
SV Jeurys Familia 2

START 8:07 DATE October 15, 2015 (Thursday)
FINISH 11:20 ATT. 54,602
TIME 3:13 WX clear 74°

LAD DP/OPP   DEFENSE   E

Enrique Hernandez   Joc Pederson   Andre Ethier

Corey Seager   Howie Kendrick

Justin Turner   (4.89 Zack Greinke)   Adrian Gonzalez

Yasmani Grandal

ALCS
Tor 93-57
KC 95-57

ALDS
Hou 2
KC 3
Tex 2
Tor 3

WC
Hou def NYY

New York Mets	Avg 206	HR 6	R/G 4.75	1	2	3	4	5	6	7	8	9	10	11	AB 12	R 13	H 14	BI 15
3 Curtis Granderson RF 427 0 0 5						3-1	7	7										
5 David Wright 3b 083 0 0 2				K	K	7	0-3	L4									
28 Daniel Murphy 2b 235 2 0 3							4-3										
52 Yoenis Cespedes CF/LF 313 2 0 4				K	8	K	K										
21 Lucas Duda 1b 133 0 0				K	88	7	C										
7 Travis d'Arnaud C 178 1 0 3				K	F7	3-1	F3										
30 Michael Conforto LF 250 1 0 2 / 12 Juan Lagares CF 333 0 1 0				7	FC	1-3											
4 Wilmer Flores SS 276 0 0 0				K	K		88										
48 Jacob deGrom P / 35 Kelly Johnson PH / 34 Noah Syndergaard P / 27 Jeurys Familia P								K									
R/ER			1/1	0/0	0/0	1/1	0/0	1/1	0/0	0/0	0/0							
H			2	0	0	1	0	2	0	0								
E			0	0	0	0	0	0	0	0								
LOB			1	0/1	0/1	1/2	0/2	0/2	2/4	0/4	2/6							

LH BENCH RH
Nieuwenhuis Reynolds
Johnson Plawecki
Colabello
Lagares

LAD PITCHERS		IP	H	R	ER	W	K	103 P
Zack Greinke		6 2/3	6	3	3	1	9	27 BF 1HR
Luis Avilan (43)		1/3	0	0	0	0	0	1 BF
Chris Hatcher (41)	8	1	0	0	0	0	1	3 BF
Kenley Jansen (74)	9	1	1	0	0	1	1	5 BF

LH LAD BULLPEN RH
Kershaw Hatcher
Avilan Baez
Anderson
Wood Peralta
Howell Garcia

My dad and my wife sat down next to me as the clock struck 8:00 PM local time, and the witching hour was upon us. My beautiful wife understood my fandom, but it was still relatively new for her. We had been married just 45 days earlier, and she was about to witness a game like she had never seen before. Every single pitch of this game was like surgery and was filled with stress like you would

Scorecard: Dodger Stadium. Mets vs Dodgers. NLDS Game 5, 2-2. Handwritten baseball scorecard.

never believe. When Curtis Granderson began the game with an infield single and was driven in by Daniel Murphy's RBI double, the exhilaration filling our third floor apartment was off the charts. But the game really began in the bottom of the first because Mets manager Terry Collins was about to be tested in a major way. Knowing what we would find out later about Jacob deGrom's competitiveness would make Terry's faith in him much more understandable, but in the moment, Collins stuck with Jake when most of us were ready to pull the plug. In the bottom of the first inning, deGrom allowed four consecutive hits to flip the score in the Dodgers' favor, 2–1. With two on and one out in an elimination game, I was ready to pull him. As good as Jake was in Game 1, we didn't know if he was simply imploding under the hot lights of a winner-take-all game. Collins didn't blink. DeGrom calmly struck out Yasmani Grandal and Kiké Hernández to strand those two runners. Okay, it's a 2–1 game, not the end of the world yet. In the second inning, deGrom issued a lead-off walk to the No. 8 hitter, Joc Pederson, and after Wilmer Flores made a defensive miscue, there were again runners on first and second with one out, but this time it was Corey Seager and Adrián González facing deGrom. While all of that trouble wasn't deGrom's fault, again the Mets were in a spot where pulling him wouldn't have been nuts. But again, Terry Collins showed faith as deGrom struck out the No. 2 and 3 hitters back to back. The third inning may have been his most magical. After Justin Turner continued to destroy Mets pitching by picking up a leadoff double, deGrom, facing yet another first-and-second, one-out jam, calmly fielded a comebacker hit by Hernández and turned a 1-6-3 double play.

This was now truly insane—deGrom was escaping jam after jam unscathed and showing the poise of a legend. At this point deGrom and Collins had won me over. I was no longer thinking about yank-ing deGrom when he was in trouble, because I now fully expected him to escape trouble time after time. And it continued! In both the fourth and fifth innings, deGrom worked his way through run-ner-on-second, one-out jams. This was a freakin' clinic. All the while, the Mets had tied the game in the fourth and then took the lead two innings later when Daniel Murphy, who had scored the tying run on Travis d'Arnaud's sac fly after stealing an uncovered third base, put the exclamation point on a very good Division Series by hitting a home run against Greinke. The only inning where deGrom didn't face major trouble would turn out to be his final inning on the rub-ber, the sixth, when he set down the Dodgers 1-2-3. At this point

I was all for him staying in the game, but Collins chose to pinch-hit for deGrom in the seventh with a runner on first and two out. That meant the Mets needed to get nine more outs to win this series while nursing a tiny one-run lead. The nerves in my stomach were hitting a fever pitch.

At this point, my wife left the room. My dad was quiet as we watched anxiously as Noah Syndergaard pitched a very solid seventh inning, striking out both Seager and Justin Turner. Jeurys Familia was given the ball in the eighth to record a Mariano Rivera–like, six-out, postseason save. Could he do it? My confidence was not high, especially knowing that the prick himself, Chase Utley, was lurking as a bat off the bench. That eventual Utley at-bat was the scariest baseball moment I may have ever faced. Leading off the ninth inning, Dodgers manager Don Mattingly went to the Utley chip as he pinch-hit for Pederson. Of all the moments from this incredible game, this at-bat is still my clearest vision and memory from this evening. The crowd at Dodger Stadium was electric and filled with "Utley!" chants as he made his first appearance in this series since he obliterated Ruben Tejada's leg. Strike one.... Ball one, a touch off the plate.... Foul ball.... And then the moment of truth. Familia threw a hanger, and Utley hit the crap out of it. When watching a game on TV, you have that split second between the swing and then seeing where the ball is going. After that beautiful swing by Utley, it felt like it took forever to then see where the ball was traveling. Luckily, it was traveling right into the glove of Curtis Granderson standing his ground in right field. When that out was recorded, there was a sigh of relief between me and my father almost like we knew without saying what we thought now. We were gonna win his game, but no way in hell would we say this out loud. Familia would then calmly get the next two outs very quickly, and I swear to you, my excitement from that final out matches any Mets game I've ever seen in my lifetime. As Howie Kendrick struck out swinging, I jumped into the air and hugged my dad. My wife came running in and she hugged me too. This was an exhilarating win, and for my money the most satisfying win of my Mets fandom. The eerie silence coming out of the TV from

Los Angeles, California, reminded me of the silence we experienced nine years earlier when the Cardinals shut Shea Stadium up. It will never make up for that loss, but being on the right side of a game like this was what sports dreams are made of. What a night, what a game, what a series. Jacob deGrom became a man that night. Terry Collins had finally earned my trust, and it was off to the NLCS.

KEEPING SCORE: The series victory over the Dodgers gave the Mets a perfect 4–0 record in the Division Series round…. Murphy hit .333 (7-for-21) with three home runs in the series and was just heating up…. The game came on the 29th anniversary of the Mets' 16-inning victory over the Astros at Houston to clinch the 1986 National League pennant.

COMPLETING THE PENNANT SWEEP

METS 8 CUBS 3
GAME 4, NATIONAL LEAGUE CHAMPIONSHIP SERIES
OCTOBER 21, 2015, at WRIGLEY FIELD, CHICAGO

WHEN A TEAM has a 3–0 lead, the series is over…right? In the NBA it's been over 100 percent of the time, and in baseball it's been over every single time with the lone exception of 2004, when the Red Sox came back against the Yankees. But when you are the ones holding the seemingly insurmountable 3–0 lead, do we really think it's over? Well, in 2015, I had a chance to experience my first example of this as a Mets fan. I remember being down 3–0 to the Braves in 1999 and trying to talk myself into how they could come back, but now we were on the other side of it. The Mets had taken a commanding 3–0 lead over the Chicago Cubs and needed one win to secure the pennant. So here is what scared me, and it had nothing to do with the 2015 Mets. When the Red Sox pulled off the only comeback from three games down in MLB history, it felt as if it had to happen that way. Remember, the Sox were still in the midst of their "curse," or championship drought, whatever you want to call it, and coming back from 3–0 down to the Yankees of all teams seemed like the perfect way to end the curse. Holding a 3–0 lead on the team with the

	1	2	3	4	5	6	7	8	9						
Mets	4	2	0	0	0	0	0	2	0						
Cubs	0	0	0	1	0	0	0	2	0						

STADIUM/CAP. Wrigley Field

NLCS Game 4
3-0 Met
Mets win NL Pennant
1st since 2000, 5th in franchise history

Murphy sets PlayOff record w/ HR in 6th straight G
NLCS MVP
Daniel Murphy

		Chicago Cubs	Ave 207	HR 15	RIG 3.63

longest championship drought in baseball history felt eerily familiar to me. There was nothing about the first three games that caused me angst, it was simply baseball history, and the fact that if the Cubs were going to shatter their curse going back to 1908, might it happen the same way it did for the Sox just 11 years earlier? That was the fear I could not fight off.

At the time, I was living with my wife of just two months when I floated an idea her way. "Hey, hon, what do you think of me flying to Chicago today to potentially see the Mets win the pennant?" She was fully supportive of me doing so but could not join me on that trip and neither could my dad. The bosses at WFAN had approved me doing the following day's show from a Chicago studio if needed, so the only thing keeping me from Wrigley Field that night was *me*. Did I want to fly to Chicago by myself and either celebrate the second pennant of my lifetime, or be stuck there for a second day with the risk that I flew to Chicago to see the beginning of an all- time collapse? It was 8:00 AM on the Wednesday morning of the game, and I had to make a final call before I began my midday show that day two hours later. I had found a flight that would land me in Chicago with a few hours to spare before Game 4, but did I really want to do this? I went back and forth debating the pros and cons, but I knew that my decision had to come really quick. Ultimately, I decided against the idea, and what I told my wife (and myself) was that, if the Mets won the pennant, I wanted to celebrate that special moment with her, like we did for the dramatic Game 5 win over the Dodgers a week earlier. In the back of my mind, I also wondered something all men have thought about—was she testing me? Did she really not want me to go, but was just telling me it was okay? After many more years of marriage, I'm now 1,000 percent sure it was *not* a test, but at the time...how the hell did I know? So I made the decision so stay. But I also think a small part of me was scared of the outcome of the game.

Much like when the Mets won the pennant 15 years earlier, the series-clinching win was one giant party. I clearly had nothing to be scared of! Lucas Duda and Travis d'Arnaud went back to back in the first inning off Jason Hammel, and then Duda struck a two-run double in the second. It was 6–0 Mets, and the rout was on. Any fear of this turning into 2004 was quickly extinguished. As my wife sat next to me, she asked me numerous times throughout the momentous evening, "Do you regret not going?" The honest answer years later... sorta. I stand by my initial thought that celebrating a pennant with my wife was indeed special. She was still getting to fully realize my crazed sports fandom, so her seeing me cry for like the fourth time in a month over the Mets was necessary! With that said, watching David Wright spray champagne on the Mets fans who made the trip did cause a little bit of envy. Partying with strangers in Chicago after advancing to the World Series could have been epic and certainly memorable. "You know what, baby," I said to my wife as we watched the Mets celebrate, "we will go to the World Series for Games 6 and 7 and either experience the beauty of a championship or the pain of defeat. So it's okay that we missed Chicago." I came oh so close to that vision, but never got the chance.

KEEPING SCORE: Since starting pitcher Steven Matz was removed from the game one batter shy of qualifying for the victory, Bartolo Colon came in to get credit for the W.... The Mets did not trail in any of the four games of the series.... Daniel Murphy homered in each game and set a postseason record by hitting a home run in six consecutive postseason games dating back to the last two games of the Division Series.... The Cubs would go on to break their curse a year later by beating the Cleveland Indians in the World Series.

DÉJÀ VU OF THE WORST KIND

ROYALS 5 METS 4 (14 INNINGS)
GAME 1, WORLD SERIES
OCTOBER 27, 2015, at KAUFFMAN STADIUM, KANSAS CITY

AFTER THE METS finished off the Chicago Cubs to win the 2015 National League pennant, I lived in ecstasy for a few days. I didn't let the future concern me, I was truly living in the moment and could enjoy advancing to just my second World Series as a fan. This was a truly surprising run that felt impossible just a few shorts months earlier, and now we were sitting back with our feet up waiting to see who the Mets would face in the World Series. Two days later, the panic started to sink in, and I know the exact moment it hit me like a ton of bricks. The moment I sat down (scorebook in hand) to watch Game 6 of the ALCS with the Royals looking to close the Blue Jays out, the fear of losing struck me like lightning. Every batter that came up, every pitch that was thrown, I started to envision those guys facing my team in a few short days. I have also learned by this point that you can't take anything for granted. Just because the Mets have this really good young rotation that seems to be on the rise doesn't mean the Mets will get another chance in the Fall Classic anytime soon. On the midday show with Joe B, a few fans even tried the whole "the Mets are playing with house money" card. I found that to be completely foolish and naïve. We are here, and you have to take advantage of this moment because the likelihood is that you won't get another crack anytime soon. We as Mets fans should know that more than anyone. I wanted the Blue Jays to win Game 6, and then in a winner-take all-game I'd decide who'd I'd rather face, but in this moment I preferred the series get extended to the limit. It did not. The Royals closed out Game 6, and our fate was sealed. The first-ever all-expansion team World Series—the New York Mets vs. the Kansas City Royals.

Since the Mets clearly weren't going to use their starters on short rest, the plan of starting Harvey in Game 1 and deGrom in Game 2 was totally fine with me. Matt's second start would be at Citi, and Jake would be poised to take the ball in a huge Game 6 on the road where he has already shown he can handle any kind of pressure. The nerves were killing me as I awaited first pitch in my Long Island City apartment, as this was the first time I'd watch a Mets World Series game on TV. In 2000, I was fortunate enough to be at all five games. When the Mets went down 1-2-3 in the top of the first, a bad feeling crept through my entire body. Throughout the entire post-season, I had seen Alcides Escobar, the Royals leadoff hitter, attack first pitches, so I was hopeful Matt would send a message early and put one close to his ear. He did not...and Escobar pounded a ball to center, where Yoenis Cespedes and Michael Conforto converged

©1996 Bob Carpenter Communications, Inc. All Rights Reserved

and it fell between them. To make matters worse, Cespedes kicked the ball to left field. As Conforto chased it down, Escobar was flying around the bases. Are you kidding me? Is the World Series going to really start with an inside-the-park home run? It did. That 1–0 deficit seemed to last forever, but to the credit of Matt Harvey, he bounced back very strongly from that unfortunate start to the game.

The Mets tied it in the fourth inning on Travis d'Arnaud's RBI single and then scored runs in the fifth on Curtis Granderson's home run and in the sixth thanks to a sac fly by Conforto to take a 3–1 lead against Royals starter Edinson Volquez. Winning Game 1 had now become a must, especially with my only other Mets World Series memory being how a Game 1 essentially cost them a series in 2000.

The Royals scratching out two runs across against Harvey in the sixth inning to tie the game was huge, and I knew it at the time. Despite the two runs Harvey gave up, I was very pleased with his outing—six innings, five hits, three runs. The Mets were able to regain the lead in the eighth as a two-out error by Royals first baseman Eric Hosmer allowed Juan Lagares to score the go-ahead run. In the bottom of the inning, the Royals put two runners on with two out against Tyler Clippard, and Terry Collins decided to go for the kill. Jeurys Familia had already shown in the playoffs that asking for more than three outs to get a save wasn't a problem, so Terry asked him to do it again. He calmly and quickly got Mike Moustakas to ground out, and the inning was over. The Mets now stood three outs away from a 1–0 series lead. These commercial breaks felt like waiting forever at the DMV—the nerves were at an all-time high.

As the bottom of the ninth inning started, all I could think about was Paul O'Neill. I mean, I couldn't shake the ghosts of the 2000 World Series as the Mets stood in the exact same place. Salvador Perez, the Royals catcher, grounded out—sorta like how Jorge Posada, the Yankees catcher, flied out to start that infamous ninth inning 15 years earlier. And then a left-handed hitting outfielder, Alex Gordon, would become my Paul O'Neill on steroids. With the count even at 1–1, Jeurys Familia tried to quick-pitch Gordon, and it quickly broke my soul. Gordon drove a ball to center field, and I dropped to my knees. My wife, now resting in the other room, would never forget the sound she heard from the living room. As that ball cleared the center-field fence, I pounded the ground and screamed, "*Fuck!*" at the top of my lungs numerous times. I couldn't believe it, yet I most certainly could believe it. I sat around for three-plus hours scared to death of 2000, and like straight out of a horror movie 2000 reappeared. I was numb for the next four innings, waiting for the inevitable funeral. The Mets pen kept it tied, and the one opportunity the Mets had that really hurts to think about was David Wright striking out with men on first and second and two out in the 11th. David was also the guy who helped put the final nail in our coffin in the 14th inning. Alcides Escobar hit a ground ball to

David, which he booted, recovered, and then made a wide throw to first. A single and an intentional walk later set up Hosmer to walk it off with a game-winning sacrifice fly. At 1:18 AM, the Mets had written a chapter in the book of losses that will haunt us forever. Much like 2000, the Mets had flushed a ninth-inning lead on the road and much like 2000, I was now fully convinced there was no way they could recover.

KEEPING SCORE: The Game 1 loss was the Mets' fifth in as many World Series openers.... It was the third Series game to go 14 innings, the most extra frames until the Red Sox and Dodgers played 18 innings in 2018.... Daniel Murphy's streak of hitting a home run in six consecutive postseason games came to an end as he went 2-for-7.... Escobar's inside-the-park home run was the first in Series play since 1929, when Mule Haas of the Philadelphia Athletics legged one out against the Chicago Cubs.

THE 60 FEET, 6 INCHES GAME

METS 9 ROYALS 3
GAME 3, WORLD SERIES
OCTOBER 30, 2015, at CITI FIELD

THERE WAS A chill in the air, and the desperation was at an all-time high as the New York Mets were scheduled to play their first home World Series game in 15 years. Despite the kick in the balls that was Game 1, followed by a slow death of a loss in Game 2, nothing could hurt the raw excitement of walking into your building for a World Series game. As much as 2000 was permeating my brain, I knew that being down 0–2 with Games 3, 4, and 5 in your building was certainly not a death sentence. I've seen teams come back from this deficit before, so why not us? The crowd was electric and was certainly not

14 V/G Royals	W-L 9-4	GB +2	H 7-1	R 2-3	E 4-2	C 0-0	W 3-2	IL 2-0			
12 H/G Mets	W-L 7-4	GB 2	H 3-1	R 4-3	E 0-0	C 4-0	W 3-2	IL 0-2			

AL STANDINGS

	R	H	E	LOB	
KC	3	7	1		5
Met	9	12	0		6

WP Noah Syndergaard 2-1
LP Yordano Ventura 0-2
SV

START 8:08 DATE October 30, 2015
FINISH 11:30 ATT 44,781
TIME 3:22 WX clear 52°

Met DP/OPP

DEFENSE

Michael Conforto — Yoenis Cespedes — Curtis Granderson

Wilmer Flores — Daniel Murphy

David Wright — (3.20 Noah Syndergaard) — Lucas Duda

Travis d'Arnaud

World Series
Met 0
KC 2

ALCS
Tor 2
KC 4

ALDS

WC
Hou def NYY

Met PITCHERS

	IP	H	R	ER	W	K	
1-1 2.77 Noah Syndergaard	6	7	3	3	2	6	
Addison Reed	7	1	0	0	0	0	
Tyler Clippard	8	1	0	0	0	0	
Jeurys Familia	9	1	0	0	0	1	

LH BENCH RH
Orsen / Colon, Butera

LH Met BULLPEN RH
Gilmartin / Niese — Robles / Colon

©1996 Bob Carpenter Communications, Inc. All Rights Reserved

beaten down from the hole we now found ourselves trying to climb out of. As the Mets took the field, a sound blared from the P.A. system that night that has stuck with me—it was theme from *Halloween* by John Carpenter. If you've never heard it, go to YouTube right now and check it out, and now imagine closing your eyes and hearing that music as Noah Syndergaard warmed up for his first World

STADIUM/CAP. Citi Field

	1	2	3	4	5	6	7	8	9
Royals	1	2	0	0	0	0	0	0	0
Mets	3	0	2	1	0	4	0	0	X

NL STANDINGS

World Series
Met 0
KC 2

Gm Met 4 14 62 Met 1
KC 5 inn KC 7

NLCS
Cub 0
Met 4

NLDS
Cub 3 Met 3
StL 1 LAD 2

WC
Cub def Pit

DEFENSE

KC DP/OPP — E

Alex Gordon — Lorenzo Cain — Alex Rios

Alcides Escobar — Ben Zobrist

Mike Moust-k-s — 3.86 Yordano Ventura — Eric Hosmer

Salvador Perez

U Everitt M Cederstrom
P
S Winters

Miszuez — Carlson
2B
3B 1B Wolf
HP

World Series Game 3
2-0 KC ✦

Met CH
Gordon safe at
3rd in 2nd is overturned

W 3
KC
No G-me — David Wright 2 for 5 1HR 4RBI

Met
No G-me

New York Mets	AVE 220	HR 15	RBI 4.36	1	2	3	4	5	6	7	8	9	10	11	AB 12	R 13	H 14	BI 15
3 Curtis Granderson RF 268 1+8																		
5 David Wright 3b 171 0+3						1-4												
28 Daniel Murphy 2b 353 7+11																		
52 Yoenis Cespedes cf 227 2+7																		
21 Lucas Duda 1b 270 1+7																		
7 Travis d'Arnaud c 186 3+7																		
30 Michael Conforto LF 050 1+3 / 12 Juan Lagares ph/cf @ 368 0+0																		
4 Wilmer Flores ss 226 0+0																		
34 Noah Syndergaard P 000 0+0																		

	1	2	3	4	5	6	7	8	9	10	11
R/ER	2|2	0|0	2|2	1|1	0|0	4|4	0|0				
H	2	0	2	3	1	3	1				
E	0	0	0	0	0	1E1	0				
LOB	0	0	2	1	1|3	2|5	1|6				

LH BENCH RH

Nieuwenhuis Lagares
Johnson Colabello
Uribe Plawecki

KC PITCHERS	IP	H	R	ER	W	K	
1-1 3.18 Yordano Ventura (30)	3⅓	7	5	5	0	1	53f
Danny Duffy (41)	4⅔	0	0	0	0	1	17BF 2HR 28f
Luke Hochevar (44)	5	1	1	0	0	2	48f
Franklin Morales (46)	⅓	2	4	4	0	0	5BF 1HBP
Kelvin Herrera (40)	⅔	1	0	0	0	1	4BF
Ryan Madson (46)	7	1	1	0	0	0	4BF
Kris Medlen (34)	8	1	0	0	0	2	3BF

LH KC BULLPEN RH

Hochevar Davis
Duffy Herrera
Hochevar
Madson
stiff
Young
Volquez
Cueto

Series start. The sound was eerie, scary, and perfectly encapsulated the moment as we were set to begin Game 3 of the World Series.

Everyone wanted the same thing...every single person in that ballpark had watched the first two games and also knew from his postseason track record that Royals leadoff hitter Alcides Escobar was going to swing at the first pitch. A few nights earlier, he had jumped all over a fastball by Matt Harvey and stroked an inside-the-park home run, so it was certainly fresh in our minds. As the crowd roared in anticipation of the first pitch, I was hoping that a 22-year-old rookie would do what needed to be done. And, boy, did he come through. The first pitch of Game 3 was far different than the first pitch of Game 1 and miles different from the first pitch to Derek Jeter in Game 4 of the 2000 Fall Classic. Noah threw a fastball up and a bit inside to put Escobar straight down on his rear end. Citi Field exploded in appreciation as someone finally did what needed to be done! I could see from my seat that a Royals player was pissed at Noah; third baseman Mike Moustakas started jawing at Syndergaard. We all loved it! With the team down 0–2 and after watching Escobar pound an inside-the-park home run that started this whole mess, it was enjoyable and therapeutic to see Escobar eat dirt and the Royals pissed. This by no means made me think the Mets were a lock to win Game 3, or even that Noah would dominate, but it was just awesome to see someone, especially a rookie, take matters into his own hands.

What's funny about this moment is how memories change reality. Even though Noah won the battle against Escobar by striking him out two pitches later, the Royals scored a run in the first inning and two more in the second against Noah. The two runs the Royals scored in the second on three singles and Travis d'Arnaud's passed ball really stung at the time, because it answered the dramatic home run David Wright had hit in the bottom of the first off Yordano Ventura, which gave the Mets a 2–1 lead. But to the Syndergaard's credit, he settled in really well after those first two innings, and the Mets took the lead back in the third when Curtis Granderson went yard for the second time in the Series. The Mets ended all the drama by blowing the entire game open in the sixth inning, highlighted by Wright's two-run single to go up 9–3. Game 3 was drama-free for the final three innings as the Mets repeated the 2000 script by winning the third game of the Series at home after losing the first two on the road. While confidence was not soaring high after the win, it certainly felt like we regained our pulse and had a chance in this battle with Kansas City. Winning Game 3 also meant the Mets needed to win just one of the next two games to ensure a trip back to Kansas City, which got my brain working. I started putting together a game plan for how my family and I could make the trip to K.C. and see Game 6 and a potential Game 7. And guess who would be in line to pitch for the Mets in a potential winner-take-all Game 7? The 22-year-old rookie who dusted Alcides Escobar and then after the game pleased Mets fans even more by suggesting that anybody who had a problem with that could meet him 60 feet, 6 inches away. That loud arrogance on the road in a Game 7? Sign me up!

KEEPING SCORE: Syndergaard's next start did come against the Royals in Kansas City—the following April, when he tossed six shutout innings in the second game of the 2016 season.... Wright's clout off Ventura, who would be killed in an automobile accident less than two years later, was the first World Series home run ever hit at Citi Field, and the third baseman became the second Mets player to have at least four RBIs in a World Series game. Rusty Staub (five ribbies) was the first in Game 4 in 1973 against the Oakland Athletics.

WHERE IT ALL WENT TO HELL

ROYALS 5 METS 3
GAME 4, WORLD SERIES
OCTOBER 31, 2015, at CITI FIELD

THIS IS THE GAME. This is the moment. This is the sequence of events that should haunt all of us, yet it doesn't. When we as Mets fans think back to what went wrong in the 2015 World Series against the Royals, there are two other games that jump out in our minds first. Blowing Game 1 in Kansas City, and how things fell apart in the Game 5 clincher are the ultimate in pain, but the truth is Game 4 derailed this series as much as the other two. It was a spooky

Halloween evening with temperatures that were pretty comfortable sitting in the low 50s. Steven Matz was asked to even the series up and would be facing the former Met (and guy who years later as general manager of the Texas Rangers would steal Jacob deGrom from us) Chris Young. Once again electricity filled the air as we had some confidence after taking Game 3 the night before to make the series 2–1 in favor of the Royals.

Right fielder Michael Conforto had been called up to the majors a few months earlier almost to act as a savior. In the weeks before dealing for Yoenis Cespedes, the Mets needed offense badly, so they summoned their first-round pick from the year before to spark the offense. Michael had a solid rookie campaign and was a key cog in this lineup for the postseason. Game 4 of the World Series would be his finest moment, even if no one wants to remember it. Conforto broke the scoreless tie by leading off the bottom of the fourth inning with a home run. Then in the bottom of the fifth inning with the Mets up 2–1, he did it again! This time Conforto hit a bomb off a lefty, Danny Duffy, who had just come in to replace Young. The Mets were up 3–1, just 12 outs away from evening the series at two games apiece and ensuring a trip back to Kansas City. Epic moments are routinely forgotten in losses, and I thought Bartolo Colon supplied one in this game. With the Mets nursing a 3–2 lead in the sixth and the tying run in scoring position with two out, Colon and Salvador Perez engaged in a pitcher-vs.-hitter battle for the ages. After 10 pitches and a lot of anxiety, Colon K'd Perez to cause a mini earthquake of excitement at Citi Field. The Mets were now only nine outs away from making this a 2–2 series. The Mets' inability to hit the Royals pen was causing me stomach pain on this evening, because I had a sneaky suspicion that their three runs just wouldn't be enough.

The stage was now set for the meltdown I was fearing. Tyler Clippard had issued back-to-back walks to Ben Zobrist and Lorenzo Cain with one out in the eighth, setting up Terry Collins to do what he absolutely needed to do. He made the call for Jeurys Familia to try and record a five-out save and face Eric Hosmer with the tying and lead runs on base. Familia quickly got Hosmer to hit a little chopper to second base, not the easiest play in the world, but certainly playable. Daniel Murphy charged in to make the play against the slow-footed Hosmer and had the ball slip under his glove. In one fell swoop the game was *over*. This error by Murphy not only tied the game 3–3, it allowed Cain to advance to third. So the Royals had runners at the corners with one out. Without much time to even think about the next batter, Mike Moustakas came to the plate, and all I could think about to salvage this disaster was getting Moose to hit a ground ball and end the inning with a double play. First pitch I got what I wanted...except his little ground ball found the hole past a diving Murphy. It was now 4–3 Royals, and one batter later it was 5–3 when Salvador Perez also singled to right. This was painful. But little did I know there would be some more pain to end this disaster.

Down 5–3 with men on first and second and one out in the ninth, following consecutive singles by Murphy and Yoenis Cespedes, Lucas Duda came to the plate against Royals closer Wade Davis. Dreams of a walk-off bomb circled my naïve head, but that's not what would happen. Instead, Duda hit a soft line drive to third base and instead of that just being the second out and Travis d'Arnaud getting a shot to be hero, Cespedes had his head up his rear end and got doubled off first base to end the game. What a gut punch. The Mets had gone from five measly outs away from tying the Series, to a collapse that featured a brutal error, soft base hits, and a mental miscue. Never forget Game 4...never forget how close the Mets came to evening this thing up and possibly changing everything. Instead it was a 3–1 hole, and our destiny of disappointment was right on track.

KEEPING SCORE: Conforto became the first rookie since Andruw Jones in 1996 to hit two home runs in a World Series game. He was also the second Mets player to homer twice in a Series game, Gary Carter being the first in Game 4 of the 1986 Fall Classic. Duffy had not allowed a home run to a left-handed batter in four years, and it was the first time Conforto had connected off a left-handed pitcher since being called up in July.

LOSING THE WORLD SERIES AT HOME

ROYALS 7 METS 2
GAME 5, WORLD SERIES
NOVEMBER 1, 2015, at CITI FIELD

I'M NOT A confident guy when it comes to my sports teams, as my former radio partner, Craig Carton (who coined the term "Roberts-itis" to describe my negative emotions), can attest. But as negative as I may be, I'm the kind of fan that never loses hope. I've seen my sports teams down 3-0, and even though logic and history would tell me it's over and deep down I would know it's over, I still hold out hope that we can be the miracle team. When the Red Sox won the World Series in 2004, they did it in an epic way by erasing a 3-0 deficit in the ALCS against the mighty Yankees, and it only seemed fitting that they would break the curse in an epic way. I guess in my mind my personal fight with losing would end also in an epic way too. Deep in my soul, the 2015 World Series was over before it really started. The way the Mets lost Game 1 was so damn bad and eerily reminiscent of the way they lost Game 1 of my only other World Series back in 2000. If that wasn't bad enough, Game 4 against the Royals also was a really, really demoralizing loss. So why would I have hope going into Game 5 of the World Series with the season on the line? I guess I'm conditioned to have an ounce of hope at all costs. As I walked into Citi Field on this November night, I asked the baseball gods for one simple thing: don't let the Royals celebrate on my field. I have seen this before, and as painful as it would be to watch the Mets lose a World Series on the road, I would rather have that experience than another home defeat. The sound of Yankees fans celebrating on our field 15 years earlier was still ringing in my ears.

My wife and I had been married for a few months, and she was not a sports fan, but she was very supportive of my insane passion. I had gone to every single postseason game with my dad, and my wife had no interest in going to any postseason game until this very night. "Is there any way to get an extra ticket for tonight?" she asked. Whatever the cost, it would be totally worth it! If the Mets lost the World Series at home, it might help to have her next to me as I walked comatose out of Citi Field. Plus, she had a legit rooting interest in this game besides wanting her husband to be happy. We had bought one-way tickets to Kansas City for the next day to see the Mets play Game 6 of the World Series. We would then book our return trip when we knew if we were going to have spend an extra day in K.C. for a potential Game 7. She was naturally excited about the prospect of seeing a city she had never been to before. She had

K
V/G Royals   W-L 10-5   GB +2   H 7-1   R 3-4   E 4-2   C 0-0   W 3-2   IL 3-1
14
H/G Mets   W-L 8-5   GB 2   H 4-2   R 4-3   E 0-0   C 4-0   W 3-2   IL 1-3

AL STANDINGS

12 inn	R	H	E	LOB		Met DP/OPP	DEFENSE	E
KC	7	10	1	7				
Met	2	4	2	6				

WP Luke Hochevar 2-0
LP Addison Reed 0-1
SV ~~~~~~~

START 8:18   DATE November 1, 2015
FINISH 12:33   ATT. 44,859
TIME 415   WX clear 61°

DEFENSE positions:
Michael Conforto, Yoenis Cespedes, Curtis Granderson, Wilmer Flores, Daniel Murphy, David Wright, 3.24 Matt Harvey, Lucas Duda, Travis d'Arnaud

World Series: Met 1 KC 3
ALCS: Tor 2 KC 4
ALDS: Hou 2 Tor 3 KC 3 Tor 3
WC: Hou 4 NYY

Kansas City Royals	Avc 264	HR 17	RIG 5.53	1	2	3	4	5	6	7	8	9	10	11	AB 12	R 13	H 14	BI 15
2 Alcides Escobar SS 344 148																	
18 Ben Zobrist 2b 311 206																	
6 Lorenzo Cain cf 246 168																	
35 Eric Hosmer 1b 300 1416																	
8 Mike Moustakas 3b 320 148																	

R/ER	0/0	0/0	1	0/0	0/0	0/0	0/0	0/0	2/2	0/0	0/0	5/4			
H	1	0	1	0	0	1	1	0	1	0	1	4			
E	0	1ES	0	0	0	0	0	0	0	0	0	1E4			
LOB	1	1/2	0/2	0/2	1/3	1/4	1/5	0/5	0/5	0/5	1/6	1/7			

LH   BENCH   RH

Met PITCHERS	IP	H	R	ER	W	K	HP
Matt Harvey 2-0 3.38	8+	5	2	2	2	9	318F
Jeurys Familia 32	9	2	0	0	2	2	6BF
Jon Niese 49	11	1	0	0	0	0	4BF
Addison Reed 43	12 1/3	3	5	4	1	0	6BF
Bartolo Colon 40	12 2/3	1	0	0	0	0	3BF

LH   Met BULLPEN   RH
Gilmartin, Niese, Matz / Reed, Familia, Clippard, Robles, deGrom, Syndergaard

©1996 Bob Carpenter Communications, Inc. All Rights Reserved

already done her research on restaurants to check out and places to see in our maiden voyage to Kansas City.

The signs from Game 5 against the Royals pointed me in the direction of a win, and a trip for me, my wife, my dad, and sister to Kansas City for Game 6. I mean, freakin' Curtis Granderson hit an 0–2 pitch from Edinson Volquez over the fence in right-center to start the bottom of the first. Shades of Len Dykstra in 1986 and even José Reyes in Game 6 against the Cardinals in the 2006 NLCS rang through my head. And then Matt Harvey dominated—he had a look on his face that made you think there was no way he would let his team lose. Nursing a 2–0 lead thanks to Granderson's homer and Lucas Duda's sixth-inning sac fly, we all remember the fateful decision by Terry Collins:

he allowed Matt to start the ninth inning. Here is why I was against it then and years later it still boils my blood. Jeurys Familia needed a clean inning to work with badly. I had visions of the night before, when bringing Familia in with guys on base was a recipe for disaster. When Matt was allowed to start the ninth, I compromised, thinking, *Okay, give him a shot. But as soon as a guy reaches base, get his ass out.* My wife whispered to me, "I guess we are going to Kansas City." A big no-no, which she soon realized as I glared back at her. You would think, after walking Lorenzo Cain, that would be the moment to pull him. But Terry allowed him to face Eric Hosmer, who hit a line drive to left field to score Cain that I can still visualize clear as day. Once he pulled Harvey for Jeurys, it was too late. Hosmer would score the tying run later in the inning when he was able to beat Lucas Duda's throw home on Salvador Perez's groundout to third. Much like Game 1, this loss would be that slow death. The offense couldn't muster a rally to break the tie in the ninth, 10th, or 11th. By the time the 12th rolled around, it was too late. Christian Colon would etch his name in Mets history as the guy who got the World Series–winning hit. To make matters worse and put an exclamation point on what was a dreadful defensive series, Daniel Murphy made yet another backbreaking error, and the Royals blew the game open. When the top of the 12th was over, the score was 7–2, and the stadium was filled with mostly Royals fans. Yes, *Royals fans.* In 2000 it was Yankees fans celebrating in my building, and here we were 15 years later, and it was a fan base from a franchise that meant nothing to me until a few weeks earlier getting to celebrate a title in my building. When Wade Davis got Wilmer Flores to strike out looking, the dream had died a miserable death.

KEEPING SCORE: Harvey had a career record of 25–18 with a 2.53 ERA and 449 Ks in 437 innings through the 2015 season. Hampered by injuries, he finished his Mets career at 34–37 with a 3.66 ERA and 612 Ks in 639⅓ innings when was traded to the Cincinnati Reds early in the 2018 season.... Granderson became the second Met to hit three home runs in a World Series, joining Donn Clendenon, who did so as the MVP of the 1969 Series.

THE BAT-FLIP GAME

METS 9 PHILLIES 8 (11 INNINGS)

SEPTEMBER 22, 2016, at CITI FIELD

I WAS NOT at this game and I have zero regrets. I guess becoming a father quickly teaches you about priorities in life. I love the Mets, and I certainly love being at games, but 11 days earlier my wife gave birth to our first son, Jett, and while I was still going to games, I was certainly being a lot more selective. This night in late September is very vivid in my mind for the on-field and off-field emotions I was feeling that evening. The Mets had stormed back to put themselves in a great position to claim one of the two wild-card spots in the National League, but had hit a major road bump. They had lost three in a row and found themselves in a three-way tie with the San Francisco Giants and St. Louis Cardinals with only 10 games left on the schedule. More worrisome than the math was how the Mets were now playing. After sweeping the awful Minnesota Twins the weekend prior, the Mets stubbed their toes against the almost-as-dreadful Atlanta Braves. At this time in 2016, the Braves were in the midst of the rebuild that would be rewarded shortly, but at this moment they were a beatable team on their way to a 90-plus-loss season. In our own building with the playoffs on the line, the Mets somehow managed to be swept by the hated Braves. After more than a month of sterling baseball, the Mets looked as if they were going to flush the hot streak and, worst of all, do it against division rivals who were crappy. This is why the Mets had now found themselves in that three-way tie going into a pivotal four-game set against the fourth-place Philadelphia Phillies, who were 14 games under .500.

My wife was bleary-eyed. We were new parents and were learning very quickly that one of the side effects of that was zero sleep. "Don't worry, baby, I got Jett tonight," I told her as the Mets got set to host the Phillies. So in our makeshift "sports room," which had a few TVs scattered everywhere, I sat down on the floor with my scorebook and my 11-day-old son, Jett, on my lap. I slowly rocked him to bed as I would ever-so-gently write in the plays from the game in my Carpenter scorebook.

This game was pressure-filled and completely wild. The score was tied in the seventh inning, but a clutch double by Yoenis Cespedes gave the Mets a 4–3 lead. Then in the next inning Addison

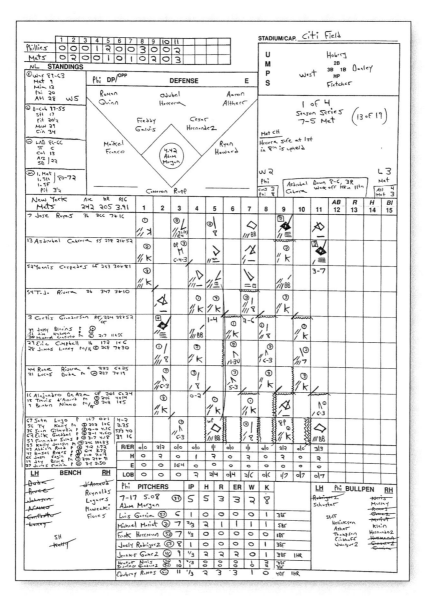

Reed imploded and blew that short-lived edge, capped off by a
Maikel Franco three-run bomb that seemingly put the Mets on the
brink of a four-game losing streak. Down to their final two outs in
the ninth inning, the returning José Reyes electrified Citi Field with
a two-run home run off Jeanmar Gomez that sent the game to extra
innings. It was becoming seemingly impossible to keep Jett sound

asleep as my body was shaking from excitement. But even though he was passed out, I felt that he was sharing this emotion with me, if not just from osmosis. The good emotions quickly went away when the Phillies regained the lead in the 11th against Jeurys Familia and Jim Henderson, including a 10-pitch walk drawn by Mets-killer Franco that put the Phillies up by two. It was now late into the evening and hope was almost gone. At least my sleeping son was going to be introduced into painful, heartbreaking baseball right out of the gate. Down 8–6 with one out in the bottom of the inning, Michael Conforto singled and José Reyes walked. Asdrubal Cabrera stepped to the plate against rookie Edubray Ramos. It was past 11:00 PM now, and I was starting to get a bit uncomfortable as I had now spent four hours sitting on the floor trying to simultaneously score a game and keep my son asleep. On a 1–0 pitch, Cabrera took a massive cut and flipped his bat far away—I knew what everyone at Citi Field knew. That beautiful white baseball flew through the dark sky like a shooting star through outer space. What's funny is that the ball didn't clear the fence by much! I think the combination of the bat flip and the swing put me into a false sense of security that it was a moon shot. But, either way, it cleared the fence for a game-winning, walk-off, three-run home run. I slowly raised Jett into the air while keeping as quiet as I could. I softly said, "Yes, yes, yes!" as Cabrera pimped his shot and slowly rounded the bases. The Mets had walked off the Phillies in the 11th for an insane back-and-forth win. I kissed Jett on the forehead as I stood in awe, watching this awesome Mets moment. Citi Field was shaking, but I was in a better place. I got to enjoy a memorable Mets win with my sleeping son. When I think back on the 2016 regular season, this is the *only* game worth remembering, and for me it was more than a game.

KEEPING SCORE: Cabrera hit 55 home runs in two-plus seasons for the Mets before they traded him to, ironically, the Phillies during the 2018 season. He would win a World Series ring with the Washington Nationals in 2019 and played in the majors until 2021 when he suited up for both the Arizona Diamondbacks and Cincinnati Reds.... The

Mets received a minor league pitcher named Franklin Kilome for Cabrera. The hard-throwing righty underwent Tommy John surgery in 2019 and made his only four appearances for the Mets in 2020.

THE PLAYOFFS?

GIANTS 3 METS 0
NATIONAL LEAGUE WILD CARD GAME
OCTOBER 5, 2016, at CITI FIELD

BETWEEN THE YEARS 2012 and 2021 (minus the pandemic-affected 2020 season), Major League Baseball had a pretty cool concept called the Wild Card Game. This system made divisional races really matter for the first time in the wild-card era because who would want their 162-game season to come down to one game? My only quibble with the Wild Card Game concept is that I believe it should count as a regular season game. Much like previous one-game playoffs in baseball history, it should fall into the same bucket as an extra game that extends the regular season. My contention from day one was that if you made the Wild Card Game and lost, it would be like not making the playoffs at all. So why confuse things? Just call it a regular season game, and let's call it a day. In 2015 the New York Yankees made the game and lost to the Houston Astros at Yankee Stadium as Dallas Keuchel outpitched Masahiro Tanaka. I was in the building that night and left believing the same thing. The Yankees had not really made the playoffs, and I had just witnessed an extra regular season game. The following year, I would be put to the test, because for the first time the Mets would be involved in this.

The 2016 season was such a bizarre one for the Mets. The off-season featured losing Daniel Murphy, who instantly morphed into a superhero who would beat the crap out of us at every turn as a member of the Washington Nationals. The forte of the previous year's Mets team was their young emerging rotation, but by September all the young guns were injured with the exception of Noah Syndergaard. DeGrom, Harvey, and Matz would all be shut down and would not return. On August 20, the Mets were 60–62 and were 5 1/12 games out of the second wild-card spot. The season appeared to be flushed down the toilet. Then, spurred by a rotation led by Syndergaard, Seth Lugo, Robert Gsellman, and the ageless Bartolo Colon, the Mets got hot. *Very hot.* Yoenis Cespedes, Asdrubal Cabrera, and the returning José Reyes sparked the Mets offense as they played red hot baseball to close August and through September to not only earn a wild-card spot, but the *top* spot, which meant hosting the game at Citi Field.

It would be the Mets against the San Francisco Giants; Noah Syndergaard vs. postseason legend Madison Bumgarner in a winner-moves-on game. Looking back on this game, here is where I think I was very right, but also dead wrong. Walking into Citi Field on that beautiful evening, I did have the playoff jitters, no doubt, and the crowd certainly acted like it was Game 7 of the World Series. I mean, the place was jumping! "Let's go, Mets!" chants filled the stadium prior to Syndergaard even taking the mound. Despite this team being in the World Series a year earlier and being completely ravaged by injuries, the crowd had that same desperation to win it had a year earlier. If the Mets had won the game, we would be destined to face the Chicago Cubs, who looked even better than the team the Mets had dispatched a year earlier. The Cubs had won 103 games during the regular season and were the odds-on favorites to win the pennant. It didn't matter if guys like Gsellman and Lugo, both rookies, were going to have to start instead of deGrom and Harvey, this crowd was feeling it.

Madison Bumgarner did everything early on to shut us up, though. Not only did he cruise through the Mets lineup through the first four innings by only allowing two base runners, but his pitch count was extremely low. It was obvious we were going to need Syndergaard to match him pitch for pitch and then hope to get Bumgarner out of the game and beat the Giants pen, because we

Baseball scorecard (©1996 Bob Carpenter Communications, Inc. All Rights Reserved)

weren't going to beat him. In the bottom of the fifth inning, second baseman T.J. Rivera led off with a double to start a potential Mets rally. By the way, let that marinate for a second. In a one-game play-off, the Mets were playing T.J. Rivera, a rookie with all of 105 major league at-bats, and he was hitting fifth in the batting order! Unfortunately, Bumgarner was not going to let a measly leadoff double

STADIUM/CAP. Citi Field

	1	2	3	4	5	6	7	8	9						
Giants	O	O	O	O	O	O	O	O	3						
Mets	O	O	O	O	O	O	O	O	O						

U M P S

Bucknor   Everitt   Wolcott
Wolf   2B   Nelson
3B 1B
HP
Winters

NL STANDINGS

WC
SF 87-75
Met 87-75

NLDS
SF/Met
Cub 103-58

LAD 91-71
Was 95-67

SF DP/OPP   DEFENSE   E

Angel
Pagan
Denard
Span
Hunter
Pence

Brandon
Crawford
Joe
Panik

Conor
Gillespie
3.65
Madison
Bumgarner
Brandon
Belt

Buster Posey

NL Wild Card Game ⚾
Reg. Season Series
4-3 Met

SF CH
Span CS in 4th
is upheld
Syndergaard 5⅔
no hit innings
Giants advance to NLDS

W 4
last post
SF
2014 WS
W KC

Madison   IP 9
Bumgarner   R 0

L 1
last post
Met
2015 WS
L KC

New York Mets	Avc	HR	RBI	1	2	3	4	5	6	7	8	9	10	11	AB 12	R 13	H 14	BI 15
7 Jose Reyes	.246	.218	4.14															
13 Asdrubal Cabrera ss																		
52 Yoenis Cespedes LF																		
3 Curtis Granderson CF																		
54 T.J. Rivera 2b																		
19 Jay Bruce RF																		
44 Rene Rivera C																		
28 James Loney 1b / 21 Eric Campbell ph																		
34 Noah Syndergaard p / 43 Addison Reed p / 56 Ty Kelly ph / 27 Jeurys Familia p																		

		1	2	3	4	5	6	7	8	9	10	11	12	13	14	15
R/ER		0/0	0/0	0/0	0/0	0/0	0/0	0/0	0/0	0/0						
H		0	0	1	1	1	0	0	1	0						
E		0	0	0	0	0	0	0	0	0						
LOB		0	0	0	1	2/3	1/4	0/4	1/5	0/5						

LH   BENCH   RH

Johnson
Conforto
De Aza

d'Arnaud
Campbell
Plawecki
Lagares

SH
Kelly

SF PITCHERS	IP	H	R	ER	W	K
7-3-1 2.14 ⑩ Madison Bumgarner	9	4	0	0	2	6

338F

LH   SF BULLPEN   RH

Okert
Smith
Lopez

Romo
Strickland
Casilla
Smardzija
Law
Cueto
Kontos

©1996 Bob Carpenter Communications, Inc. All Rights Reserved

affect him, because he calmly and quickly struck out Jay Bruce, got Rene Rivera to ground out, and after an intentional walk, struck out Noah Syndergaard. In the top of the sixth we were treated to our Endy Chavez moment. With a runner on second and two outs, Brandon Belt smoked a ball to deep center field. Curtis Granderson, who was playing center field these days but certainly wasn't the defensive center fielder he was back in the day, darted back and made an incredible over-the-shoulder catch as he pounded into the wall. It saved a run from scoring and, knowing the Mets were facing Bumgarner, saved the game in the moment. The crowd roared as loud as it would get on this October night. Ten years earlier, when Endy Chavez made his insane catch in the NLCS, I naïvely thought that meant the Mets would win the game and the pennant, but this time a wiser Evan had a different reaction. I turned to my dad and said, "You know what this means." My dad glanced back at me waiting to hear what witty line I had in my arsenal. "Dad, it means we are completely fucked."

Syndergaard came out of the game after seven brilliant innings and 108 pitches with the score still tied 0–0. Addison Reed did his best Houdini act in the eighth by loading the bases, but came up big when he struck out Hunter Pence to keep them loaded. Meanwhile, the Mets had no shot against Bumgarner, who through eight innings had allowed only four hits and two walks. In a no-brainer move, Terry Collins went to Jeurys Familia to keep the game scoreless in the ninth inning. If the Mets could just keep it right there, we were getting closer to finally seeing Bumgarner, who was now past 100 pitches, have to exit this game, and at that point we would have a legit shot to win this classic. After Familia gave up a leadoff double to Brandon Crawford, struck out Angel Pagan, and issued a walk to Joe Panik we had entered the pivotal moment of the evening. First and second with one out and the batter was Conor Gillaspie. So here was my wild thought: walk Gillaspie. My reasoning for this was, you force Giants manager Bruce Bochy to make a decision. Does he trust the hitting of Bumgarner, or would he pinch-hit for him? We all know Madison was considered one of the better hitting pitchers, but let's put this in perspective. During the regular season that year, he hit .186 with 3 home runs. So, yes, he's one of the better hitting pitchers in baseball, but he's still a .186 hitter whom you would have up with bases loaded and one out. Fuck it—I was so desperate to get Bumgarner out of this game I was willing to do it. Terry Collins was not. The result was Gillaspie hitting a three-run home run. Turn out the lights. Bumgarner would calmly get the final three outs, and the Mets season was kaput. I walked out of Citi Field dejected and depressed. My stomach pain certainly told me this was a playoff game, and I had the playoff loss hurts inside. Little did I know the Mets wouldn't taste October baseball again for six more years. With all of that said—it wasn't the playoffs! I may be hardheaded on this, but you can't spend only three hours in the playoffs. Even more than thinking about Bumgarner and Gillaspie, the thing that brings me the most pain from this night is that stupid banner that still hangs from Citi Field. It says "2016 Wild Card"...to me it was just losing Game 163.

KEEPING SCORE: Syndergaard appeared in five postseason games for the Mets (four starts) and went 2–1 with a 2.42 ERA.... Bumgarner ended up throwing 119 pitches.... The Giants would lose to the Cubs in the Division Series, three games to one.

FAREWELL TO DAVID WRIGHT

METS 1 MARLINS 0 (13 INNINGS)

SEPTEMBER 29, 2018, at CITI FIELD

IN 2004, it was a depressing time to be a New York Mets fan. The team sucked, and you could tell early on that the squad we were watching would not be a part of the Mets' future. But there was one beacon of light from that otherwise forgettable waste of a season. On July 21 in a game against the Montreal Expos, a 21-year-old third baseman from Virginia named David Wright made his major league debut. Through the spring and early summer of 2004, I had started to keep my eye on this guy who was tearing up Double A Binghamton and eventually would have some early success in Triple A Norfolk— because when your team sucks, that's what you do! You hope for the

160
V/G Marlins W-L 63-96 GB 26½ H 38-43 R 25-53 E 26-48 C 13-17 W 15-18 IL 9-11

161
H/G Mets W-L 75-85 GB 15 H 35-44 R 40-41 E 38-36 C 13-20 W 16-17 IL 8-12

AL STANDINGS

1. B-J-s 107-53
   WC-NYY 2
   TB 17
   Tor 34
   B-I 60's
2. B-Cle 90-70
   Min 14
   Det 30
   CWS 28
   KC 33
3. B-Hou 101-58
   WC-O-K 5½
   Se 14½
   LAA 22½
   Tex 34½
1. NYY 77-61
2. O-K 16-64

13inn	R	H	E	LOB
Mia	0	5	0	6
Met	1	11	0	14

WP Daniel Zamora 1-0 ☆ 1st ML win ☆
LP Jarlin García 3-3
SV ~~~~~~~

START 7:12 DATE September 29, 2018
FINISH 11:26 ATT. 43,928
TIME 4:14 WX Clear 59°

Met DP/OPP DEFENSE E

Michael Conforto
Austin Jackson
Brandon Nimmo
Jose Reyes
Jeff McNeil
David Wright
4.14 Steven Matz
Jay Bruce
Kevin Plawecki

Miami Marlins	Avg	HR	P/G	1	2	3	4	5	6	7	8	9	10	11	AB 12	R 13	H 14	BI 15
	239	128	3.70															

LH	BENCH	RH

Met PITCHERS	IP	H	R	ER	W	K
Steven Matz 20-26 4.05	6	3	0	0	1	8
Tyler Bashlor	7	1	0	0	0	1
Drew Smith	8	1	0	0	0	1
Anthony Swarzak	9	1	1	0	0	1
Jerry Blevins	10	1	0	0	1	0
Jacob Rhame	11	2	1	0	0	1

LH Met BULLPEN RH

future, and David Wright was clearly our future. When the Mets lost free agent pitcher Mike Hampton to the school districts of Denver, Colorado, after the 2000 season, the Mets received a compensatory draft pick that they would use on David Wright. Thank you, Denver school system!

David became the face of the team and eventually the captain. The injuries he suffered late in his career are nothing but heartbreaking. He was not a perfect player, and I certainly had moments when I criticized him and compared him to other stars who were better, but he was more than anything else *our* guy. I was so happy when the Mets locked him up to a long-term contract a year before free agency because flaws and all, there was no way David Wright should have been allowed to play in any other uniform but the Mets. There was nobody in my lifetime who would go down as a career Met, and other than Ed Kranepool, there was nobody in Mets history who could fit that bill...and that made David even more special. When he came back after missing four months in 2015 and had a major impact on the pennant-winning team, it was freakin' awesome. David was good when he played in 2015 and did hit a World Series home run in the only game the Mets would win in the 2015 Fall Classic. But in 2016 he was a shell of his former self due to a back injury. He didn't play in 2017 and wasn't going to play in 2018, either. It was damn sad. David Wright was still only 35 years old in 2018, and we all knew the sad truth—he was never going to play another game for the Mets.

On September 13, 2018, well over two years since his last major league appearance, a surprise announcement was made—David would return to start one last game as a Met before officially retiring. We as Mets fans would get one last chance to show him our love before he finally ended the dream of a full-time comeback. This was so unorthodox, but a rare great move by the Wilpon regime. If anyone deserved a chance to suit up one last time before an adoring home crowd, it was David Wright. In an otherwise gloomy season, a Saturday night in September against the lousy Marlins in what would have been a meaningless game instantly became the hottest ticket since the postseason two years earlier. I walked into Citi that night with my wife, who wanted to join me for the occasion, and as much as my father respected David, this was clearly not as meaningful to him as it was to the younger generation of Mets fans. The place was *packed*. It didn't have the overall electricity a full house would normally have, other than when Wright appeared. The crowd chanted his name before the game, during the game, and throughout the evening. It was cool to have José Reyes playing shortstop next to David like the old days, and while I didn't appreciate it or realize it at the time, looking back on my scorecard, it's awesome to see key cogs of the future in Jeff McNeil and Brandon Nimmo in the game as well. If only the Mets had called up Pete Alonso when they should have, we really would have had the perfect mix of past and future together.

Seeing Wright at the plate was sort of surreal because it had been so long. Facing Trevor Richards, a rookie right-hander, he drew a walk in his first plate appearance, which drew boos from the home crowd. He received a standing ovation before and after his at-bat, and a rousing hand when he fielded a routine ground ball to end the second inning. But the most memorable moment was his final swing. On the second pitch he saw from Richards in the fourth inning, David popped up a foul ball wide of first base. Peter O'Brien calmly made the catch and was booed unmercifully by the crowd, who pleaded with him to drop the ball and extend David's at-bat. What made it worse was that Mets manager Mickey Callaway then pulled David from the game. So Peter O'Brien received villainous boos for the rest of the evening and for the rest of his major league career.

The game itself would be a journey deep into the evening, when it finally ended after 13 innings and more than four hours of base-ball, it was Austin Jackson who delivered the game-winning hit to secure the Mets' 1–0 win. No one remembers that and no one cares... it was all about David. It was a sad night and a celebratory night all rolled into one. We walked out of the stadium that evening to a cho-rus of "Thank You, David!" chants. David Wright truly was the face of an era, and now it was over.

KEEPING SCORE: Wright was a seven-time All-Star, won two Gold Gloves and two Silver Sluggers, and was named the fourth captain in Mets history in 2013. He retired as the team's all-time leader in sev-eral categories, including at-bats (5,998), hits (1,777), runs scored (949), total bases (2,945), doubles (390), and RBIs (970). His 242 home runs place him second, 10 behind Darryl Strawberry.

I HAD TO BE IN THE BUILDING

METS 7 NATIONALS 6
AUGUST 9, 2019, at CITI FIELD

THE METS were playing really good baseball and were on a six-game winning streak as they were set to open a weekend set against the Washington Nationals. The Mets trailed the Nats by 2½ games for the first wild-card spot in the National League and sat just a half-game behind the Milwaukee Brewers for the second spot. Citi Field was set to be packed in anticipation of the biggest series the team had played in three years, but I was not planning on going. At this point I would go to a few weeknight games with my father or a friend and then take my family to a Saturday or Sunday game, but I had made an effort to avoid Friday nights. It wasn't about not liking Free Shirt Fridays or anything kooky, it was simply a good night to watch the game from home with my family, and that was my plan for this evening. But something happened while I was at work that I couldn't and still can't explain. It was almost like a voice was talking to me like I was Ray Kinsella in *Field of Dreams*...something odd was imploring me to go to this game. I sent a text over to my wife basically asking permission: "Hunny I know I told you I wasn't going tonight, but I have this strange feeling...is it ok if I go." My wife, Sylvia, is the best. She didn't hesitate in replying, "Go to the game and have fun." With my season tickets already being used for the night, I quickly jumped online and scooped up two tickets.

If I thought that the inner voice telling me to go was trying to warn me about a no-hitter, well I was sadly mistaken. Trea Turner led the game off with an infield hit, so this wasn't going to be that kind of special. My dad once told me that something told him to be near a TV the night Tom Seaver took a perfect game into the ninth against the Cubs in 1969 before Jimmy Qualls broke it up. This was clearly not going to be a night like that. Marcus Stroman was making his Citi Field debut and his second Mets start since they had

115
VIG Nationals W-L 61-53 GB 5½ H 31-25 R 30-28 E 30-22 C 5-11 W 18-16 IL 8-4
116
HIG Mets W-L 59-56 GB 8 H 32-20 R 27-36 E 27-24 C 12-15 W 10-13 IL 10-4

AL STANDINGS

	R	H	E	LOB
Was	6	13	0	8
Met	7	11	0	6

WP Luis Avilan 3-0
LP Sean Doolittle 6-4
SV

START 7:11 DATE Friday August 9, 2019
FINISH 10:31 ATT. 39,602
TIME 320 WX Clear 80°

Met DP/OPP DEFENSE

J.D. Davis — Michael Conforto — Jeff McNeil
Amed Rosario — Joe Panik
Todd Frazier — 4.39 Marcus Stroman — Pete Alonso
Wilson Ramos

©1996 Bob Carpenter Communications, Inc. All Rights Reserved

acquired him a few weeks earlier from the Toronto Blue Jays in a pre-deadline deal. Stroman gave up three runs in the fourth inning, but the Mets' bats responded immediately when Pete Alonso and J.D. Davis went back to back against Stephen Strasburg to tie up the game. In the top of the fifth inning, something happened to me

	1	2	3	4	5	6	7	8	9
Nationals	0	0	0	3	0	0	2	0	1
Mets	0	0	3	0	0	0	0	4	

STADIUM/CAP. Citi Field

NL STANDINGS

Was DP / OPP — DEFENSE — E

Juan Soto — Victor Robles — Adam Eaton

Trea Turner — Brian Dozier

Anthony Rendon — 4.40 Stephen Strasburg — Matt Adams

Kurt Suzuki

U M P S — Reyburn — 2B — Blakney — 3B 1B Gibson — HP — Carlson

1 of 3 Season Series P-5 Met (14 of 19)

Met CH
Soto safe at 1st in 7th is upheld

W 3
Was — Todd Frazier — Trying 3R HR in 9th — Met
Day off — Day off

New York Mets	Ave	HR	R/G		1	2	3	4	5	6	7	8	9	10	11	AB 12	R 13	H 14	BI 15
	254	170	4.82																
6 Jeff McNeil RF	340	15	52																
1 Amed Rosario SS	278	12	48																
30 Michael Conforto CF	261	25	64																
20 Pete Alonso 1B	260	37	83																
28 J.D. Davis LF	305	17	35																
40 Wilson Ramos C	287	12	58																
21 Todd Frazier 3B	247	14	46																
2 Joe Panik 2B	235	3	27																

R/ER	0	0	0	0	0	0	3	3	0	0	0	0	0	0	0	0	4	4
H	0	0	0	2	0	2	0	1	6
E	0	0	0	0	0	0	0	0	0
LOB	0	0	0	1	0	1	2	3	0	3	1	4	2	6

LH — BENCH — RH
Guillorme — Nido — Lagares — Althorr

Was PITCHERS	IP	H	R	ER	W	K	97 P
Stephen Strasburg	108-57 3.20 ㉗	7	4	3	3	2	6
Daniel Hudson ㊼	8	1	1	0	0	0	1
Sean Doolittle ㉛	9 2/3	6	4	4	0	0	

LH — W-S BULLPEN — RH
Grace — Rodney, Strickland, Hudson, Guerra, Suaro, Rainey
Corbin — Sanchez, Fedde, Ross

©1996 Bob Carpenter Communications, Inc. All Rights Reserved

that's very rare at a ballpark. I must've eaten something earlier that upset my stomach, and I found myself spending the next inning and a half in the men's room. I awkwardly scored the game in the bathroom stall while listening to Howie Rose describe the action. Did my inner voice tell me to go to this game as a practical joke so I could score the game from the shitter for 20 minutes!?

The Nationals scored twice in the seventh and added an insurance run in the top of the ninth to open up a 6–3 lead going into the bottom of the ninth. The Mets had given me no sign that something magical was about to happen, but in a lightning flash it did. It took Sean Doolittle only nine pitches for the Mets to get a double, single, and a dramatic Todd Frazier three-run bomb to left field that tied the game. When Todd crushed the 2–1 pitch, the entire ballpark in one motion jumped to its feet. I began leaning my neck, as if that somehow could keep the ball fair. The ball was hit so high and so deep down the left-field line that it took forever to see if it was actually going to stay fair and tie the game. It did, and Citi Field exploded like it hadn't in years. Random high fives and hugs took place in my section as we celebrated this shocking comeback.

The Doolittle implosion continued and was capped off by Michael Conforto ripping a ball over right fielder Adam Eaton's head to score Juan Lagares and end the game. The Mets had come back from a three-run deficit in the ninth and did it in record pace. In showing the highlights to my son Jett the next day, he repeated over and over, "Conforto no shirt on." His teammates had ripped Michael's shirt off in excitement. For years to come, this game was known in the Roberts household as the "Conforto no shirt" game. Years earlier I was not in attendance (nor did I score) the Wilmer Flores walk-off game against Washington, but from afar this felt the same. The Mets were right in the middle of the NL playoff race and had just won an insane game against a division rival. I legit walked out of Citi Field that night thinking we were going to go on some type of long playoff run like 2015. And for the sake of the voice that told me to show up, the story would be much better if they had. They did not. The 2019 Mets would blow a ton of heartbreaking games and fall a few games short of the wild-card. The Nationals would be the magic team, because they were the ones that won a wild-card game, Division Series, NLCS, and eventually the seventh game of the World Series. On this August night, I thought it would be us, if not only because of that win, but because of that voice. I will now and forever ignore that damn voice.

KEEPING SCORE: The Mets would defeat the Nationals the next night for their 15th win in 16 games before losing the series finale. The hot streak moved them from nine games under .500 to five games over at 61–56.... The Mets ended the season 10 games over with 86 victories, three less than the Brewers and seven less than the Nationals, the two wild-card teams.

The
2020s

"GREATEST DAY
IN METS HISTORY"

METS 4 YANKEES 3 (SECOND GAME)

AUGUST 28, 2020, at YANKEE STADIUM

I SPRINTED upstairs to my home studio as fast I could. It was late at night on a Friday in August, during the heart of the COVID-19 pandemic, but I was as excited as I had been in years. I couldn't wait to turn on the microphone so I could proudly proclaim this day the greatest moment in Mets history. Okay, okay, I quickly couched that into the greatest day in Mets history that doesn't include winning a championship. I was damn excited...but why? Did my view on this night age well or terribly? Let's explore.

The year 2020 is obviously one none of us will ever forget. Like everything else in life, sports were greatly affected and so damn bizarre that we will never forget the oddities of that season. It was already weird enough that baseball was having a 60-game season with zero fans in attendance. But there were other quirks of the 2020 campaign that we never expected to see. The Mets and Yankees were playing a doubleheader at Yankee Stadium in which, in the second game, the Mets would act as the home team. Since there were no fans in attendance, there was no point of doing what they had done before in pulling off a two-stadium double dip. During the

2020 season, under the guise of player safety, doubleheaders would be seven-inning games. So when the Mets made a dramatic sixth-inning comeback in Game 1, it was really the eighth, er, let's just call it late in the game. The Mets were down 4–0 and then proceeded to take batting practice against Chad Green in the sixth and won the game 6–4. A little after 8:40, the Mets and Yankees were set to play Game 2 under the same seven-inning rule, but this time the Mets would bat last and act as the home team. It was in the midst of this game that there was major breaking news related to the Mets.

At 9:53 PM, a tweet from David Faber of CNBC read:

> Steve Cohen has entered exclusive negotiations to buy the NY Mets and is expected to reach a deal to purchase the team within days, according to people familiar with the process. Other bidders, including the group led by Alex Rodriguez, are no longer in pursuit of the club.

I freaked out...Mets Twitter freaked out. Our dream owner, the billionaire Steve Cohen, was going to save us from the Wilpon era! The game felt secondary as the idea of Cohen buying the Mets—which had seemed dead a few weeks earlier—was back in play.

In the final opportunity for the Mets, the bottom of the seventh came around, and the Mets were trailing the Yankees 3–2 and facing closer Aroldis Chapman. Jeff McNeil drew a walk, and Amed Rosario was sent in to pinch-hit for Luis Guillorme. At this moment, I wasn't fully comprehending the oddity of what could potentially happen right now. The Mets could walk off the Yankees at Yankee Stadium. Amed, wearing No. 42 like everyone else in honor of the great Jackie Robinson, crushed a 2–0 slider from Chapman to deep left field. As the ball clanked against the empty left-field seats in dead silence, I'll never forget what Gary Cohen said: "Gives the Mets the lead...ehhh, the win." Even Gary was confused! Take everything in that quick moment and try to explain it to someone living a few years or even a few months earlier. Amed Rosario hit a walk-off home run on the road, with no one in the ballpark in the bottom of the seventh inning.

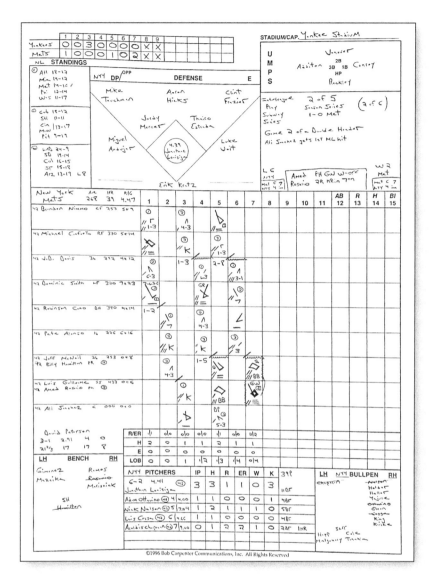

Nothing made sense. The Mets had swept a doubleheader from the Yankees with two dramatic wins and were about to be bought by the richest man in the universe. I was on cloud nine.

So when I proclaimed this day and moment the greatest non-championship moment in franchise history, was I nuts? Obviously, the excitement over the win and sweep turned out to be a fart in the wind. The Mets finished eight games under .500 and missed the expanded playoffs in 2020 as it turned out to be another wasted season. While it was cool to beat the Yankees, winning a Subway Series game had become less meaningful over the years and with no one in attendance and being unable to hang out with anyone in the isolation era of Covid, who was I bragging to? But the news of Steve Cohen buying the Mets has changed the franchise in an MLB-altering way. So I stand by my excitement! Steve Cohen bought the Mets, and for most of us that is without a doubt a Mount Rushmore moment in the history of the franchise.

KEEPING SCORE: The game-winning shot by Rosario was the first walk-off homer by a visiting player since 1899 and the first walk-off of any kind by a visiting team since 1906.... The doubleheader was made necessary after the previous weekend's scheduled series at Citi Field had to be postponed after a Mets player (reportedly Tomas Nido) and another member of the organization contracted the coronavirus during a series in Miami. Another doubleheader was played at Yankee Stadium on August 30 (the Yankees won both games), and the third postponed game was made up at Citi Field on September 3 (won by the Mets on Pete Alonso's 10th-inning home run).... Cohen officially completed the purchase of the Mets on November 6, 2020, for $2.4 billion.

THE RETURN

PHILLIES 5 METS 3

APRIL 5, 2021, at CITIZENS BANK PARK, PHILADELPHIA

IT WAS EARLY March 2020, and Joe Benigno and I had just finished a few days of shows at spring training. Instead of flying back to New York immediately, my wife was supposed to meet me in Florida, where we would spend a few days together in the warm weather. Things were changing because Sylvia had some concerns about this Covid thing that people were starting to talk about. So she stayed home, and I would use my extra day in Florida to catch a spring training game between the Mets and Astros in West Palm Beach. A day earlier, I had secretly pulled up to the Astros' spring facility late at night, where I would put a giant asterisk poster next to the sign that read "2017 World Series Champions." I was so proud of my juvenile prank and quickly snapped a picture before running off into the Florida evening. The next day I watched the Mets and Astros play baseball before I boarded a plane back to New York. What I didn't realize in the moment was that baseball was on the verge of a four-month shutdown, and I wouldn't be in another stadium for over a year.

After the bizarre 2020 baseball season, things were supposed to be normal in 2021...or at least a little bit normal. Baseball would have a 162-game season in 2021, but the season would begin with stadiums that were 10 percent filled. Hey, 10 percent is better than 0 percent, so even if we weren't back to packed houses, the fact people would be in the stands felt like a huge step forward. The Mets were scheduled to open the post-Covid season in Washington, but we were quickly reminded that we weren't actually post-Covid quite yet. The Nationals were hit with a virus outbreak, and the entire opening series was canceled. So, while the baseball world was back, the Mets had to wait. But this delay created an opportunity. In 2021, my Opening Day streak of games attended was about to end due to my afternoon radio show commitments, but was there a loophole? Now that the Mets' opening series in Washington was canned, their season opener would now be on a Monday night in Philadelphia. I asked my bosses if it was okay for me to do my show, *Carton & Roberts*, from Philly before attending the night game. They approved, and it was on! I was going to my first baseball game in over a year and, via a technicality, keeping my Opening Day streak alive. During our afternoon show, news broke that the Jets had traded quarterback Sam Darnold to the Carolina Panthers, which became the big topic of the day. At night, I met my dad and father-in-law after my show and made the short drive from the WIP studios to Citizens Bank Park. As we walked into the building with our masks securely on, it was a surreal feeling. It had been such a long time since any of us could have this experience—that old simple feeling of walking into a ballpark, smelling the hot dogs and hearing the sounds of the crowd. It was a little emotional thinking about what society had gone through over the last year...it wasn't about baseball, it was about how life as we once knew it was shut down for such an absurdly long period of time. This was a small step toward being back. Obviously, a socially distanced crowd with a 10 percent capacity isn't being "back," but it was an important step.

It didn't take long to get all the feels back of a real baseball game with the same stresses. Jacob deGrom was his typical Jake self. He put guys on base early but would always find a way to wiggle out of trouble. Shortstop Francisco Lindor, who had been acquired from Cleveland during the off-season, was making his Mets debut with the huge pressures of a massive contract and All-Star expectations. In the fourth inning, RBI singles by James McCann and deGrom against Matt Moore gave the Mets a 2–0 lead that they would nurse for the next few innings. DeGrom allowed just three hits and struck out seven in six scoreless innings but was pulled after only 77 pitches, which was annoying but understandable. Coming off the short 2020 season, there was an early concern about how pitchers would adjust from a small workload to a traditional amount of innings the following season. So there was an expectation that guys would be handled more conservatively than normal.

The Mets needed their pen now to protect the two-run lead, and Miguel Castro did his job with a clean seventh inning. But in his Mets debut, Trevor May made a freakin' mess in the eighth. With the bases loaded and one out, Mets manager Luis Rojas brought Aaron Loup in to face Bryce Harper. Harper got hit by a pitch that made it 2–1, and then J.T. Realmuto tied the game with an RBI single. The death of this game would come on the very next pitch from an unlikely source. Alec Bohm hit a chopper to the sure-handed Luis Guillorme at third base. Luis made a throw home that was wild and off the outstretched glove of James McCann, which allowed two runs to score. The 10 percent–filled stadium in Philly erupted as the Phillies took a 4–2 lead. Pain...back in the ballpark with pain. We would get one more tease, because in the ninth down 5–3, Pete Alonso, as the tying run, would drive one to deep right field before it was caught by Harper in front of the wall to end it. The sting of losing a tough game and being in the building was back! As we filed out of Citizens Bank Park to begin our trek back to New York, I was filled with mixed emotions. The game sucked. The feeling of losing was awful—but, man, was it cool to be back! Our first step back to baseball normalcy was on, and the familiar pain of losing was my welcome back gift.

KEEPING SCORE: It was the Mets' first Opening Day loss since 2016.... They opened their home season three days later with a 3–2 win over the Miami Marlins before 8,492 fans.... The Mets held a five-game lead in the National League East at the end of July but went 21–37 the rest of the way to finish in third place with a 77–85 record, and manager Luis Rojas was let go.

THE COMBINED NO-HITTER

METS 3 PHILLIES 0

APRIL 29, 2022, at CITI FIELD

WHEN I GOT home from doing my *Carton & Roberts* show on this Friday in 2022, I was exhausted. It wasn't from working with Craig, it was from the fact that I got zero sleep the night before. With two kids, it wasn't the one-year-old giving us trouble but our five-year-old, who was dealing with nightmares and having big issues sleeping through the night. Because of that, the night before was very difficult for Dad, as I barely got any shut-eye. I trudged my way through a four-and-a-half-hour show before finally getting home close to 8:00 PM after dealing with Friday traffic. My method of watching games usually followed the same script. I would get home, debrief with my wife on our days, and eat some dinner. At about 9:00 PM I would start the Mets game off the DVR, which featured the luxury of skipping through commercials, allowing me to get through the game in a timely fashion. Depending on what time I got home, some evenings I would actually catch up on the game. Otherwise, I would finish within a reasonable time of the game actually ending. But on this night, everything would be different...far different.

I've got my own weird rules when it comes to DVRing sports. I shut my phone down to avoid the outside world until I catch up and am live on a game, and usually I have zero issues. The one thing I can't do is wait until the following morning to watch a game. I tried it once years ago, and I couldn't sleep as I would twist and turn imagining the result in my head. But on this night, my rules would be tested. I was *so damn* exhausted I couldn't keep my eyes open, and trying to watch this Mets-Phillies April showdown while scoring it felt like an impossible task without sleep. So the rule of not sleeping the night was about to be tested as I passed out at 9:00 PM. But my passion and craziness for the New York Mets was no match for my shut-eye as I popped out of bed at around 1:00 AM needing to know

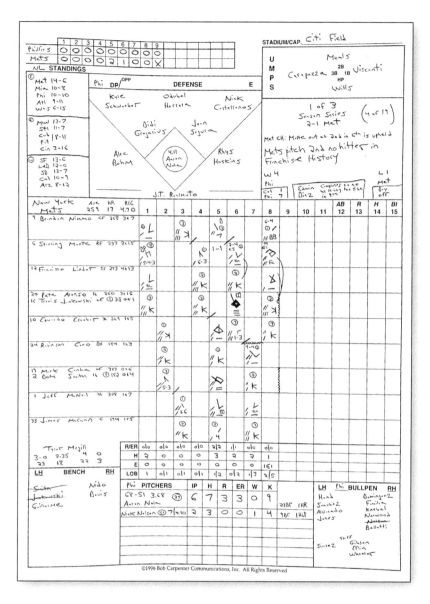

what had happened. I got up and opened my scorebook and began putting it together in anticipation of the game that probably ended hours ago. It was Tylor Megill facing Aaron Nola as the 14–6 Mets took on the 10–10 Phillies on a Friday night at Citi Field. The game felt very normal as the 0–0 game moved along into the fifth inning. The Mets struck first against Nola as Jeff McNeil singled home two

'21
V/G Phillies W-L 10-10 GB 4 H 8-5 R 2-5 E 2-5 C 1-2 W 5-2 IL 2-1
'21
H/G Mets W-L 14-6 GB +3 Min H 5-2 R 9-4 E 5-2 C 2-1 W 7-3 IL 0-0

AL STANDINGS

	R	H	E	LOB
Phi	0	0	0	5
Met	3	10	0	5

WP Tylor Megill 4-0
LP Aaron Nola 1-3
SV Edwin Diaz 4

START 7:14 DATE April 29, 2022 (Friday)
FINISH 10:32 ATT. 32,416
TIME 318 WX Clear 61°

Met DP / OPP

DEFENSE

Mark Cunha — Brandon Nimmo — Starling Marte

Francisco Lindor — Jeff McNeil

Eduardo Escobar — 2.13 Tylor Megill — Pete Alonso

James McCann

AL STANDINGS

© NYY 13-6
Tor 13-7
TB 11-8
Bos 8-12
Bal 6-13

② Min 11-8
KC 7-10
CWS 7-11
Cle 7-12
Det 6-12

③ LAA 13-7
Sea 11-8
Hou 10-9
Oak —
Tex 6-13

Philadelphia Phillies	Ave 256	HR 19	RIC 4.80	1	2	3	4	5	6	7	8	9	10	11	AB 12	R 13	H 14	BI 15
2 Jean Segura 2b 257 2+5																		
17 Rhys Hoskins 1b 206 1+6																		
3 Bryce Harper DH 275 3+14																		
8 Nick Castellanos RF 317 3+12																		
10 J.T. Realmuto c 210 1+3																		
12 Kyle Schwarber lf 164 4+11																		
28 Alec Bohm 3b 335 2+14																		
18 Didi Gregorius ss 311 0+5																		
37 Odubel Herrera cf 2+5 / 7 Johan Camargo 1b 261 1+6																		

Aaron Nola	R/ER	0|0	0|0	0|0	0|0	0|0	0|0	0|0	0|0	0|0		
1-2 3.74 4 0	H	0	0	0	0	0	0	0	0	0		
2½ 14 25 5	E	0	0	0	0	0	0	0	0	0		
LH BENCH RH	LOB	0	1	0|1	0|1	2|3	1|4	0|4	1|5	0|5		

Vierling
Stubbs

SH
Camargo
Quinn

Met PITCHERS	IP	H	R	ER	W	K	88 P		LH Met BULLPEN RH
7-6 4.07 ② Tylor Megill	5	0	0	0	3	5	18 BF		Rodriguez / Diaz
Drew Smith ② 6 0.00	1⅓	0	0	0	1	4	5 BF		Shreve / Ottavino
Joely Rodriguez 2 ③ 7 6.75	1	0	0	0	2	0	4 BF		Lugo Smith
Seth Lugo ④ 8 4.70	⅔	0	0	0	0	0	4 BF		Loper / Williams
Edwin Diaz ⑤ 9 2.00	1	0	0	0	0	3	3 BF		Reid-Foley

SI-off
Scherzer
Bassitt
Carrasco

runs, and then Pete Alonso hit a bomb in the sixth to give the Mets a 3–0 lead. It was another solid outing by Tylor Megill, who danced around a little bit of trouble to pitch five scoreless innings, but his pitch count had ballooned up to 88 pitches courtesy of three walks and a bunch of full counts.

I used to be a guy who would notice no-hitters in the first inning, but after the Johan no-no of 2012 and watching Chris Heston do it to the Mets in 2015, I guess I had become more like a normal human being in not going batshit crazy over any sign of a no-hitter. So the first I noticed of this occurrence that night was when I started filling in Megill's pitching line: 5 innings pitched, 0 runs, and *zero* hits. *Wow*, I thought to myself. It didn't feel like a no-no because the Phillies had numerous base runners, but here we were into the sixth inning, and the Mets were actually no-hitting the Phillies. The three relievers who followed would find the same script as Megill—issue walks, put guys on base, but find a way through it. Drew Smith, Joely Rodriguez, and Seth Lugo were able to navigate the sixth, seventh, and eighth innings and keep the Phillies out of the hit column. I was starting to get very nervous—did I want to see this happen? I'm not only *not* at the game, but I'm watching this *hours* after it had concluded. I could simply hit fast-forward and find out the answer in seconds if I wanted, or I could simply break the DVR rule and check my phone. The answer to this agonizing question was right in front of me if I wanted.

The Mets' bottom of the eighth inning took what seemed like forever as they put a few guys on base, threatening to open up on their seemingly comfortable 3–0 lead. As Edwin Diaz warmed up to pitch the ninth inning, I was so torn as to what I wanted to see. My sleeping wife was to my left, and I'm surprised she didn't wake up as I began hosting a radio show out loud, debating what I was rooting for in the top of the ninth inning. When Edwin Diaz began the ninth inning by striking out Bryce Harper, my gut told me the result. *Holy shit*, I thought. I was about to witness a no-hitter on tape delay. The crowd was electric through the TV as Diaz pumped in more heat and sliders that made Nick Castellanos look like a fool. The Mets were now one out away, and the drama was quickly eradicated as Diaz struck out J.T. Realmuto on three pitches. The crowd was in a frenzy, the Mets rushed out of the dugout, and my answer was given to me hours after it actually happened. The Mets had pitched a combined no-hitter. I kept saying "Wow, Wow, Wow!" as I woke up my wife to tell her the news. "That's great, baby," she responded deep in sleep. When I checked my phone, I had 40 new text messages, including one from my dad asking if I was alive. I sat in awe staring at my TV trying to soak in this insane moment, even if it was hours after it happened.

I was not mad, I was not sad, but maybe I was a tad jealous to not have experienced this moment in person. But screw that. My memory was certainly unique in that I watched this no-hitter at 2:00 o'clock in the morning. It did help that this wasn't the first no-hitter in Mets history. Not being there in person for Johan would have eaten at my soul, but since the Mets got that out of the way, missing the second, especially one that was a combined no-hitter, made it an easier pill to swallow. The other baseball thought that jumped out at me from this game was how awesome Edwin Diaz was. Edwin was trying to prove to Mets fans that he wasn't the flake he appeared to be from his early Mets struggles, and easily striking out three very good hitters in front of an electric crowd to secure the no–hitter, I thought was a great sign of things to come: 2022 felt special.

KEEPING SCORE: This was first of four no-hitters thrown in 2022. The Phillies were also held hitless in Game 4 of the World Series by four Houston Astros pitchers.... It was also the second no-hitter caught by James McCann, who was behind the plate for Lucas Giolito's gem against the Pittsburgh Pirates while playing for the Chicago White Sox in 2020.

LIVING THE DREAM

METS 5 DODGERS 3
SEPTEMBER 1, 2022, at CITI FIELD

THE METS were 83–48 as they got set to open up the month of September by closing out a three- game series against the 90–39 Los Angeles Dodgers. But what made this Thursday late afternoon special wasn't the magnitude of the game. My oldest son, Jett, was in the midst of a streak of going to games with me and doing an incredible job for a five-year-old! He was scoring games with me and really paying attention to what was going on in front of him. That didn't mean there weren't moments when I would need his iPad to get him through a nine-inning game, but he had definitely come a long way for someone his age. A year earlier, I wouldn't have dared to take him to Citi by myself, but in 2022 it had become the norm. History was repeating itself from my dad and me as a kid, as Jett was becoming a mini Mets super fan. But on this 4:00 PM start at the end of the summer in 2022, it wasn't just me and Jett at Citi, we were joined by my wife, Sylvia, and my almost two-year-old son, Spence. Spence had been to one other game during the season, and it had not gone well! The combination of summer sun and too much milk caused Spence to not have the greatest time at the ballpark. But we were feeling lucky enough to give it one more try as the latter part of the season approached. Spence was overall a very calm baby, which was quite different than Jett, who had not been the easier to take to the park. So as the Mets and Dodgers engaged in the rubber game of what was a very entertaining three-game series, I was bringing the family!

My wife and my two sons...this was the American dream, wasn't it? Spence was in awe of the ballpark, the sounds and the airplanes overhead, while Jett was following Dad in scoring this showdown between the two best teams in the NL. The game was entertaining too, as Clayton Kershaw and Chris Bassitt were locked in a duel that had the Mets trailing 2–1 going into the bottom of the sixth inning. With the Dodgers being very careful with Kershaw, the Mets got him out of the game after just 74 pitches and promptly took advantage of the Dodgers' pen when Francisco Lindor tied the game with an RBI double and Darin Ruf's sacrifice fly gave them the lead. The Mets added some insurance an inning later when Brandon Nimmo doubled home a run and then scored on Starling Marte's RBI single. As he had done a few times during the season, Buck Showalter went to the dominant Edwin Diaz early, bringing him in with a 5–2 lead in the eighth inning when the Dodgers were sending up 3-4-5 in the order. Along with Diaz's dominance, came the infatuation Mets fans had with his intro song as performed by Timmy Trumpet. In honor of this craze, Trumpet himself was on hand for the series and played a live rendition of "Narco" much to the enjoyment of the nearly 40,000 people filling up Citi Field. Both my sons loved it, especially Jett, who had recently asked me for an Edwin Diaz jersey, which he sported at the game. This was not the dominant Diaz we were used to in 2022, as he put the first two guys on base by walking Freddie Freeman and hitting Will Smith. Then he got a couple of 400-foot outs on deep fly balls hit by Max Muncy and Justin Turner, the second a sac fly, cutting the Mets' lead to two runs. But he survived the eighth inning by striking out Gavin Lux, and Adam Ottavino easily recorded the final three outs to secure the Mets' 5–3 win. From a baseball standpoint, the Mets had sent a message to the rest of the NL, that they were legit good.

The Mets took the series 2–1 and the overall season series from the Dodgers 4–3 as they maintained their lead in the NL East. Little did I know the Mets would struggle against the soft schedule the rest of the way and eventually relinquish their division lead. But my best memory from this game was the company. Just one month short of turning two, Spence did an incredible job, seeming to clap when exciting things would happen and appearing to genuinely enjoy his afternoon at the park for the first time. When the game ended after three hours and 14 minutes, it seemed like he was ready for more! Jett had completed going to three straight games and wasn't getting sick of it. I love going to Mets games, but what I enjoyed more than anything was being at the games with my wife and my boys. I think that Thursday afternoon was the true American dream...baseball with the family.

KEEPING SCORE: The Mets lost two of three games at Citi Field to the last-place Nationals immediately following the Dodgers series, and were swept by another sub-.500 team, the Chicago Cubs, less than two weeks later.... They finished the season with 101 victories, the same as the Braves, but lost the season series 10–9 and the division title (which would have given them a first-round bye in the playoffs) by dropping all three games at Atlanta in the next-to-last series of the season and had to settle for a wild-card berth.

THE FAREWELL
WE DIDN'T REALIZE

METS 7 PADRES 3
GAME 2, NATIONAL LEAGUE WILD CARD SERIES
OCTOBER 8, 2022, at CITI FIELD

THE 2022 METS' 101-win season was on the verge of ending in a dumpster fire. They had a marvelous regular season that was spoiled by getting swept by the Braves on the final weekend of the regular season, which cost the team the division that they led virtually the entire season. The booby prize for blowing that lead was facing the San Diego Padres in the newly created best-of-three Wild Card Series. Throughout the regular season, the 2022 Mets felt magical, as if something special awaited us in October. That feeling was squelched by the divisional debacle. Obviously going on an October run could quickly make us forget about the September swoon we just witnessed, but all the good feelings of the regular season had dissipated, and my confidence level was very low. It got worse when the series began with Max Scherzer being booed off the mound as the Mets got destroyed 7–1 in Game 1. Now we were facing a quick elimination in Game 2. Buck Showalter caused some controversy (though I agreed with it) by starting one of his aces in Game 1 with the potential of holding back his second ace for Game 3 or potentially the next round. But that strategy would only go into effect if the Mets had won Game 1, which they had not. So Jacob deGrom, who had only made 11 starts during the regular season, was asked to save the Mets' season in his first postseason start since the magical year of 2015.

Francisco Lindor set a strong tone with a leadoff home run off Blake Snell, but deGrom would promptly give it back in the third inning when Trent Grisham hit his second home run in as many days. The Mets retook the lead in the fourth on Brandon Nimmo's

©1996 Bob Carpenter Communications, Inc. All Rights Reserved

RBI single to knock out Snell, but again deGrom would give it right back in the fifth, and it looked like it could get even worse than that. After the Padres tied it 2–2 on Jurickson Profar's run-scoring hit, they had men on first and third with just one out and their 3-4 hitters coming up. But from that moment, Jake flipped the switch and came up huge. He struck out Manny Machado and Josh Bell back-to-back

STADIUM/CAP. Citi Field

	1	2	3	4	5	6	7	8	9
Padres	0	0	1	0	1	0	0	0	1
Mets	1	0	0	1	1	0	4	0	X

Wild Card Series Game 2
1-0 SD

©1996 Bob Carpenter Communications, Inc. All Rights Reserved

to end the threat and then pitched a nice and easy 1-2-3 sixth inning. I wanted deGrom to pitch the seventh, but Buck went super aggressive and went right to his closer, Edwin Diaz. As the trumpets blared over Citi Field, we all realized how desperate Buck Showalter was by going to Edwin this early. Diaz did his job by getting five outs and handing the ball over to Adam Ottavino. In the meantime the Mets had broken the game open with four runs in the seventh, keyed by Jeff McNeil's two-run double off reliever Adrián Morejón.

As this game stretched deep into the night in the days before a pitch clock, I had a lot of time to think, and one thought popped into my head that depressed the shit out of me. Was this the final time Jacob deGrom was going to be pitching for the Mets? Some of my fellow Mets fans had begun to turn on the ace...why, you ask? He missed the second half of 2021 and the first half of 2022, so the missed time pissed a lot of fans off. He also came up very small in a huge start against Oakland a few weeks earlier, and while he wasn't bad in his Atlanta start, he did give up three home runs and was the losing pitcher in the first game of that crucial series. There was also a theory that he didn't want to be in New York anymore. I didn't buy any of this shit, because I still saw Jacob deGrom as the most dominant pitcher in baseball who unfortunately had bad injury luck over the last two years. I also still viewed him as the man with the biggest balls on the mound—just look at this game. But more than any of that, he was *my* guy. I'm a fan of the laundry more than individual players, but deGrom broke through on that for me. A lot of it was the disrespect I felt he faced during his tenure here. From the beginning, Jacob was not appreciated the way he should have been, and even on the way out I thought the sentiment from some Mets fans was embarrassing.

A few short months later, my fears were realized when deGrom signed a five-year deal with the Texas Rangers. I was bitter toward the Mets for what they offered Jake and how they were so willing to let him walk without taking into account the emotional attachment fans might have with a lifelong Met. He was replaced by Justin Verlander, who while a great pitcher was a hired gun and not a guy who grew up in the organization. It still bothers me that the Mets let deGrom go so easily, and it especially bothered me how some fans were eager to blame Jake for the departure and rewrite history on what he did as a Met.

The Mets won this game, but even walking out of Citi Field that night, I had an uneasy feeling. I wasn't confident about winning a winner-take-all Game 3, and I wasn't confident I would ever see Jacob deGrom pitch for the Mets again. Unfortunately, I was right about both.

KEEPING SCORE: The Mets were held to just one hit (a fifth-inning single by Pete Alonso) by Joe Musgrove and two relievers in Game 3 the next night, and a season that had looked so magical just a few weeks earlier was over way too soon. The Padres, who had finished 22 games behind the Los Angeles Dodgers (winners of 111 games) in the NL West, went on to upset them in the Division Series before losing to the Philadelphia Phillies, who finished 14 games behind the Mets in the East, in the NLCS.... DeGrom's Mets legacy includes four All-Star appearances, two Cy Young Awards, and the best ERA (2.52) in team history.

The
MISSING SCORECARDS

Since scoring became an obsession during the 1992 Mets season, I haven't missed much. In fact, I started racking my brain to think of the games that I somehow missed for whatever reason. Over the course of 30-plus years, I have come up with three games that are clearly missing pieces to my scoring puzzle.

RETURN TO NEW YORK BASEBALL

METS 3 BRAVES 2

SEPTEMBER 21, 2001, at SHEA STADIUM

LIKE ALL AMERICANS, we remember everything about September 11, 2001. For me, I was living in the Washington, D.C., area while working for XM Satellite Radio, and 9/11 was actually supposed to be the same week we launched the channel I was on. After hearing about the "accident" on the radio, I soon learned that what we were witnessing was evil in its darkest form as we were brutally attacked and all we could do was watch in horror. I remember feverishly trying to call my family back in New York to no avail because cell service was down everywhere. In the days that followed, there would be no sports and really no normal life as we all came to grips with what we had just experienced. The Mets returned to playing baseball on September 17 when they went to Pittsburgh to play the Pirates and promptly swept the Pirates to jump over .500 for the first time since being 2–1 in the opening moments of the regular season. They were then set to return to New York to play the Braves on Friday, September 21. I did my radio show that day and then boarded Amtrak to return to New York for the first time since the attack. As I boarded the train, I had my transistor radio in hand ready to listen to the return of baseball in New York. I didn't pick up the signal of WFAN until well into my trip and was able to listen to the final five innings on the radio with a terrible signal that kept going in and out as my train rumbled toward Penn Station in New York. When Mike Piazza came to the plate to face Steve Karsay in the bottom of the eighth inning, I was somewhere in New Jersey and heard the legendary voice of Bob Murphy describe arguably the most poignant home run in baseball history. The Piazza home run in the return of baseball after 9/11 has gone down in Mets history and New York history, and while I don't have a scorecard to mark the moment, I, like most New Yorkers, remember exactly how I felt when that ball cleared the center-field fence.

THE WILMER FLORES GAME

METS 2 NATIONALS 1 (12 INNINGS)
JULY 31, 2015, at CITI FIELD

I WAS emotionally spent! The Mets had just traded Wilmer Flores, not traded Wilmer Flores, watched Wilmer cry on the field, blew a ninth-inning lead to the Padres in the rain, and topped it all off with a last-second trade for Yoenis Cespedes. As I drove home from my Friday radio show, which was broadcast from New York Giants camp while the Mets had pulled off the deal for Cespedes, I was physically and emotionally tired. When I got back to my Long Island City apartment to the loving arms of my fiancée (now wife), Sylvia, I lost it and started bawling like a baby. I wasn't necessarily crying over the Mets, I think I just need to let the emotion out and a good cry every once in a while is a good thing. "Listen, baby, I can't score tonight's game," I explained to her, as if I needed permission or had to explain to my fiancée at the time why I wasn't doing something she had grown accustomed to. I lay in bed as I watched the Mets battle the Washington Nationals. Matt Harvey was utterly brilliant, but Terry Collins let Matt stay in just a tad too long (sound familiar?).

With two outs in the eighth inning, Harvey hit a batter and then gave up back-to-back hits, which allowed the Nationals to tie the game. Deep into the summer night, the Mets and Nationals battled to keep the score tied 1–1. Finally, leading off the bottom of the 12th inning against Felipe Vazquez (then known as Felipe Rivero), Wilmer Flores drove a ball to deep left field. The ball cleared the fence, and the Mets had pulled off a dramatic 2–1 win in walk-off fashion, but what made it insanely special was who walked it off. The man who cried on the field just a few days earlier was now the hero of a win that would spark the Mets on their way to a runaway of the NL East. I was so excited I woke up my sleeping fiancée to tell her the amazing news.

MAX SCHERZER'S DOMINANCE

NATIONALS 2 METS 0

OCTOBER 3, 2015, at CITI FIELD

THE 2015 regular season was winding to a close as the Mets were playing a doubleheader against the Washington Nationals on the penultimate day of the season. It was a split doubleheader, and in the opener I went to the ballpark by myself to see the Mets lose 3–1 as they dropped their fourth straight game. The nightcap was Mets Blanket Night, and the giveaway certainly fit the weather because it was a crisp evening. My wife had worked during the day and was joining me for the second game of the day-night doubleheader, but we were having second thoughts as we pulled into the parking lot. "Listen, baby," I said to her, "we have been to a ton of games, and the result doesn't matter; we really don't have to go." She took me up on the chance to skip the game but was intrigued by the blanket! So I let her stay in the car as I waited in line to get the blanket and then promptly leave. Even though I had two tickets for the game, the Citi Field ticket taker was not going to allow me to take a second blanket, so I went back to the car with only one. My wife was not going to go for this—as she has warned me, every once in a while she shows her Latina temper, and today was going to be one of those days. She marched back to wait in line and get that second blanket, where she would then give the ticket taker a piece of her mind. We got the blanket and went home. Who cares about the meaningless game, right? Well, the Nationals' Max Scherzer proceeded to throw one of the most brilliant games of his Hall of Fame–bound career. Max pitched nine innings, allowed *zero* hits, *zero* walks, and struck out 17 guys. The one Mets base runner came in the sixth inning when Kevin Plawecki reached on an error by Washington third baseman Yunel Escobar. The Mets had been no-hit for the second time during the 2015 season, and this time it had come in historic fashion. It was Scherzer's second no-hitter of the season, as he became the first pitcher since Nolan Ryan in 1973 to accomplish the feat. "Are you mad you missed this?" Sylvia asked. The honest answer was I wasn't, but I would have been if not for that error. Missing a perfect game would have been tough, but now that I was a veteran of multiple no-hitters in person, I was okay with it. What would have really annoyed me was not getting that awesome Mets blanket, but luckily, we got two of them!

ACKNOWLEDGMENTS

THIS BOOK isn't written nor do I have a career without the love and support of my parents. From teaching me how to never take no for an answer and driving 100 mph so I could make Opening Day 1996, my mom is the best. She also allowed me and my dad to attend around 80 Mets games per season without batting an eye. I'm working at James Garfield's childhood home as a tour guide without her. My dad taught me everything I knew about the Mets and baseball and certainly helped cultivate the passion I still maintain to this day. And to my sister, Stacy—even though she once stuffed a Twinkie in my face to torture her little brother—she never once destroyed all my scorebooks, and that is greatly appreciated.

My wife, Sylvia, is the greatest significant other a man could create. I scored a baseball game on our third date, and she should have ran out of Citi Field that afternoon, but instead she fell in love. My sons, Jett and Spence, remind me after every Mets loss that it's just a game, and looking into their eyes I know what truly matters.

My former radio partner Craig Carton likes to take credit for stuff, but he was truly the one who put this idea in my head. Thank you, Craig, for being an awesome co-host and giving me the belief that this kind of book could actually happen.

Thank you to my agent, Maury Gostrand, who helped take this wild idea and make it reality. My first WFAN radio partner was the great Joe Benigno, and we had a wild 14-year run at WFAN that I will never forget. A lot of the stories in this book come while working with him.

Tiki Barber made the transition to afternoon drive so much easier because he's a dedicated professional, a damn good radio host, and one of the sweetest guys you'll ever meet. I also want to thank Tom Lugauer and Shaun Morash, who have done an excellent job on our afternoon radio show and help maintain the success we previously had.

One of my closest friends, Patrick Meagher, not only helped come up with the idea for the title of this book, we also spent countless hours in one of our apartments drinking beer, talking about girls all while I would score a Mets game.

Mark Chernoff gave me a shot to fill in for Mike Breen in 1993 and gave me a full-time job at WFAN in 2007. This book isn't being written without a boss that put me in position to succeed.

Chris Olivero is the most straightforward boss I've ever worked for and knows almost as much pro wrestling history as I do.

Spike Eskin has been a pleasure to work with and shares my distrust for Ben Simmons.

Thanks to my in-laws, Jose and Silvia Rodriguez. Upon having children and getting married, it was going to be impossible to remain as crazy as I was in going to games. While I certainly can't go to 80 per season anymore, their love and support has made it a thousand times easier to still spend nights at Citi Field.

To Ken, Alex, Jesse, and everyone at Triumph, I can't thank you guys enough. As a first-time author, I had no idea what I was doing, and you guys made the process very easy. Thank you.